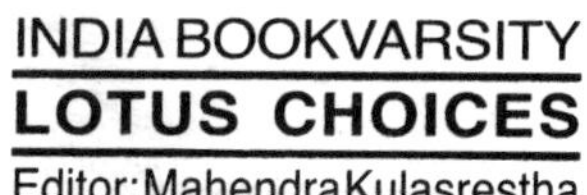

The ABC of HINDU CULTURE

John Dowson

A Book of Hindu Culture in Dictionary Form, Containing References to Religion, Mythology, Geography, History and Literature

4735/22, Prakash Deep Building,
Ansari Road, Darya Ganj,
New Delhi-110002

THE ABC OF HINDU CULTURE

John Dowson

Source: ***A Classical Dictionary of Hindu Mythology and Religion,*** **by John Dowson, published in England in the 19th century**

The ABC of HINDU CULTURE

New First Edition—2012
ISBN: 978-81-8382-289-3(H/B)

Published by:
LOTUS PRESS PUBLISHERS & DISTRIBUTORS
Unit No. 220, Second Floor, 4735/22, Prakash Deep Building,
Ansari Road, Darya Ganj, New Delhi-10002
Ph.: 011-23280047, 32903912 • Mob.: 098118-38000
E-mail: lotus_press@sify.com

Printed at: **Concept Imprint,** Delhi

Editorspeak

ABC Means Dictionary

Dictionaries of cultures is a nice and much useful concept, but, unfortunatey, has yet to gain recognition by the writing and publishing world. Many years ago, when my publishing house published our first book on the subject in Hindi, the present writer, as editor, felt specially pleased, and congratulated its author for having penned it so laboriously—though now while doing this present book, which was published nearly two centuries ago, I feel quite deflated; and also suspect that the author might as well have copied from this and other such works which would have been easily available to him, without recognising their compiler's singular contribution so long ago.

Our English counterpart, a few years later, published dictionaries of Hinduism, Buddhism, Islam, etc., by new foreign scholars which also are doing rather well though they are much shorter and compact. I think these can be still shorter, and redone, with suitable illustrations, for schools and colleges, and even general consumption. History as an academic subject could make special use of these.

John Dowson's work is astonishingly exhaustive and authentic and in its current paperback editions—one of which I'm using for this condensation; there may be more because of its being in public domain—seems to be doing rather well. There is not much information regarding the author, but for this that he was professor of Hindustani at the Staff College—but where and in what country and city is not mentioned—, a member of Royal Asiatic Society, and was 'Late' when this work was published—in which year is again not mentioned; but it is clear from the preface that he took great pains at working on this volume, and was also eager to have illustrations for it despite the heavy expenses 'if the work is approved'. Alas, he perhaps did not live long enough to see his labours appearing in print!

I would like to think that the British Council or some such body would come forward to do the needful, or at least publish biographical notes on this as well as other similar scholars devoted to such pioneer work in those early times, something on the lines of what Max Muller Bhawan has done about the German contributors to Indology in those times (or have they already done, of which I'm ignorant?)

So here we have in the present volume perhaps one of the best compilations with as comprehensive notes as possible, with all the versions of every tale available in several texts, carefully comparing them with each other, which could benefit even the experts in Indology to an extent. Amen!

Authorspeak

This Work

In this work an endeavor has been made to supply the long-felt need of a Hindu Classical Dictionary. The late Professor Wilson projected such a work, and announced his intention of preparing one for the Oriental Translation Fund, but he never accomplished his design. This is not the first attempt to supply the void. Mr. Garrett, Director of Public Instruction in Mysore, published in India a few years ago as *A Classical Dictionary of India*, but it is of a very miscellaneous character, and embraces a good deal of matter relating to the manners and customs of the present time. It has not obtained favour in Europe, and it cannot be considered as any obstacle in the way of a more complete and systematic work.

The main portion of this work consists of mythology, but religion is bound up with mythology, and in many points the two are quite inseparable. Of history, in the true sense, Sanskrit possesses nothing, or next to nothing, but what little has been discovered here finds its place.

This work is derived entirely from the publications of European scholars. I have not resorted to original Sanskrit authorities. My remaining span of life would at the best be quite insufficient for an investigation of their manifold and lengthy volumes.

There is nothing in this book for which authority is not to be found in some one or more of the many works upon Hindu literature and religion, but the aim has been to condense and bring together in a compact form that information which lies scattered in many volumes. Hindu mythology is so extensive, and the authorities are often so at variance with each other that I cannot but feel diffident of the success of my labours. I have worked diligently and carefully, I hope also intelligently.

It is unnecessary to specify all the works that have been used in the compilation of this book. But the mainstays throughout have been the 'Original Sanskrit Texts' of Dr. Muir and the works of the late professor H.H. Wilson, including his translation of the Rigveda, and more especially that of the Vishnu Purana. I have also levied numerous contributions from the writings of Williams, Max Muller, Roth, Bohthlingk, Lassen, Weber, Whitney, Wollheim da Fonseca, and many others too numerous to mention.

Contents

A 11
B 40
C 63
D 71
E 92
G 93
H 99
I 105
J 111
K 117
L 145
M 150
N 176
O 186
P 186
R 210
S 228
T 268
U 273
V 277
Y 316

The ABC of Hindu Culture

A

ABHIMANYU: Son of Arjun by his wife Subhadra, and known by the metronymic Saubhadra. He killed Lakshmana, the son of Duryodhana, on the second day of the great battle of the Mahabharata, but on the thirteenth day he himself fell fighting heroically against fearful odds. He was very handsome. His wife was Uttara, daughter of the Raja of Virata. His son, Parikshit, succeeded to the throne of Hastinapura.

ADITI: 'Free, unbounded.' Infinity; the boundless heaven as compared with the finite earth; or, according to M. Muller, the visible infinite, visible by the naked eye; the endless expanse beyond the earth, beyond the clouds, beyond the sky." In the Rigveda she is frequently implored "for blessings on children and cattle, for protection and for forgiveness." Aditi is called Devamatri, 'mother of the gods,' and is represented as being the mother of Daksha and the daughter of Daksha. On this statement Yaska remarks in the Nirukta:—"How can this be possible? They may have had the same origin; or according to the nature of the gods, they may have been born from each other and derived their substance from one another." Eight sons were born from the body of Aditi; she approached the gods with seven but cast away the eighth Martanda (the sun). These seven were the Adityas. In the Yajurveda Aditi is addressed as "Supporter of the sky, sustainer of the earth, sovereign of this world, wife of Vishnu;" but in the Mahabharata and Ramayana, as well as in the Puranas, Vishnu is called the sun of Aditi. In the Vishnu Purana she is said to be the daughter of Daksha and wife of Kasyapa, by whom she was mother of Vishnu, in his dwarf incarnation (wherefore he is sometimes called Aditya), and also of Indra, and she is called "the mother of the gods" and "the mother of the world." Indra acknowledged her as mother, and Vishnu, after receiving the adoration of Aditi, addressed her in these words: "Mother goddess, do thou show favour unto me and grant me thy blessing." According to the Matsya Purana, a pair of earrings was produced at the churning of the ocean, which Indra gave to Aditi, and several of the Puranas tell a story of these earrings being stolen and carried off to the city of Pragjyotisha by the Asura king Naraka, from whence they were brought back and restored to her by Krishna. Devaki, the mother of Krishna, is represented as being a new birth of manifestation of Aditi.

ADITYA: In the early Vedic times the Adityas were six, or more frequently seven, celestial deities, of which Varuna was chisf, consequently he was the Aditya. They were sons of Aditi, who had eight sons, but she approached the gods with seven, having cast away the eighth, Martanda (the sun). In aftertimes the number was increased to twelve, as representing the sun in the twelve months of the year. Aditya is one of the names of the sun. Dr. Muir quotes the following from Professor Roth:—"There (in the highest heaven) dwell and reign those gods who bear in common the name of Adityas We must, however, if we would discover their earliest character, abandon the conceptions which in a later age, and even in that of the heroic poems, were entertained regarding these deities. According to this conception they were twelve months. But for the most ancient period we must hold fast the primary signification of their name. They are the inviolable, imperishable, eternal beings. Aditi, eternity, or the eternal, is the element which sustains or is sustained by them. . . .The eternal and violable element in which the Adityas dwell, and which forms their essence, is the celestial light. The Adityas, the gods of this light, do not therefore by any means coincide with any of the forms in which light is manifested in the universe. They are neither sun, nor moon, nor stars, nor dawn, but the eternal sustainers of this luminous life, which exists, as it were, behind all these phenomena."

The names of the six Adityas are Mitra, Aryaman, Bhaga, Varuna, Daksha, and Ansa. Daksha is frequently excluded, and Indra, Savitri (the sun), and Dhatri are added. Those of the twelve Adityas are variously given, but many of them are names of the sun.

AGASTYA: A Rishi, the reputed author of several hymns in the Rigveda, and a very celebrated personage in Hindu story. He and Vasishtha are said in the Rigveda to be the offspring of Mitra and Varuna, whose seed fell from them at the sight of Urvasi; and the commentator Sayana adds that Agastya was born in a water-jar as "a fish of great lustre," whence he was called Kalasi-suta, Kumbha-sambhava, and Ghatodbhava. From his parentage he was called Maitra-varuni and Aurvasiya; and as he was very small when he was born; not more than a span in length, he was called Mana. Though he is thus associated in his birth with Vasishtha, he is evidently later in date, and he is not one of the Prajapatis. His name Agastya, is derived by a forced etymology from a fable which represents him as having commanded the Vindhya mountains to prostrate themselves before him, through which they lost their primeval altitude; or rather, perhaps, the fable has been invented to account for his name. This miracle has obtained for him the epithet Vindhya-kata; and he acquired another name, Pitabdhi, or

Samudra-chuluka, 'Ocean-drinker,' from another fable, according to which he drank up the ocean because it had offended him, and because he wished to help the gods in their wars with the Daityas when the latter had hidden themselves in the waters. He was afterwards made regent of the star Canopus, which bears his name. The Puranas represent him as being the son of Pulastya, the sage from whom the Rakshasas sprang. He was one of the narrators of the Brahma Purana and also a writer on medicine.

The Mahabharata relates a legend respecting the creation of his wife. It says that Agastya saw his ancestors suspended by their heels in a pit, and was told by them that they could be rescued only by his begetting a son. Thereupon he formed a girl out of the most graceful parts of different animals and passed her secretly into the palace of the king of Vidarbha. There the child grew up as a daughter of the king, and was demanded in marriage by Agastya. Much against his will the king was constrained to consent, and she became the wife of the sage. She was named Lopamudra, because the animals had been subjected to loss (lopa) by her engrossing their distinctive beauties, as the eyes of the deer. She was also called Kausitaki and Varaprada. The same poem also tells a story exhibiting his superhuman power, by which he turned King Nahusha into a serpent and afterwards restored him to his proper form.

It is in the Ramayana that Agastya makes the most distinguished figure. He dwelt in a hermitage on Mount Kunjara, situated in a most beautiful country to the south of the Vindhya mountains, and was chisf of the hermits of the south. He kept the Rakshasas who infested the south under control, so that the country was "only gazed upon and not possessed by them." His power over them is illustrated by a legend which represents him as eating up a Rakshasa named Vatapi who assumed the form of a ram, and as destroying by a flash of his eye the Rakshasa's brother, Ilvala, who attempted to avenge him. Rama in his exile wandered to the hermitage of Agastya with Sita and Lakshmana. The sage received him with the greatest kindness, and became his friend, adviser, and protector. He gave him the bow of Vishnu; and when Rama was restored to his kingdom, the sage accompanied him to Ayodhya.

The name of Agastya holds a great place also in Tamil literature, and he is "venerated in the south as the first teacher of science and literature to the primitive Dravidian tribes;" so says Dr. Caldwell, who thinks "we shall not greatly err in placing the era of Agastya in the seventh, or at least in the sixth century B.C." Wilson also had previously testified to the same effect: "The traditions of the south of India ascribe to Agastya a principal share in the formation of the Tamil language and literature, and the general tenor of the legends relating to him denotes his having been instrumental in the introduction of the Hindu religion and literature into the Peninsula."

AGNI: (Nom. Agnis = Ignis.) Fire, one of the most ancient and most sacred objects of Hindu worship. He appears in three phases—in heaven as the sun, in mid-air as lightning, on earth as ordinary fire. Agni is one of the chisf deities of the Vedas, and great numbers of the hymns are addressed to him, more indeed than to any other god. He is one of the three great deities—Agni, Vayu (or Indra), and Surya—who respectively preside over earth, air, and sky, and are all equal in dignity. "He is considered as the mediator between men and gods, as protector of men and their homes, and as witness of their actions; hence his invocation at all solemn occasions, at the nuptial ceremony. Fire has ceased to be an object of worship, but is held in honour for the part it performs in sacrifices." Agni is represented as having seven tongues, each of which has a distinct name, for licking up the butter used in sacrifices.

He is guardian of the south-east quarter, being one of the eight lokapalas, and his region is called Pura-jyotis.

In a celebrated hymn of the Rigveda attributed to Vasishtha, Indra and other gods are called upon to destroy the Kravyads 'the flesh-eaters,' or Rakshas enemies of the gods. Agni himself is also a Kravyad, and as such he takes an entirely different character. He is represented under a form as hideous as the beings he is invoked to devour. He sharpens his two iron tusks, puts his enemies into his mouth and swallows them. He heats the edges of his shafts and sends them into the hearts of the Rakshasas.

"He appears in the progress of mythological personification as a son of Angiras, as a king of the Pitris or Manes, as a Marut, as a grandson of Sandila, as one of the seven sages or Rishis, during the reign of Tamasa the fourth Manu," and as a star. In the Mahabharata Agni is represented as having exhausted his vigour by devouring too many oblations, and desiring to consume the whole Khandava forest as a means of recruiting his strength. He was prevented by Indra, but having obtained the assistance of Krishna and Arjuna, he baffled Indra and accomplished his object. In the Vishnu Purana he is called Abhimani, and the eldest son of Brahma. His wife was Swaha; by her he had three sons, Pavaka, Pavamanas, and Suchi, and these had forty-five sons; altogether forty-nine persons, identical with the forty-nine fires, which forty-nine fires the Vayu Purana endeavours to discriminate. He is described in the Harivansa as clothed in black, having smoke for his standard and head-piece, and carrying a flaming javelin. He has four hands, and is borne in a chariot drawn by red horses, and the seven winds are the wheels of his car. He is accompanied by a ram, and sometimes he is represented riding on that animal. The representations of him vary.

The names and epithets of Agni are many—Vahni, Anala, Pavaka, Vaiswanara, son of Viswanara, the sun; Abja-hasta, 'lotus in hand;' Dhuma-ketu, 'whose sign is smoke;' Hutasa or Huta-bhuj, 'devourer of offerings;' Suchi or Sukra, 'the bright;' Rohitaswa, 'having red horses;' Chhaga-ratha, 'ramrider;' Jata-vedas; Sapta-jihva, 'seven-tongued;' Tomaradhara, 'javelin-bearer.'

AITAREYA: The name of a Brahmana, an Aranyaka, and an Upanishad of the Rigveda. The Brahmana has been edited and translated by Dr. Haug; the text of the Aranyaka has been published in the Bibliotheca Indica by Rajendra Lal, and there is another edition. The Upanishad has been translated by Dr. Roer in the same series. "The Aitareya Aranyaka consists of five books, each of which is called Aranyaka. The second and third books form a separate Upanishad, and a still further subdivision here takes place, in as much as the four last sections of the second book, which are particularly consonant with the doctrines of the Vedanta system, pass as the Aitareyopanishad." —Weber

AMRITA: 'Immortal', A god. The water of life. The term was known to the Vedas, and seems to have been applied to various things offered in sacrifice, but more especially to the soma juice. It is also called Nirjara and Piyusha. In later times it was the water of life produced at the churning of the ocean by the gods and demons, the legend of which is told with some variations in the Ramayana, the Mahabharata, and the Puranas. The gods, feeling their weakness, having been worsted by the demons, and being, according to one authority, under the ban of a holy sage, repaired to Vishnu, beseeching him for renewed vigour and the gift of immortality. He directed them to churn the ocean for the Amrita and other precious things which had been lost. The story as told in the Vishnu Purana has been rendered into verse by Professor Williams thus:-

The gods addressed the mighty Vishnu thus—
'Conquered in battle by the evil demons,
We fly to thee for succour, soul of all;
Pity, and by thy might deliver us!'
Hari, the lord, creator of the world,
Thus by the gods implored, all graciously
Replied—'Your strength shall be restored, ye gods;
Only accomplish what I now command.
Unite yourselves in peaceful combination
With these your foes; collect all plants and herbs
Of diverse kinds from every quarter; cast them
Into the sea of milk; take Mandara,
The mountain, for a churning stick, and Vasuki,
The serpent, for a rope; together churn
The ocean to produce the beverage—
Source of all strength and immortality—
Then reckon on my aid; I will take care
Your foes shall share your toil, but not partake
In its reward, or drink the immortal draught!
Thus by the god of gods advised, the host
United in alliance with the demons.

Straightway they gathered various herbs and cast them
Into the waters, then they took the mountain
To serve as churning-staff, and next the snake
To serve as cord, and in the ocean's midst
Hari himself, present in tortoise-form,
Became a pivot for the churning-staff.
Then did they churn the sea of milk; and first
Out of the waters rose the sacred Cow,
God-worshipped Surabhi, eternal fountain
Of milk and offerings of butter; next,
While holy Siddhas wondered at the sight,
With eyes all rolling, Varuni uprose,
Goddess of wine.

Then from the whirlpool sprang
Fair Parijata, tree of Paradise, delight

Of heaveuly maidens, with its fragrant blossoms
Perfuming the whole world. Th' Apsarasas,
Troop of celestial nymphs, matchless in grace,
Perfect in loveliness, were next produced.
Then from the sea uprose the cool-rayed moon,
Which Mahadeva seized; terrific poison
Next issued from the waters; this the snake-gods
Claimed as their own.
Then, seated on a lotus,
Beauty's bright goddess, peerless Sri, arose
Out of the waves; and with her, robed in white,
Came forth Dhanwnntari, the gods' physician.
High in his hand he bore the cup of nectar—
Life-giving draught—longed for by gods and demons!.
Then had the demons forcibly borne off
The cup, and drained the precious beverage,
Had not the mighty Vishnu interposed.
Bewildering them, he gave it to the gods;
Whereat, incensed, the demon troops assailed
'The host of heaven, but they with strength renewed,
Quaffing the draught, struck down their foes, who fell
Headlong through space to lowest depths of hell!"

There is an elaborate article on the subject in Goldstucker's Dictionary. In after-times, Vishnu's bird Garuda is said to have stolen the Amrita, but it was recovered by Indra.

ANGIRAS: A Rishi to whom many hymns of the Rigveda are attributed. He was one of the seven Maharshis or great Rishis, and also one of the ten Prajapatis or progenitors of mankind. In later times Angiras was one of the inspired lawgivers, and also a writer on astronomy. As an astronomical personification he is Brihaspati, the regent of the planet Jupiter, or the planet itself. He was also called "the priest of the gods," and "the lord of sacrifice." There is much ambiguity about the name. It comes from the same root as agni, 'fire,' and resembles that word in sound. This may be the reason why the name Angiras is used as an epithet or synonym of Agni.

The name is also employed as an epithet for the father of Agni, and it is found more especially connected with the hymns addressed to Agni, Indra, and the luminous deities. According to one statement, Angiras was the son of Uru by Agneyi, the daughter of Agni, although, as above stated, the name is sometimes given to the father of Agni. Another account represents that he was born from the mouth of Brahma. His wives were Smriti, 'memory,' daughter of Daksha; Sraddha, 'faith,' daughter of Kardama; and Swadha 'oblation,' and Sati, 'truth,' two other daughters of Daksha. His daughters were the Richas or Vaidik hymns, and his sons were the Manes called Havishmats. But he had other sons and daughters, and among the former were Utathya, Brihaspati, and Markandeya. According to the Bhagavata Purana, "he begot sons possessing Brahminical glory on the wife of Rathi-tara, a Kshatriya who was childless, and these persons were afterwards called descendants of Angiras."

ANGIRASAS: Descendants of Angiras. "They share in the nature of the legends attributed to Angiras. Angiras being the father of Agni, they are considered as descendants of Agni himself, who is also called the first of the Angirasas. Like Angiras, they occur in hymns addressed to the luminous deities, and, at a later period, they become for the most part personifications of light, of luminous bodies, of divisions of time, of celestial phenomena, and fires adapted to peculiar occasions, as the full and change of the moon, or to particular rites, as the Aswamedha, Rajasuya, etc. —Goldstucker

In the Satapatha Brahmana they and the Adityas are said to have descended from Prajapati, and that" they strove together for the priority in ascending to heaven."

Some descendants of Angiras by the Kshatriya wife of a childless king are mentioned in the Puranas as two tribes of Angirasas who were Brahmins as well as Kshatriyas.

The hymns of the Atharvaveda are called Angirasas, and the descendants of Angiras were specially charged with the protection of sacrifices performed in accordance with the Atharvaveda. From this cause, or from their being associated with the descendants of Atharvan, they were called distinctively Atharvangirasas.

ANIRUDDHA: 'Uncontrolled', Son of Pradyumna and grandson of Krishna. He married his cousin, Subhadra. A Daitya princess named Usha, daughter of Bana, fell in love with him, and had him brought by magic influence to her apartments in her father's city of Sonitapura. Bana sent some guards to wize him, but the valiant youth, taking an iron club, slew his assailants. Bana then brought his magic powers to bear and secured him. On discovering whither Aniruddha had been carried, Krishna, Balarama, and Pradyumna went to rescue him. A great battle was fought; Bana was aided by Siva and by Skanda, god of war, the former of whom was overcome by Krishna, and the latter was wounded by Garuda and Pradyumna. Bana was defeated, but his life was spared at the intercession of Siva, and Aniruddha was carried home to Dwaraka with Usba as his wife. He is also called Jhashanka and Ushapati He had a son named Vajra.

APASTAMBA: An ancient writer on ritual and law, author of Sutras connected with the Black Yajurveda and of a Dharma-sastra. He is often quoted in law-books. Two recensions of the Taittiriya Sanhita are ascribed to him or his school. The Sutras have been translated by Buhler, and are being reprinted in the Sacred Books of the East by Max Muller.

APSARAS: The Apsarases are the celebrated nymphs of Indra's heaven. The name, which signifies 'moving in the water,' has some-analogy to that of Aphrodite. They are not prominent in the Vedas, but Urvasi and a few others are mentioned. In Manu they are said to be the creations of the seven Manus. In the epic poems they become prominent, and the Ramayana and the Puranas attribute their origin to the churning of the ocean. It is said that when they came forth from the waters neither the gods nor the Asuras would have them for wives, so they became common to all. They have the appellations of Suranganas, 'wives of the gods,' and Sumad-atmajas, 'daughters of pleasure.'

> *"Then from the agitated deep up sprung*
> *The legion of Apsarases, so named*
> *That to the watery element they owed*
> *Their being. Myriads were they born, and all*
> *In vesture heavenly clad, and heavenly gems:*
> *Yet more divine their native semblance, rich*
> *With all the gifts of grace, of youth and beauty.*
> *A train innumerous followed; yet thus fair,*
> *Nor god nor demon sought their wedded love:*
> *Thus Raghava! they still remain—their charms*
> *The common treasure of the host of heaven."*

—Ramayana, Wilson

In the Puranas various ganas or classes of them are mentioned with distinctive names. The Vayu Purana enumerates fourteen, the Harivansa seven classes. They are again distinguished as being *daivika*, 'divine,' or *laukika*, 'worldly.' The former are said to be ten in number and the latter thirty-four, and these are the heavenly charmers who fascinated heroes, as Urvasi, and allured austere sages from their devotions and penances, as Menaka and Rambha. The Kasi-khanda says, "there are thirty-five millions of them, but only one thousand and sixty are the principal." The Apsarases, then, are fairylike beings, beautiful and voluptuous. They are the wives or the mistresses of the Gandharvas, and are not prudish in the dispensation of their favours. Their amours on earth have been numerous, and they are the rewards in Indra's paradise held out to heroes who fall in battle. They have the power of changing their forms; they are fond of dice, and give luck to whom they favour. In the Atharvaveda they are not so amiable; they are supposed to produce madness (love's madness?), and so there are charms and incantations for use against them. There is a long and exhaustive article on the Apsarases in Goldstucker's Dictionary, from which much of the above has been adapted. As regards their origin he makes the following speculative observations:—"Originally these divinities seem to have been personifications of the vapours which are attracted by the sun and form into mist or clouds; their character may be thus interpreted in the few hymns of the Rigveda where mention is made of them. At a subsequent period...(their attributes expanding with those of their associates the Gandharvas), they became divinities which represent phenomena or objects both of a physical and ethical kind closely associated with that life" (the elementary life of heaven).

ARANYAKA: 'Belonging to the forest.' Certain religious and philosophical writings which expound the mystical sense of the ceremonies, discuss the nature of God. They are attached to the Brahmanas, and intended for study in the forest by Brahmins who have retired from the distractions of the world. There are four of them extant: 1. Brihad; 2. Tattiriya; 3. Aitareya; and 4. Kaushitaki Aranyaka. The Aranyakas are closely connected with the Upanishads, and the names are occasionally used interchangeably: thus the Brihad is called indifferently Brihad Aranyaka or Brihad Aranyaka Upanishad; it is attached to the Satapatha Brahmins. The Aitareya Upanishad is a part of the Aitareya Brahmins, and the Kaushitaki Aranyaka consists of three chapters, of which the third is the Kaushitaki Upanishad. "Traces of modern ideas (says Max Muller) are not wanting in the Aranyakas, and the very fact that they are destined for a class of men who had retired from the world in order to give themselves up to the contemplation of the highest problems, shows an advanced and already declining and decaying society, not unlike the monastic age of the Christian world....In one sense the Aranyakas are old, for they reflect the very dawn of thought; in another they are modern, for they speak of that dawn with all the experience of a past day. There are passages in these works unequalled in any language for grandeur, boldness, and simplicity. These passages are the relics of a better age. But the generation which became the chronicler of those Titanic wars of thought was a small race; they were dwarfs, measuring the footsteps of departed giants."

ARJUNA: 'White.' The name of the third Pandu prince. All the five brothers were of divine paternity, and Arjuna's father was Indra, hence he is called Aindri. A brave warrior, high-minded, generous, upright, and handsome, the most prominent and the most amiable and interesting of the five brothers. He was taught the use of arms by Drona, and was his favourite pupil. By his skill in arms he won Draupadi at her Swayamvara. For an involuntary transgression he imposed upon himself twelve years' exile from his family, and during that time he visited Parsurama, who gave him instruction in the use of arms. He at this period formed a connectjon with Ulupi, a Naga princess, and by her had a son named Iravat. He also married Chitrangada, the daughter of the king of Manipura, by whom he had a son named Babhruvahana. He visited Krishna at Dwaraka, and there he married Subhadra, the sister of Krishna. By her he had a son named Abhimanyu.

Afterwards he obtained the bow Gandiva from the god Agni, with which to fight against Indra, and he assisted Agni in burning the Khandava forest. When Yudhishthira lost the kingdom by gambling, and the five brothers went into exile for thirteen years, Arjuna proceeded on a pilgrimage to the Himalayas to propitiate the gods, and to obtain from them celestial weapons for use in the contemplated war against the Kauravas. There he fought with Siva, who appeared in the guise of a Kirata or mountaineer; but Arjuna, having found out the true character of his adversary, worshipped him, and Siva gave him the Pasupata, one of his most powerful weapons. Indra, Varuna, Yama, and Kuvera came to him, and also presented him with their own peculiar weapons. Indra, his father, carried him in his car to his heaven and to his capital Amaravati, where Arjuna spent some years in the practice of arms. Indra sent him against the Daityas of the sea, whom he vanquished, and then returned victorious to Indra, who "presented him with a chain of gold and a diadem, and with a war-shell which sounded like thunder."

In the thirteenth year of exile he entered the service of Raja Virata, disguised as an eunuch, and acted as music and dancing master, but in the end he took a leading part in defeating the king's enemies, the king of Trigarta and the Kaurava princes, many of whose leading warriors he vanquished in single combat. Preparations for the great struggle with the Kauravas now began. Arjuna obtained the personal assistance of Krishna, who acted as his charioteer, and, before the great battle began, related to him the Bhagavadgita. On the tenth day of the battle he mortally wounded Bhishma, on the twelfth he defeated Susarman and his four brothers; on the fourteenth he killed Jayadratha; on the seventeenth, he was so stung by some reproaches of his brother, Yudhishthira, that he would have killed him had not Krishna interposed. On the same day he fought with Kama, who had made a vow to slay him. He was near being vanquished when an accident to Kama's chariot gave Arjuna the opportunity of killing him.

After the defeat of the Kauravas, Aswatthama, son of Drona, and two others, who were the sole survivors, made a night attack on the camp of the Pandavas, and murdered their children. Arjuna pursued Aswatthama, and made him give up the precious jewel which he wore upon his head as an amulet.

When the horse intended for Yudhishthira's Aswamedha sacrifice was let loose, Arjuna, with his army, followed it through many cities and countries, and fought with many Rajas. He entered the country of Trigarta, and had to fight his way through. He fought also against Vajradatta, who had a famous elephant, and against the Saindhavas. At the city of Manipura he fought with his own son, Babhruvahana, and was killed; but he was restored to life by a Naga charm supplied by his wife Ulupi. Afterwards he penetrated into the Dakshina or south country, and fought with the Nishadas and Dravidians: then went westwards to Gujarat, and finally conducted the horse back to Hastinapura, where the great sacrifice was performed.

He was subsequently called to Dwaraka by Krishna amid the internecine struggles of the Yadavas, and there he performed the funeral ceremonies of Vasudeva and of Krishna. Soon after this he retired from the world to the Himalayas. (See Mahabharata.) He had a Son named Iravat by the serpent nymph Ulupi; Bhabhruvahana, by the daughter of the king of Manipura, became king of that country; Abhimanyu, born of his wife Subhadra, was killed in the great battle, but the kingdom of Hastinapura descended to his son Parikshit. Arjuna has many appellations: Bibhatsu, Guda-kesa, Dhananjaya, Jishnu, Kiritin, Paka-sasani, Phalguna, Savya-sachin, Swetavahana, and Partha.

ARYABHATA: The earliest known Hindu writer on algebra, and, according to Colebrooke, "if not the inventor, the improver of that analysis," which has made but little advance in India since. He was born, according to his own account, at Kusumapura (Patna), in A.D. 476, and composed his first astronomical work at the early age of twenty-three. His larger work, the *Arya Siddhanta*, was produced at a riper age. He is probably the Andubarius (Ardubarius?) of the *Chronichon*

Paschale, and the Arjabahr of the Arabs. Two of his works, the *Dasagitisutra* and *Aryashtasata*, have been edited by Kern under the title of *Aryabhatiya*. There is another and later astronomer of the same name, distinguished as Laghu Aryabhata, i.e., Aryabhata the Less.

ASHTAVAKRA: A Brahmin, the son of Kahoda, whose story is told in the Mahabharata. Kahoda married a daughter of his preceptor, Uddalaka, but he was so devoted to study that he neglected his wife. When she was far advanced in her pregnancy, the unborn son was provoked at his father's neglect of her, and rebuked him for it. Kahoda was angry at the child's impertinence, and condemned him to be born crooked; so he came forth with his eight (ashta) limbs crooked (vakra); hence his name. Kahoda went to a great sacrifice at the court of Janaka, king of Mithila. There was present there a great Buddhist sage, who challenged disputations, upon the understanding that whoever was overcome in argument should be thrown into the river. This was the fate of many, and among them of Kahoda, who was drowned.

In his twelfth year Ashtavakra learned the manner of his father's death, and set out to avenge him. The lad was possessed of great ability and wisdom. He got the better of the sage who had worsted his father, and insisted that the sage should be thrown into the water. The sage then declared himself to be a son of Varuna, god of the waters, who had sent him to obtain Brahmins for officiating at a sacrifice by overpowering them in argument and throwing them into the water. When all was explained and set right, Kahoda directed his son to bathe in the Samanga river, on doing which the lad became perfectly straight.

A story is told in the Vishnu Purana that Ashtavakra was standing in water performing penances when he was seen by some celestial nymphs and worshipped by them. He was pleased, and told them to ask a boon. They asked for the best of men as a husband. He came out of the water and offered himself. When they saw him, ugly and crooked in eight places, they laughed in derision. He was angry, and as he could not recall his blessing, he said that, after obtaining it, they should fall into the hands of thieves.

ASOKA: A celebrated king of the Maurya dynasty of Magadha, and grandson of its founder, Chandragupta. This king is the most celebrated of any in the annals of the Buddhists. In the commencement of his reign he followed the Brahminical faith, but became a convert to that of Buddha, and a zealous encourager of it. He is said to have maintained in his palace 64,000 Buddhist priests, and to have erected 84,000 columns (or topes) throughout India. A great convocation of Buddhist priests was held in the eighteenth year of his reign, which was followed by missions to Ceylon and other places. He reigned for thirty-six years, from about 234 to 198 B.C., and exercised authority more or less direct from Afghanistan to Ceylon. This fact is attested by a number of very curious Pali inscriptions found engraven upon rocks and pillars, all of them of the same purport, and some of them almost identical in words, the variations showing little more than dialectic differences.

That found at Kapur-di-giri, in Afghanistan, is in the Bactrian Pali character, written from right to left; all the others are in the Indian Pali character, written from left to right. The latter is the oldest known form of the character now in use in India, but the modern letters have departed so far from their proto types that it required all the acumen and diligence of James Prinsep to decipher the ancient forms. These inscriptions show a great tenderness for animal life, and are Buddhist in their character, but they do not enter upon the distinctive peculiarities of that religion. The name of Asoka never occurs in them; the king who set them up is called Piyadasi (Sans.

Priyadarsi), 'the beautiful,' and he is entitled Devanampiya, 'the beloved of the gods.' Buddhist writings identify this Piyadasi with Asoka, and little or no doubt is entertained of the two names representing the same person.

One of the most curious passages in these inscriptions refers to the Greek king Antiochus, calling him and three others: Turamayo, Antakana, Mako, and Alikasunari, which represent Ptolemy, Antigonus, Magas, and Alexander. The date of Asoka is not exactly that of Antiochus the Great, but it is not very far different; and the corrections required to make it correspond are no more than the inexact manner in which both Brahminical and Buddhist chronology is preserved may well be expected to render necessary.

ASURA: 'Spiritual, divine.' In the oldest parts of the Rig. veda this term is used for the supreme spirit, and is the same as the Ahura of the Zoroastrians. In the sense of 'god' it was applied to several of the chisf deities, as to Indra, Agni, and Varuna. It afterwards acquired an entirely opposite meaning, and came to signify, as now, a demon or enemy of the gods. The word is found with this signification in the later parts of the Rigveda, particularly in the last book, and also in the Atharvaveda. The Brahmanas attach the same meaning to it, and record many contests between the Asuras and the gods. According to the Taittiriya Brahmana, the breath (asu) of Prajapati became alive, and "with that breath he created the Asuras." In another part of the same work it is said that Prajapati "became pregnant. He created Asuras from his abdomen." The Satapatha Brahmana accords with the former statement, and states that "he created Asuras from his lower breath." The Taittiriya Aranyaka represents that Prajapati created gods, men, fathers, Gandharvas, and Apsarases" from water, and that the Asuras, Rakshasas, and Pisachas sprang from the drops which were spilt. Manu's statement is that they were created by the Prajapatis. According to the Vishnu Purana, they were produced from the groin of Brahma (Prajapati). The account of the Vayu Purana is: "Asuras were first produced as sons from his (Prajapati's) groin. Asu is declared by Brahmins to mean breath. From it these beings were produced; hence they are Asuras." The word has long been used as a general name for the enemies of the gods, including the Daityas and Danavas and other descendants of Kasyapa, but not including the Rakshasas descended from Pulastya. In this sense a different derivation has been found for it: the source is no longer asu, 'breath,' but the initial a is taken as the negative prefix, and a-sura signifies 'not a god;' hence, according to some, arose the word sura, commonly used for a 'god.'

ASWAMEDHA: 'The sacrifice of a horse.' This is a sacrifice which, in Vedic times, was performed by kings desirous of offspring. The horse was killed with certain ceremonies, and the wives of the king had to pass the night by its carcass. Upon the chisf wife fell the duty of going through a revolting formality which can only be hinted at. Subsequently, as in the time of the Mahabharata, the sacrifice obtained a high importance and significance. It was performed only by kings, and implied that he who instituted it was a conqueror and king of kings. It was believed that the performance of one hundred such sacrifices would enable a mortal king to overthrow the throne of Indra, and to become the ruler of the universe and sovereign of the gods. A horse of a particular colour was consecrated by the performance of certain ceremonies, and was then turned loose to wander at will for a year. The king, or his representative, followed the horse with an army, and when the animal entered a foreign country, the ruler of that country was bound either to fight or to submit. If the liberator of the horse succeeded in obtaining or enforcing the submission of all the countries over which it passed, he returned in triumph with the vanquished Rajas in his train; but if he failed, he was disgraeed and his pretensions ridiculed. After the successful return a great festiyal was held, at which the horse was sacrificed, either really or figuratively.

ASWATTHAMA: Son of Drona and Kripa, and one of the generals of the Kauravas. Also called by his patronymic Draunayana. After the last great battle, in which Duryodhana was mortally wounded, Aswatthama with two other warriors, Kripa and Kritavarman, were the sole survivors of the Kaurava host that were left effective. Aswatthama was made the commander. He was fierce in his hostility to the Pandavas, and craved for revenge upon Dhrishtadyumna, who had slain his father, Drona. These three surviving Kauravas entered the Pandava camp at night. They found Dhrishtadyumna asleep, and Aswatthama stamped him to death as he lay. He then killed Sikhandi, the other son of Drupada, and he also killed the five young sons of the Pandavas and carried their heads to the dying Duryodhana.

He killed Parikshit, while yet unborn in the womb of his mother, with his celestial weapon Brahmastra, by which he incurred the curse of Krishna, who restored Parikshit to life. On the next morning he and his comrades fled, but Draupadi clamoured for revenge upon the murderer of her children. Yudhishthira represented that Aswatthama, was a Brahmin, and pleaded for his life. She then consented to forego her demand for his blood if the precious and protective jewel which he wore on his head were brought to her. Bhima, Arjuna, and Krishna then went in pursuit of him. Arjuna and Krishna overtook him, and compelled him to give up the jewel. They carried it to Draupadi, and she gave it to Yudhishthira, who afterwards wore it on his head.

ASWINS, ASWINAU (dual), ASWINI KUMARAS: 'Horsemen.' Two Vedic deities, twin sons of the Sun or the sky. They are ever young and handsome, bright, and of golden brilliancy, agile, swift as falcons, and possessed of many forms; and they ride in a golden car drawn by horses or birds, as harbingers of Ushas, the dawn. "They are the earliest bringers of light in the morning sky, who in their chariot hasten onwards before the dawn and prepare the way for her." —Roth.

As personifications of the morning twilight, they are said to be children of the sun by a nymph who concealed herself in the form of a mare; hence she was called Aswini and her son Aswins. But inasmuch as they precede the rise of the sun, they are called his parents in his form Pushan. Mythically, they are the parents of the Pandu princes Nakula and Sahadeva. Their attributes are numerous, but relate mostly to youth and beauty, light and speed, duality, the curative power, and active benevolence. The number of hymns addressed to them testify to the enthusiastic worship they received. They were the physicians of Swarga, and in this character are called Dasras and Nasatyas, Gadagadau and Swar-vaidyau; or one was Dasra and the other Nasatya. Other of their appellations are Abdhijau, 'ocean, born;' Pushkara-srajau, 'wreathed with lotuses-Badaveyau, sons of the submarine fire, Badava. Many instances are recorded of their benevolence and their power of healing. They restored the sage Chyavana to youth, and prolonged his life when he had become old and decrepit, and through his instrumentality they were admitted to partake of the libations of soma, like the other gods, although Indra strongly opposed them. The Aswins, says Muir, "have been a puzzle to the oldest commentators," who have differed widely in their explanations. According to different interpretations quoted in the Nirukta, they were "heaven and earth," "day and night," "two kings, performers of holy acts." The following is the view taken of them by Professor Goldstucker, as printed in Muir's Texts, vol. v.:—

"The myth of the Aswins is, in my opinion, one of that

class of myths in which two distinct elements, the cosmical and the human or historical, have gradually become blended into one. It seems necessary, therefore, to separate these two elements in order to arrive at an understanding of the myth. The historical or human element in it, I believe, is represented by those legends which refer to the wonderful cures effected by the Aswins, and to their performances of a kindred sort; the cosmical element is that relating to their luminous nature. The link which connects both seems to be the mysteriousness of the nature and effects of the phenomena of light and of the healing art at a remote antiquity. That there might have been some horsemen or warriors of great renown, who inspired their contemporaries with awe by their wonderful deeds, and more especially by their medical skill, appears to have been also the opinion of some old commentators mentioned by Yaska in the Nirukta. For some 'legendary writers,' he says, took them for 'two kings, performers of holy acts,' and the view seems likewise borne out by the legend in which it is narrated that the gods refused the Aswins' admittance to a sacrifice on the ground that they had been on too familiar terms with men. It would appear, then, that these Aswins, like the Ribhus, were originally renowned mortals, who, in the course of time, were translated into the companionship of the gods.

"The luminous character of the Aswins can scarcely be a matter of doubt, for the view of some commentators, recorded by Yaska, according to which they are identified with heaven and earth,' appears not to be countenanced by any of the passages known to us. Their very name, it would seem, settles this point, since Aswa, the horse, literally 'the pervader,' is always the symbol of the luminous deities, especially of the sun.

"It seems to be the opinion of Yaska that the Aswins represent the transition from darkness to light, when the intermingling of both produces that inseparable duality expressed by the twin nature of these deities. And this interpretation, I hold, is the best that can be given of the character of the cosmical Aswins. It agrees with the epithets by which they are invoked, and with the relationship in which they are placed. They are young, yet also ancient, beautiful, bright, swift, etc.; and their negative character, the result of the alliance of light with darkness, is, I believe, expressed by Dasra, the destroyer, and also by the two negatives in the compound Nasatya (na + a-satya); though their positive character is again redeemed by the ellipsis of 'enemies, or diseases' to Dasra, and by the sense of Nasatya, not untrue, i.e., truthful."

ATRI: 'An eater.' A Rishi, and author of many Vedic hymns. " A Maharshi or great saint, who in the Vedas occurs especially in hymns composed for the praise of Agni, Indra, the Aswins, and the Viswedevas. In the epic period he is considered as one of the ten Prajapatis or lords of creation engendered by Manu for the purpose of creating the universe; at a later period he appears as a mind-born son of Brahma, and as one of the seven Rishis who preside over the reign of Swayambhuva, the first Manu, or, according to others, of Swarochisha, the second, or of Vaivaswata, the seventh. He married Anasuya, daughter of Daksha, and their son was Durvasas."—Goldstucker. In the Ramayana an account is given of the visit paid by Rama and Sita to Atri and Anasuya in their hermitage south of Chitrakuta. In the Puranas he was also father of Soma, the moon, and the ascetic Dattatreya by his wife Anasuya. As a Rishi he is one of the stars of the Great Bear.

AVATARA: 'A descent.' The incarnation of a deity, especidally of Vishnu. The first indication, not of an Avatara, but of what subsequently developed into an Avatara, is found in the Rigveda in the "three steps" of "Vishnu, the unconquerable preserver," who strode over this universe," and "in three places planted his step." The early commentators understood the "three places" to be the earth, the atmosphere, and the sky; that in the earth Vishnu was fire, in the air lightning, end in the sky the solar light. One commentator, Aurnavabha, whose name deserves mention, took a more philosophical view of the matter, and interpreted "the three steps "as being" the different positions of the sun at his rising, culmination, and setting." Sayana, the great commentator, who lived in days when the god Vishnu had obtained pre-eminence, understood "the three steps" to be "the three steps" taken by that god in his incarnation of Vamana the dwarf, to be presently noticed. Another reference to "three strides" and to a sort of Avatara is made in the Taittiriya Sanhita, where it is said, "Indra, assuming the form of a she-jackal, stepped all round the earth in three strides. Thus the, gods obtained it."

Boar Incarnation: In the Taittiriya Sanhita and Brahmana, and also in the Satapatha Brahmana, the creator Prajapati, afterwards known as Brahma, took the form of a boar for the purpose of raising the earth out of the boundless waters. The Sanhita says, "This universe was formerly waters, fluid. On it Prajapati, becoming wind, moved. He saw this earth. Becoming a boar, he took her up. Becoming Viswakarman, he wiped the moisture from her. She extended. She became the extended one Prithvi. From this the earth derives her designation as 'the extended one.' The Brahmana is in accord as to the illimitable waters, and adds, "Prajapati practised arduous devotion saying, How shall this universe be developed? He beheld a lotus leaf standing. He thought, There is somewhat on which this lotus leaf rests. He, as a boar—having assumed that form—plunged beneath towards it. He found the earth down below. Breaking off a portion of her, he rose to the surface, He then extended it on the lotus leaf. Inasmuch as he extended it, that is the extension of the extended one the earth. This became *abhut.* From this the earth derives its name of Bhumi." Further, in the Taittiriya Aranyaka it is said that the earth was "raised by a black boar with a hundred arms." The Satapatha Brahmana states, "She the earth was only so large, of the size of a span. A boar called Emasha raised her up. Her lord, Prajapati, in consequence prospers him with this pair and makes him complete." In the Ramayana also it is stated that Brahma "became a boar and raised up the earth."

Kurma or Tortoise: In the Satapatha Brahmana it is said that "Prajapati, having assumed the form of a tortoise (Kurma), created offspring. That which he created he made (*akarot*); hence the word Kurma."

Fish Incarnation: The earliest mention of the fish Avatara occurs in the Satapatha Brahmana, in connection with the Hindu legend of the deluge. Manu found, in the water which was brought to him for his ablutions, a small fish, which spoke to him and said, "I will save thee" from a flood which shall sweep away all creatures. This fish grew to a large size, and had to be consigned to the ocean, when he directed Manu to construct a ship and to resort to him when the flood should rise. The deluge came, and Manu embarked in the ship. The fish then swam to Manu, who fastened the vessel to the fish's horn, and was conducted to safety. The Mahabharsta repeats this story with some variations.

The incarnations of the boar, the tortoise, and the fish are thus in the earlier writings represented as manifestations of Prajapati or Brahma. The "three steps" which form the germ of the dwarf incarnation are ascribed to Vishnu, but even these appear to be of an astronomical or mythical character rather than glorifications of a particular deity. In the Mahabharsta Vishnu has become the most prominent of the gods, and some of his incarnations are more or less distinctly noticed; but it is in the Puranas that they receive their full development. According to the generally received account, the inarnations of Vishnu are ten in number, each of them being assumed by Vishnu, the great preserving power, to save the world from some great danger or trouble.

1. Matsya: 'The fish.' This is an appropriation to Vishnu of the ancient legend of the fish and the deluge, as related in the Satapatha Brahmana, and quoted above. The details of this Avatara vary slightly in different Puranas. The object of the incarnation was to save Vaivaswata, the seventh Manu, and progenitor of the human race, from destruction by a deluge. A small fish came into the hands of Manu and besought his protection. He carefully guarded it, and it grew rapidly until nothing but the ocean could contain it. Manu then recognised its divinity, and worshipped the deity Vishnu thus incarnate. The god apprised Manu of the approaching cataclysm, and bade him prepare for it. When it came, Manu embarked in a ship with the Rishis, and with the seeds of all existing things." Vishnu then appeared as the fish with a most stupendous horn. The ship was bound to this horn with the great serpent as with a rope; and was secured in safety until the waters had subsided. The Bhagavata Purana introduces a new feature. In one of the nights of Brahma, and during his repose, the earth and the other worlds were submerged in the ocean. Then the demon Haya-griva drew near, and carried off the Veda which had issued from Brahma's mouth. To recover the Veda thus lost, Vishnu assumed the form of a fish, and saved Manu as above related. But this Purana adds, that the fish instructed Manu and the Rishis in "the true doctrine of the soul of the eternal Brahma;" and, when Brahma awoke at the end of this dissolution of the universe, Vishnu slew Hayagriva and restored the Veda to Brahma.

2. Kurma: 'The tortoise.' The germ of this Avatara is found in the Satapatha Brahmana, as above noticed. In its later and developed form, Vishnu appeared in the form of a tortoise in the Satya-yuga, or first age, to recover some things of value which had been lost in the deluge. In the form of a tortoise he placed himself at the bottom of the sea of milk, and made his back the base or pivot of the mountain Mandara. The gods and demons twisted the great serpent Vasuki round the mountain, and, dividing into two parties, each took an end of the snake as a rope, and thus churned the sea until they recovered the desired objects. These were—(1.) Amrita, the water of life; (2.) Dhanwantari, the physician of the gods and bearer of the cup of Amrita; (3.) Lakshmi, goddess of fortune and beauty, and consort of Vishnu; (4.) Sura, goddess of wine; (5.) Chandra, the moon; (6.) Rambha, a nymph, and pattern of a lovely and amiable woman; (7.) Uchchaih-sravas, a wonderful and model horse; (8.) Kaustubha, a celebrated jewel; (9.) Parijata, a celestial tree; (10.) Surabhi, the cow of plenty; (11.) Airavata, a wonderful model elephant; (12.) Sankha, a shell, the conch of victory; (13.) Dhanus, a famous bow; and (14.) Visha, poison.

3. Varaha: 'The boar.' The old legend of the Brahmanas concerning the boar which raised the earth from the waters has been appropriated to Vishnn. A demon named Hiranyaksha had dragged the earth to the bottom of the sea. To recover it Vishnu assumed the form of a boar, and after a contest of a thousand years he slew the demon and raised up the earth.

4. Narasinha, or Nrisinha: 'The man-lion.' Vishnu assumed this form to deliver the world from the tyranny of Hiranyakasipu, a demon who, by the favour of Brahma, had become invulnerable, and was secure from gods, men, and animals. This demon's son, named Prahlada, worshipped Vishnu, which so incensed his father that he tried to kill him, but his efforts were all in vain. Contending with his son as to the omnipotence and omnipresence of Vishnu, Hiranyakasipu demanded to know if Vishnu was present in a stone pillar of the hall, and struck it violently. To avenge Prahlada, and to vindicate his offended majesty, Vishnu came forth from the pillar as the Narasinha, half-man and half-lion, and tore the arrogant Daitya king to pieces.

These four incarnations are supposed to have appeared in the Satya-yuga, or first age of the world.

5. Vamana: 'The dwarf.' The origin of this incarnation is "the three strides of Vishnu," spoken of in the Rigveda, as before explained. In the Treta-yuga, or second age, the Daitya king Bali had, by his devotions and austerities, acquired the dominion of the three worlds, and the gods were shorn of their power and dignity. To remedy this, Vishnu was born as a diminutive son of Kasyapa and Aditi The dwarf appeared before Bali, and begged of him as much land as he could step over in three paces. The generous monarch complied with the request. Vishnu took two strides over heaven and earth; but respecting the virtues of Bali, he then stopped, leaving the dominion of Patala, or the infernal regions, to Bali.

The first five incarnations are thus purely mythological; in the next three we have the heroic element, and in the ninth the religious.

6. Parasurama: 'Rama with the axe.' Born in the Treta, or second age, as son of the Brahmin Jamadagni, to deliver the Brahmins from the arrogant dominion of the Kshatriyas.

7. Rama or Ramachandra: 'The moon-like or gentle Rama, the hero of the Ramayana.' He was the son of Dasaratha, king of Ayodhya, of the Solar race, and was born in the Treta-yuga, or second age, for the purpose of destroying the demon Ravana.

8. Krishna: ' The black or dark coloured.' This is the most popular of all the later deities, and has obtained such pre-eminence, that his votaries look upon him not simply as an incarnation, but as a perfect manifestation of Vishnu. When Krishna is thus exalted to the full godhead, his elder brother, Balarama takes his place as the eighth Avatara.

9. Buddha: The great success of Buddha as a religious teacher seems to have induced the Brahmins to adopt him as their own, rather than to rccognise him as an adversary. So Vishnu is said to have appeared as Buddha to encourage demons and wicked men to despise the Vedas, reject caste, and deny the existence of the gods, and thus to effect their own destruction.

10. Kalki: 'The white horse.' This incarnation of Vishnu is to appear at the end of the Kali or Iron Age, seated on a white horse, with a drawn sword blazing like a comet, for the final destruction of the wicked, the renovation of creation, and the restoration of purity.

The above are the usually recognised Avataras, but the number is sometimes extended, and the Bhagavata Purana, which is the most fervid of all the Puranas in its glorification of Vishnu, enumerates twenty-two incarnations:—(1.) Purusha, the male, the progenitor; (2.) Varaha, the boar; (3.) Narada, the grea: sage; (4.) Nara and Narayana; (5.) Kapila, the great sage; (6.) Dattatreya, a sage; (7.) Yajna, sacrifice; (8.) Rishabha, a righteous king, father of Bharata; (9.) Prithu, a king; (10.) Matsya, the fish; (11.) Kurma, the tortoise; (12 and 13) Dhanwantari, the physician of the gods; (14.) Narasinha, the man-lion; (15.) Vamana, the dwarf; (16.) Parasurama; (17.) Veda-Vyasa; (18.) Rama; (19.) Balarama; (20.) Krishna; (21.) Buddha; (22.) Kalki. But after this it adds—"The incarnations of Vishnu are innumerable, like the rivulets flowing from an inexhaustible lake. Rishis,Manus, gods, sons of Manus, Prajapatis, are all portions of him."

B

BALARAMA: (Balabhadra and Baladeva are other forms of this name.) The elder brother of Krishna. When Krishna is regarded as a full manifestation of Vishnu, Balarama is reeognised as the seventh Avatara or incarnation in his place. According to this view, which is the favourite one of the Vaishnavas, Krishna is a full divinity and Balarama an incarnation; but the story of their birth, as told in the Mahabharata, places them more upon an equality. It says that Vishnu took two hairs, a white and a black one, and that these became Balarama and Krishna, the children of Devaki. Balarama was of fair complexion, Krishna was very dark. As soon as Balarama was born, he was carried away to Gokula to preserve his life from the tyrant Kansa, and he was there nurtured by Nanda as a child of Rohini. He and Krishna grew up together, and he took part in many of Krishna's boyish frcaks and adventures.

His earliest exploit was the killing of the great Asura Dhenuka, who had the form of an ass. This demon attacked him, but Balarama seized his assailant, whirled him round by his legs till he was dead, and cast his carcass into a tree. Another Asura attempted to carry off Balarama on his shoulders, but the boy beat out the demon's brains with his fists. When Krishna wenl to Mathura, Balarama accompanied him, and manfully supported him till Kansa was killed. Once, when Balarama was intoxicated, he called upon the Yamuna river to come to him, that he might bathe; but his command not being heeded, he plunged his ploughshare into the river, and dragged the waters whithersoever he went, until they were obliged to assume a human form and beseech his forgiveness. This action gained for him the title Yamuna-bhid and Kalindi-karshana, breaker or dragger of the Yamuna. He killed Rukmin in a gambling brawl. When Samba, son of Krishna, was detained as a prisoner at Hastinapur by Duryodhana, Balarama demanded his release, and, being refused, he thrust his ploughshare under the ramparts of the city, and drew them towards him, thus compelling the Kaura-vas to give up their prisoner. Lastly, he killed the great ape Dwivida, who had stolen his weapons and derided him.

Such are some of the chisf incidents of the life of Balarama, as recited in the Puranas, and as popular among the votaries of Krishna. In the Mahabharata he has more of a human character. He taught both Duryodhana and Bhima the use of the mace. Though inclining to the side of the Pandavas, he refused to take an active part either with them or the Kauravas. He witnessed the combat between Duryodhana and Bhima, and beheld the foul blow struck by the latter, which made him so indignant that he seized his weapons, and was with difficulty restrained by Krishna from falling upon the Pandavas. He died just before Krishna, as he sat under a banyan tree in the outskirts of Dwaraka.

Another view is held as to the origin of Balarama. According to this, he was an incarnation of the great serpent Sesha, and when he died the serpent is said to have issued from his mouth.

The "wine-loving" Balarama (Madhu-priya or Priya-madhu) was as much addicted to wine as his brother Krishna was devoted to the fair sex. He was also irascible in temper, and sometimes quarrelled even with Krishna: the Puranas represent them as having a serious difference about the Syamantaka jewel. He had but one wife, Revati, daughter of King Raivata, and was faithful to her. By her he had two sons, Nisatha and Ulmuka. He is represented as of fair complexion, and, as Nila-vastra, 'clad in a dark-blue vest.' His especial weapons are a club (*khetaka* or *saunanda*), the ploughshare (hala), and the pestle (*musala*), from which he is called Phala and Hala, also Halayudha, 'plough-armed;' Halabhrit, 'plough-bearer;' Langali and Sankarshana, 'ploughman;' and Musali, 'pestle-holder.' As he has a palm for a banner, he is called Tala-dhwaja. Other of his appellations are Guptachara, 'who goes secretly;' Kampala and Samvartaka.

BALI: A good and virtuous Daitya king. He was son of Virochana, son of Prahlada, son of Hiranyakasipu. His wife was Vindhyavali. Through his devotion and penance he defeated Indra, humbled the gods, and extended his authority over the three worlds: The gods appealed to Vishnu for protection, and ho became manifest in his Dwarf Avatara for the purpose of restraining Bali. This dwarf craved from Bali the boon of three steps of ground, and, having obtained it, he stepped over heaven and earth in two strides; but then, out of respect to Bali's kindness and his grandson Prahlada's virtues, he stopped short, and left to him Patala, the infernal regions. Bali is also called Mahabali, and his capital was Mahabalipura. The germ of the legend of the three steps is found in the Rigveda, where Vishnu is represented as taking three steps over earth, heaven, and the lower regione, typifying perhaps the rising, culmination, and Setting of the sun.

BHAGAVAD-GITA: 'The song of the Divine One.' A celebrated episode of the Mahabharata, in the form of a metrical dialogue, in which the divine Krishna is the chisf speaker, aud expounds to Arjuna his philosophical doctrines. The author of the work is unknown, but he "was probably a Brahmin, and nominally a Vaishnava, but really a philosopher and thinker, whose mind was cast in a broad mould." This poem has been interpolated in the Mahabharata, for it is of much later date than the body of that epic; it is later also than the six Darsanas or philosophical schools, for it has received inspiration from them all, especially from the Sankhya, Yoga, and Vedanta. The second or third century A.D. has been proposed as the probable time of its appearance.

Krishna, as a god, is a manifstation of Vishnu; but in this song, and in other places, he is held to be the supreme being. As man, he was related to both the Pandavas and the Kauravas, and in the great war between these two families he refused to take up arms on either side. But he consented to act as the Pandava Arjuna's charioteer. When the opposing hosts were drawn up in array against each other, Arjuna, touched with compunction for the approaching slaughter of kindred and friends, appeals to Krishna for guidance. This gives the occasion for the philosophical teaching.

The poem is divided into three sections, each containing six chapters, the philosophical teaching in each being somewhat distinct, but undoubtedly the main design of the poem, the sentiments expressed in which have exerted a powerful influence throughout India for the last so many years, is to inculcate the doctrine of Bhakti (faith), and to exalt the duties of caste above all other obligations, including those of friendship and kindred. So Arjuna is told to do his duty as a soldier without heeding the slaughter of friends. In the second division of the poem the Pantheistic doctrines of the Vedanta are more directly inculcated than in the other sections. Krishna here, in the plainest language, claims adoration as one with the great universal spirit pervading and constituting the universe. The langnage of this poem is exceedingly beautiful, and its tone and sentiment of a very lofty character, so that they have a striking effect even in the prose translation. It was one of the earliest Sanskrit works translated into English by Wilkins; but a much more perfect translation, with an excellent introduction, has since been published by Mr. J. Cockburn Thompson, from which much of the above has been borrowed. There are several other translations in French, German, etc.

BHAGAVATA PURANA: The Purana "in which ample details of duty are described, and which opens with an extract from the Gayatri; that in which the death of the Asura Vritra is told, and in which the mortals and immortals of the Saraswata Kalpa, with the events that then happened to them in the world, are related, that is celebrated as the Bhagavata, and consists of 18,000 verses." Such is the Hindu description of this work. "The Bhagavata," says Wilson, "is a work of great celebrity in India, and exercises a more direct and powerful influence upon the opinions and feelings of the people than perhaps any other of the Puranas. It is placed fifth in all the lists, but the Padma ranks it as the eighteenth, as the extracted substance of all the rest. According to the usual specification, it consists of 18,000 slokas, distributed amongst 332 chapters, divided into twelve skandhas or books. It is named Bhagavata from its being dedicated to the glorification of Bhagavata or Vishnu." The most popular and characteristic part of this Purana is the tenth book, which narrates in detail the history of Krishna, and has been translated into perhaps all the vernacular languages of India. Colebrooke concurs in the opinion of many learned Hindus that this Purana is the composition of the grammarian Vopadeva, who lived about six or seven centuries ago at the court of Hemadri, Raja of Devagiri (Deogarh or Daulatabad), and Wilson sees no reason for calling in question the tradition which assigns the work to this writer. This Purana has been translated into French by Burnouf, and has been published with the text in three volumes folio, and in other forms.

BHARADWAJA: A Rishi to whom many Vedic hymns are attributed. He was the son of Brihaspati and father of Drona, the preceptor of the Pandavas. The Taittiriya Brahmana says that "he lived through three lives" (probably meaning a life of great length), and that "he became immortal and ascended to the heavenly worm, to union with the sun." In the Mahabharata he is represented as living at Hardwar; in the Ramayana he received Rama and Sita in his hermitage at Prayaga, which was then and afterwards much celebrated. According to some of the Puranas and the Harivansa, he became by gift or adoption the son of King Bharata, and a story is told about his birth to account for his name: His mother, the wife of Utathya, was pregnant by her husband and by Brihaspati. Dirghatamas, the son by her husband, kicked his half-brother out of the womb before his time, when Brihaspati said to his mother, 'Bhara-dwa-jam,' 'Cherish this child of two fathers.'

BHARATA: 1. A hero and king from whom the warlike people called Bharatas, frequently mentioned in the Rigveda, were descended. The name is mixed up with that of Viswamitra. Bharata's sons were called Viswamitras and Viswamitra's sons were called Bharatas.

2. An ancient king of the first Manwantara. He was devoted to Vishnu, and abdicated his throne that he might continue constant in meditation upon him. While at his hermitage, he went to bathe in the river, and there saw a doe big with young frightened by a lion. Her fawn, which was brought forth suddenly, fell into the water, and the sage rescued it. He brought the animal up, and becoming excessively fond of it, his abstraction was interrupted. In the course of time he died, watched by the deer with tears in its eyes, like a son mourning for his father; and he himself, as he expired, cast his eyes upon the deer and thought of nothing else, being wholly occupied with one idea." For this misapplied devotion he was born again as a deer with the faculty of recollecting his former life. In this form he lived an austere retired life, and having atoned for his former error, was born again as a Brahmin. But his person was ungainly, and he looked like a crazy idiot. He discharged servile offices, and was a palankin-bearer; but he had true wisdom, and discoursed deeply upon philosophy and the power of Vishnu. Finally, he obtained exemption from future birth. This legend is "a sectarial graft upon a Pauranik stem."

3. Son of Dasaratha by his wife Kaikeyi, and half-brother of Ramachandra. He was educated by his mother's father, Aswapati, king of Kekaya, and married Mandavi, the cousin of Sita. His mother, through maternal fondness, brought about the exile of Rama, and endeavoured to secure her own son's succession to the throne, but Bharata refused to supplant his elder brother. On the death of his father Bharata performed the funeral rites, and went after Rama with a complete army to bring him back to Ayodhya and place him on the throne.

He found Rama at Chitrakuta, and there was a generous contention between them as to which should reign. Rama refused to return until the period of his exile was completed, and Bharata declined to be king; but he returned to Ayodhya as Rama's representative, and setting up a pair of Rama's shoes as a mark of his authority, Bharata ruled the country in his brother's name. "He destroyed thirty millions of terrible gandharvas" and made himself master of their country.

4. A prince of the Puru branch of the Lunar race. Bharata was son of Dushyanta and Sakuntala. Ninth in descent from him came Kuru, and fourteenth from Kuru came Santanu. This king had a son named Vichitravirya, who died childless, leaving two widows. Krishna Dwaipayana was natural brother to Vichitravirya. Under the law he raised up seed to his brother from the widows, whose sons were Dhritarashtra and Pandu, between whose descendants, the Kauravas and Pandavas, the great war of the Mahabharata was fought. Through their descent from Bharata, these princes, but more especially the Pandavas, were called Bharatas.

5. A sage who is the reputed inventor of dramatic entertainments.

BHARTRIHARI: A celebrated poet and grammarian, who is said to have been the brother of Vikramaditya. He wrote three Satakas or Centuries of verses, called—(1.) Sringara-sataka, on amatory matters; (2.) Niti-sataka, on polity and ethics; and (3.) Vairagya-sataka, on religious austerity. These maxims are said to have been written when he had taken to a religious life after a licentious youth. He was also author of a grammatical work of high repute called Vakya-padiya, and the poem called Bhattikavya is by some attributed to him. The moral verses were translated into French so long ago as 1670. The text with a Latin translation was printed by Schisfner and Weber. There is a translation in German by Bohlen and

Schutz, in French by Fauche, and of the erotic verses by Regnaud; in English by Professor Tawney in the Indian Antiquary.

BHASKARACHARYA: (Bhaskara + Acharya.) A celebrated mathematician and astronomer, who was born esrly in the eleventh century A.D. He was author of the Bijaganita on arithmetic, the Lilavati on algebra, and the Siddhanta Siromani on astronomy. It has been claimed for Bhaskara that he "was fully acquainted with the principle of the Differential Calculus. This claim Dr. Spottiswoode considers to be overstated, but he observes of Bhaskara: "It must be admitted that the penetration shown by Bhaskara in his analysis is in the highest degree remarkable that the formula which he establishes, and his method of establishing it, bear more than a mere resemblance—they bear a strong analogy—to the corresponding process in modern astronomy; and that the majority of scientific persons will learn with surprise the existence of such a method in the writings of so distant a period and so distant a region."

BHAVISHYA PURANA: This Purana, as its name implies, should be a book of prophecies foretelling what will be. The copies discovered contain about 7000 stanzas. The work is far from agreeing with the declared character of a Purana, and is principally a manual of rites and ceremonies. Its deity is Siva. There is another work, containing also about 7000 verses, called the Bhavishyottara Purana, a name which would imply that it was a continuation or supplement of the former, and its contents are of a similar character.

BHIMA, BHIMASENA: 'The terrible.' The second of the five Pandu princes, and mythically son of Vayu, 'the god of the wind.' He was a man of vast size, and had great strength. He was wrathful in temper, and given to abuse, a brave warrior, but a fierce and cruel foe, coarse in taste and manners, and a great feeder, so that he was called Vrikodara, 'wolf's belly.' Half of ihe food of the family was allotted to him, and the other half sufficed for his four brothers and their mother. The weapon he generally used was a club, which suited his gigantic strength, and he had been trained in the use of it by Drona and Balarama. His great strength excited the envy of his cousin Duryodhana, who poisoned him and threw his body into the Ganges; but it sank to the realm of the serpents, where it was restored to health and vigour, and Bhima returned to Hastinapura. At the passage of arms at Hastinipura, he and Duryodhana engaged each other with clubs; but the mimic combat soon turned into a fierce personal conflict, which Drona had to put an end to by force.

It was at this same meeting that he reviled Karna, and heaped contempt upon him, increasing and converting into bitter hatred the enmity which Karna had previously entertained against the Pandavas. When he and his brothers were in exile, and an attempt was made, at the instigation of Duryodhana, to burn them in their house, it was he who barricaded the house of Purochana, the director of the plot, and burnt him as he had intended to burn them. Soon after this he met the Asura Hidimba, whom he killed, and then married his sister Hidimbaa. He also slew another Asura named Vaka, whom he seized by the legs and tore asunder; afterwards he killed his brother, Kirmira, and other Asuras. This brought the Asuras to submission, and they engaged to refrain from molesting mankind.

After the Pandu princes were established at Indraprastha, Bhima fought in single combat with Jarasandha, king of Magadha, who had refused to recognise their supremacy. As 'son of the wind,' Bhima was brother of Hanuman, and was able to fly with great speed. By this power of flight, and with the help of Hanuman, he made his way to Kuvera's heaven, high up in the Himalayas. When Jayadratha failed in his attempt to carry off Draupadi, he was pursued by Arjuna and Bhima. The latter overtook him, dragged him by the hair from his chariot to the ground, and kicked him till he became senseless. At Arjuna's remonstrance Bhima refrained from killmg him; but he cut off all his hair except five locks, and compelleted him to acknowledge publicly that he was the slave of the Pandavas. Bhima refused to listen to his brother's plea for Jayadratha's release, but at Draupadi's intercession he let him go free.

In the second exile of the Pandavas, they went to the Raja of Virata, whose service they entered. Bhima, holding a ladle in one hand and a sword in the other, undertook the duties of cook; but he soon exhibited his prowess by fighting with and killing a famous wrestler named Jimuta. Draupadi had entered into the service of the queen as a waiting-maid, and attracted the admiration of the king's brother-in-law, Kichaka. When she rejected his advances, he insulted and brutally assaulted her. Her husbands did not seem disposed to avenge her, so she appealed to Bhima, as she was wont when she sought revenge. Draupadi made an assignation with Kichaka, which Bhima kept, and after a sharp struggle with the disappointed gallant, he broke his bones to atoms, and made his body into a large ball of flesh, so that no one could tell how he had been killed or who had killed him. Draupadi was judged to have had a share in his death, and was condemned to be burnt alive; but Bhima drew his hair over his face, so that no one could recognise him and, tearing up a large tree for a club, he rushed to the rescue. He was taken for a mighty Gandharva, the crowd fled, and Draupndi was released. Kichaka had been the general of the forces of Virata and the mainstay of the king. After his death, Susarman, king of Trigarta, aided and abetted by the Kauravas and others, determined to attack Virata. The Raja of Virata was defested and made prisoner, but Bhima pursued Su-sarman and overcame him, rescued the prisoner, and made the conqueror captive.

In the great battle between the Kauravas and Pandavas, Bhima took a very prominent part. On the first day he fought against Bhishma; on the second he slew the two sons of the Raja of Magadha, and after them their father, killing him and his elephant at a single blow. In the night between the fourteenth and fifteenth day of the battle, Bhima fought with Drona until the rising of the sun; but that redoubted warrior fell by the hand of Dhrishtadyumna, who continued the combat till noonday. On the seventeenth day he killed Duhsasana, and drank his blood, as he had long before vowed to do, in retaliation of the insults Duhsasana had offered to Draupadi. On the eighteenth and last day of the battle Duryodhana fled and hid himself in a lake. When he was discovered, he would not come out until he had received a promise that he should not have to fight with more than one man at a time. Even then he delayed until he was irritated by the abuse and the taunts of the Pandavas, Bhima and Duryodhana fought as usual with clubs. The battle was long and furious; the parties were equally matched, and Bhima was getting the worst of it, when, he struck an unfair blow which smashed Duryodhana's thigh, and brought him to the ground. Thus he fulfilled his vow and avenged Draupadi. In his fury Bhima kicked his prostrate foe on the head, and acted so brutally that his brother Yudhishthira struck him in the face with his fist, and directed Arjuna to take him away. Balarama was greatly incensed at the foul play to which Bhima had resorted, and would have attacked the Pandavas had he not been modified by Krishna. He declared that Bhima should thenceforward be called Jihma-yodhin, 'the unfair fighter.'

After the conclusion of the war, the old king, Dhritarashtra, asked that Bhima might be brought to him. Krishna, who knew the blind old man's sorrow for his son, whom Bhima had killed, and suspecting his intention, placed before him an iron statue, which Dhritarashtra crushed in his embrace. Dhritarashtra never forgave Bhima, and he returned the ill feeling with insults, which ended in the old king's retiring into the forest.

Bhima's last public feat was the slaughter of the horse in the sacrifice which followed Yudhishthira's accession to the throne. Apart from his mythological attributes, the character of Bhima is natural and distinct. A man of burly form, prodigious strength, and great animal courage, with coarse tastes, a gluttonous appetite, and an irascible temper; jovial and jocular when in good humor, but abusive, truculent, and brutal when his passions were roused. His repartees were forcible though coarse, and he held his own even against Krishna when the latter made personal remarks upon him.

By his Asura wife Hidimba a he had a son named Ghatotkacha; and by his wife Balandhara, princess of Kasi, he also had a son named Sarvatraga or Sarvaga. Other appellations of Bhima are Bhimasena, Bahusalin, 'the large armed,' Jarasandha-jit, 'van. quisher of Jarasandha.'

BHISHMA: 'The terrible.' Son of King Santanu by the holy river goddess Ganga, and hence called Santanava, Gangeya, and Nadija, 'the riverborn.' When King Santanu was very old he desired to marry a young and beautiful wife. His son Santanava or Bhishma found a suitable damsel, but her parents objected to the marriage because Bhishma was heir to the throne, and if she bore sons they could not succeed. To gratify his father's desires, he made a vow to the girl's parents that he would never accept the throne, nor marry a wife, nor become the father of children. Santanu then married the damsel, whose name was Satyavati, and she bore him two sons.

At the death of his father, Bhishma placed the elder son upon the throne, but he was headstrong and was soon killed in battle. The other son, named Vichitraviryya, then succeeded, and Bhishma acted as his protector and adviser. By force of arms Bhishma obtained iwo daughters of the king of Kasi and married them to Vichitravirya, and when that prince died young and childless, Bhishma acted ss guardian of his widows. By Bhishma's arrangement, Krishna Dwaipayana, who was born of Satyavati before her marriage, raised up seed to his half-brother. The two children were Pandu and Dhritarashtra. Bhishma brought them up and acted for them as regent of Hastina-pura. He also directed the training of their respective children, the Pandavas and Kauravas. On the rupture taking place between the rival families, Bhishma counselled moderation and peace. When the war began he took the side of the Kauravas, the sons of Dhritarashtra, and he was made commander-in-chisf of their army. He laid down some rules for mitigating the horrors of war, and he stipulated that he should not be called upon to fight against Arjuna. Goaded by the reproaches of Duryodhana, he attacked Arjuna on the tenth day of the battle. He was unfairly wounded by Sikhandi, and was pierced with innumerable arrows from the hands of Arjuna, so that there was not a space of two fingers' breadth left unwounded in his whole body, and when he fell from his chariot he was upheld from the ground by the arrows and lay as on a couch of darts. He was mortally wounded, but he had obtained the power of fixing the period of his death, so he survived fifty-eight days, and delivered several long didactic discourses. Bhishma exhibited throughout his life a self-denial, devotion, and fidelity which remained unsullied to the last. He is also known by the appellation Tarpanchchhu, and as Talaketu, 'palm banner.'

BHRIGU: A Vedic sage. He is one of the Prajapatis and great Rishis, and is regarded as the founder of the race of the Bhrigus or Bhargavas, in which was born Jamadagni and Parasurama. Manu calls him son, and says that he confides to him his Smriti. According to the Mahabharata he officiated at Daksha's celebrated sacrifice, and had his beard pulled out by

Siva. The same authority also tells the following story:—It is related of Bhrigu that he rescued the sage Agastya from the tyranny of King Nahusha, who had obtained superhuman powers. Bhrigu crept into Agastya's hair to avoid the potent glance of Nahusha, and when that tyrant attached Agastya to his chariot and kicked him on the head to make him move, Bhrigu cursed Nahusha, and he was turned into a serpent. Bhrigu, on Nahusha's supplication, limited the duration of his curse.

In the Padma Purana it is related that the Rishis, assembled at a sacrifice, disputed as to which deity was best entitled to the homage of a Brahmin. Being unable to agree, they resolved to send Bhrigu to test the characters of the various gods, and he accordingly went. He could not obtain access to Siva because that deity was engaged with his wife; finding him, therefore, to consist of the property of darkness, Bhrigu sentenced him to take the form of the Linga, and pronounced that he should have no offerings presented to him, nor receive the worship of the pious and respectable. His next visit was to Brahma, whom he beheld surrounded by sages, and so much inflated with his own importance as to treat Bhrigu with great inattention, betraying his being made up of foulness. The Muni therefore excluded him from the worship of the Brahmins. Repairing next to Vishnu, he found the deity asleep, and, indignant at his seeming sloth, Bhrigu stamped upon his breast with his left foot and awoke him; instead of being offended, Vishnu gently pressed the Brahmin's foot and expressed himself honoured and made happy by its contact; and Bhrigu, highly pleased by his humility, and satisfied of his being impersonated goodness, proclaimed Vishnu as the only being to be worshipped by men or gods, in which decision the Munis, upon Bhrigu's report, concurred."—Wilson.

BRAHMA, BRAHMAN (neuter): The supreme soul of the universe, self-existent, absolute, and eternal, from which all thinge emanate, and to which all return. This divine essence is incorporeal, immaterial, invisible, unborn, uncreated, without beginning and without end, illimitable, and inappreciable by the sense until the film of mortal blindness is removed. It is all-pervading and infinite in its manifestations, in all nature, animate and inanimate, in the highest god and in the meanest creature. This supreme soul receives no worship, but it is the object of that abstract meditation which Hindu sages practise in order to obtain absorption into it. It is sometimes called Kalahansa.

There is a passage in the Satapatha Brahmana which represents Brahma (neuter) as the active creator.

The Veda is sometimes called Brahma.

BRAHMA (Masculine): The first member of the Hindu triad; the supreme spirit manifested as the active creator of the universe. He sprang from the mundane egg deposited by the supreme first cause, and is the Prajapati, or lord and father of all creatures, and in the first place of the Rishis or Prajapatis.

When Brahma has created the world it remains unaltered for one of his days, a period of 2,160,000,000 years. The world and all that is therein is then consumed by fire, but the sages, gods, and elements survive. When he awakes he again restores creation, and this process is repeated until his existence of a hundred years is brought to a close, a period which it requires fifteen figures to express. When this period is ended he himself expires, and he and all the gods and sages, and the whole universe are resolved into their constituent clements. His name is invoked in religious services, but Pushkara , near Ajmer, is the only place where he receives worship, though Professor Williams states that he has heard of homage being paid to him at Idar.

Brahma is said to be of a red colour. He has four heads; originally he had five, but one was burnt off by the fire of Siva's central eye because he had spoken disrespectfully. Hence he is called Chaturanana or Chaturmukha, 'four-faced,' and Ashtakarna, 'eight-eared.' He has four arms; and in his hands he holds his sceptre, or a spoon, or a string of beads, or his bow Parivita, or a water jug, and the Veda. His consort is Saraswati, goddess of learning, also called Brahmin His vehicle is a swan or goose, from which he is called Hansavahana. His residence is called Brahmavrinda.

The name Brahma is not found in the Vedas and Brahmanas, in which the active creator is known as Hiranyagarbha, Prajapati, etc.; but there is a curious passage in the Satapatha Brahmana which says: "He (Brahma, neuter) created the gods. Having created the gods, he placed them in these worlds: in this world Agni, Vayu in the atmosphere, and Surya in the sky."

Two points connected with Brahma are remarkable. As the father of men he performs the work of procreation by incestuous intercourse with his own daughter, variously named Vach or Saraswati (speech), Sandhya (twilight), Satarupa (the hundred-formed), etc. Secondly, that his powers as creator have been arrogated to the other gods Vishnu and Siva, while Brahma has been thrown into the shade. In the Aitareya Brahmana it is said that Prajapati was in the form of a buck and his daughter was Rohit, a deer. According to the Satapatha Brahmana and Manu, the supreme soul, the self-existent lord, created the waters and deposited in them a seed, which seed becarne a golden egg, in whish he himself was born as Brahma, the progenitor of all the worlds. As the waters (Nara) were" the place of his movement, he (Brahma) was called Narayana." Here the name Narayana is referred distinctly to Brahma, but it afterwards became the name of Vishnu.

The account of the Ramayana is that all was water only, in which the earth was formed. Thence arose Brahma, the self-existent, with the deities. He then, becoming a boar, raised up the earth and created the whole world with the saints, his sons. Brahma, eternal and perpetually undecaying, sprang from the ether; from him was descended Marichi ; the son of Marichl was Kasyapa. From Kasyapa sprang Vivaswat, and Manu is declared to have been Vivaswat's son." A later recension of this poem alters this passage so as to make Brahma a mere manifestation of Vishnu. Instead of "Brahma, the self-existent, with the deities," it substitutes for the last three words, "the imperishable Vishnu." The Vishnu Purana says that the "divine Brahma called Narayana created all beings," that Prajapati "had formerly, at the commencement of the (previous) kalpas, taken the shape of a fish, a tortoise, etc., (so now), entering the body of a boar, the lord of creatures entered the water." But this "lord of creatures" is clearly shown to be Vishnu, and these three forms, the fish, the tortoise, and the boar, are now counted among the Avataras of Vishnu.

This attribution of the form of a boar to Brahma (Prajapati) had been before made by the Satapatha Brahmana, which also says, "Having assumed the form of a tortoise, Prajapati crested offspring." The Linga Purana is quite exceptional among the later works in ascribing the boar form to Brahma. The Mahabharata represents Brahma as springing from the navel of Vishnu or from a lotus which grew thereout; hence he is called Nabhija, 'navel-born;' Kanja, 'the lotus;' Sarojin, 'having a lotus;' Abjaja, Abjayoni, and Kanjaja, 'lotus-born' This is, of course, the view taken by the Vaishnavas. The same statement appears in the Ramayana, although this poem gives Brahma a more prominent place than usual. It represents Brahma as informing Rama of his divinity, and of his calling him to heaven in "the glory of Vishnu." He bestowed boons on Rama while that hero was on earth, and he extended his favours also to Ravana and other Rakshasas who were descendants of his son Pulastya.

In the Puranas also he appears as a patron of the enemies of the gods, and it was by his favour that the Daitya King Bali obtained that almost universal dominion which required the incarnation of Vishnu as the dwarf to repress. He is further represented in the Ramayana as the creator of the beautiful Ahalya, whom he gave as wife to the sage Gautama. Brahma, being thus inferior to Vishnu, is represented as giving homage and praise to Vishnu himself and to his form Krishna, but the Vaishnava authorities make him superior to Rudra, who, they say, sprang from his forehead. The Saiva authorities make Mahadeva or Rudra to be the creator of Brahma, and represent Brahma as worshipping the Linga and as acting as the charioteer of Rudra.

Brahma was the father of Daksha, who is said to have sprung from his thumb, and he was present at the sacrifice of that patriarch, which was rudely disturbed by Rudra. Then he had to humbly submit and appease the offended god. The four Kumaras, the chisf of whom was calleu Sanatkumara or by the patronymic Vaidhatra, were later creations or sons of Brahma.

Brahma is also called Vidhi, Vedhas, Druhina, and Srashtri, 'creator;' Dhatai and Vidhatri, 'sustainer;' Pitamaha, 'the great father;' Lokesa, lord of the world;' Parameshta, 'supreme in heaven;' Sanat, 'the ancient;' Adikavi, 'the first poet;' and Drughana, 'the axe or mnllet.'

BRAHMIN: The first of the four castes; the sacerdotal class, the members of which may be, but are not necessarily, priests. A Brahmin is the chisf of all created beings; his person is inviolate; he is entitled to all honour, and enjoys many rights and privileges. The Satapatha Brahmana declares that "there are two kinds of gods; first the gods, then those who are Brahmins, and have learnt the Veda and repeat it: they are human gods." The chisf duty of a Brahmin is the study and teaching of the Vedas, and the performance of sacrifices and other religious ceremonies; but in modern times many Brahmins entirely neglect these duties, and they engage in most of the occupations of secular life. Under the law of Manu, the life of a Brahmin was divided into four asramas or stages:—

1. Brahmachari: The student, whose duty was to pass his

days in humble and obedient attendance upon his spiritual preceptor in the study of the Vedas.

2. Grihastha: The householder; the married man living with his wife as head of a family engaged in the ordinary duties of a Brahmin, reading and teaching the Veda, sacrificing and assisting to sacrifice, bestowing alms and receiving alms.

3. Vanaprastha: The anchorite, or "dweller in the woods," who, having discharged his duties as a man of the world, has retired into the forest to devote himself to self-denial in food and raiment, to mortifications of various kinds, to religious meditation, and to the strict performance of all ceremonial duties.

4. Sannyasi: The religious mendicant, who, freed from all forms and observances, wanders about and subsists on alms, practising or striving for that condition of mind which, heedless of the joys and pains, cares and troubles of the flesh, is intent only upon the deity and final absorption.

The divisions and subdivisions of the Brahmin caste are almosl innumerable. It must suffice here to notice the great divisions of north and south, the Pancha Gauda and the Pancha Dravida. The five divisions of Gauda, or Bengal, arc the Brahmins of— 1. Kanyakubja, Kanauj; 2. Saraswata, the north-west, about the Saraswati or Sarsati river; 3. Gauda; 4. Mithila, North Bihar: 5. Utkala, Orissa. The Pancha Dravida are the Brahmins of— 1. Maharashtra, the Mahratta country; 2. Telinga, the Telugu country; 3. Dravida, the Tamil country; 4. Karnata, the Kannada country; 5. Gurjjara, Gujerat.

BRAHMANA: 'Belonging to Brahmins.' Works composed by and for Brahmins. That part of the Veda which was intended for the use and guidance of Brahmins in the use of the hymns or the Mantra, and therefore of later production; but the Brahmana, equally with the Mantra, is held to be Sruti or revealed word. Excepting its claim to revelation, it is a Hindu

Talmud. The Brahmana collectively is made up of the different Brahmanas, which are ritualistic and liturgical writings in prose. They contain the details of the Vedic ceremonies, with long explanations of their origin and meaning; they give instructions as to the use of particular verses and metres; and they abound with curious legends, divine and human, in illustration. In them are found "the oldest rituals we have, the oldest linguistic explanations, the oldest traditional narratives, and the oldest philosophical speculations." As literary productions they are not of a high order, but some "striking thoughts, bold expressions, sound reasoning, and curious traditions are found among the mass of pedantry and grandiloquence."

Each of the Sanhitas or collection of hymns has its Brahmanas, and these generally maintain the essential character of the Veda to which they belong. Thus the Brahmanas of the Rig are specially devoted to the duties of the Hotri, who recites the richas or verses, those of the Yajur to the performance of the sacrifices by the Adhwaryu, and those of the Saman to the chanting by the Udgatri. The Rig has the Aitareya Brahmana, which is perhaps the oldest, and may date as far back as the seventh century B.C. This is sometimes called Aswalayana. It has another called Kaushitaki or Sankhayana. The Taittiriya Sanhita of the Yajurveda has the Taittiriya Brahmana, and the Vajasaneyi Sanhita has the Satapatha Brahmana, one of the most important of all the Brahmanas. The Samaveda has eight Brahmanas, of which the best known are the Praudha or Panchavinsa, the Tandya, and the Shadvinsa. The Atharva has only one, the Gopatha Brahmana. In their fullest extent the Brahmanas embrace also the treatises called Aranyakas and Upanishads.

BRAHMA PURANA: In all the lists of the Puranas the Brahma stands first, for which reason it is sometimes entitled the Adi or "First" Purana. It was repeated by Brahma to Marichi, and is said to contain 10,000 stanzas, but the actual number is betwesn 7000 and 8000. It is also called the Saura Purana, because "it is, in great part, appropriated to the worship of Surya, the Sun." "The early chapters give a description of the croation, an account of the Manwantaras, and the history of the Solar and Lunar dynasties to the time of Krishna in a summary manner, and in words which are common to it and several other Puranas. A brief description of the universe succeeds; and then come a number of chapters relating to the holincss of Orissa, with ita templcs and sacred groves, dedicated to the sun, to Siva, and Jagannatha, the latter especially.

These chapters are characteristic of this Purana, and show its main object to be the promotion of the worship of Krishna as Jagannatha. To thcse particulars succeeds a life of Krishna, which is word for word the same as that of the Vishnu Purana; and the compilation terminates with a particular detail of the mode in which Yoga or contemplative devotion, the object of which is still Vishnu, is to be performed. There is little in this which corresponds with the definition of a Panchalakshana Purana, and the mention of the temple of Orissa, the date of the original construction of which is recorded, shows that it could not have been compiled earlier than the thirteenth or fourteenth century." This Purana has "a supplementary or concluding section called the Brahmottara Purana, which contains about 3000 stanzas. This bean still more entirely the character of a Mahatmya or local legend, being intended to celebrate the sanctity of the Balaja river, conjectured to be the same as the Banas in Marwar. There is no clue to ita date, but it is clearly modern, grafting personagcs and fictions of its own invention on a few hints from older aulhorities."—Wilson.

BRIHASPATI: In the Rigveda the names Brihaspati and Brahmanaspati alternate, and are equivalent to each other. They are names "of a deity in whom the action of the worshipper upon the gods is personified. He is the suppliant, the sacrificer, the priest, who intercedes with gods on behalf of men and protects mankind against the wicked. Hence he appears as the prototype of the priests and priestly order; and is also designated as the Purohita (family priest) of the divine community. He is called in one place 'the father of the gods,' and, a widely extended creative power is ascribed to him. He is also designated as 'the shining' and 'the gold-coloured,' and as 'having the thunder for his voice.'"

In later times he is a Rishi. He is also regent of the planet Jupiter, and the name is commonly used for the planet itself. In this character his car is called Nitighosha 'and is drawn by eight pale horses. He was son of the Rishi Angiras, and he bears the patronymic Angirasa. As preceptor of the gods he is called Animishacharya, Chakshas, Ijya, and Indrejya. His wife, Tara, was carried on by Soma, the moon, and this gave rise to a war called the Tarakamaya. Soma was aided by Usanas, Rudra, and all the Daityas and Danavas, while Indra and the gods took the part of Brihaspati. "Earth, shaken to her centre," appealed to Brahma, who interposed and restored Tara to her husband. She was delivered of a son which Brihaspati and Soma both claimed, but Tara, at the command of Brahma to tell the truth, declared Soma to be the father, and the child was named Budha. There is an extraordinary story in the Matsya and Bhagavata Puranas of the Rishis having milked the earth through Brihaspati. Brihaspati was father of Bharadwaja, by Mamata, wife of Utathya. An ancient code of law bears the name of Brihaspati, and he is also represented as being the Vyasa of the "fourth, Dwapara age." There was a Rishi of the name in the second Manwantara, and one who was founder of an heretical sect. Other epithets of Brihaspati are Jiva, 'the living,' Didivis, 'the bright,' Dhishna, 'the intelligent,' and, for his eloquence, Gishpati, 'lord of speech.'

BUDHA: 'Wise, intelligent.' The planet Mercury, son of Soma, the moon, by Rohini, or by Tara, wife of Brihaspati. He married Ila, daughter of the Manu Vaivaswata, and by her had a son, Puraravas. Budha was author of a hymn in the Rigveda. From his parents he is called Saumya and Rauhineya. He is also called Praharshana, Rodhana, Tunga, and Syamanga, 'black-bodied.' The intrigue of Soma with Tara was the cause of a great quarrel, in which the gods and the Asuras fought against each other. Brahma compelled Soma to give up Tara, and when she returned to her husband she was pregnant. A son was born, who was so beautiful that Brihaspati and Soma both claimed him. Tara for a long time refused to tell his paternity, and so excited the wrath and nearly incurred the curse of her son. At length, upon the command of Brahma, she declared Soma to be the father, and he gave the boy the name of Budha. This name is distinct from Buddha.

C

CHAMUNDA: An emanation of the goddess Durga, sent forth from her forehead to encounter the demons Chanda and Munda. She is thus described in the Markandeya Purana:—

"From the forehead of Ambika (Durga), contracted with wrathful frowns, sprang swiftly forth a goddess of black and formidable aspect, armed with a scimitar and noose, bearing a ponderous mace, decorated with a garland of dead corpses, robed in the hide of an elephant, dry and withered and hideous, with yawning mouth, and lolling tongue, and bloodshot eyes, and filling the regions with her shouts." When she had killed the two demons, she bore their heads to Durga, who told her that she should henceforth be known, by a contraction of their names, as Chamunda"

CHANDRAGUPTA: This name was identified by Sir W. Jones with the Sandracottus or Sandrocyptus mentioned by Arrian and the other classical historians of Alexander's campaign; and somewhat later on as having entered into a treaty with Seleucus Nicator through the ambassador Megasthenes. The identification has been contested, but the chisf writers on Indian antiquities have admitted it as an established fact, and have added confirmatory evidence from various sources, so that the identity admits of no reasonable doubt. This identification is of the utmost importance to Indian chronology; it is the only link by which Indian history is connected with that of Greece, and everything in Indian chronology depends upon the date of Chandragupta as ascertained from that assigned to Sandracottus by the classical writers. His date, as thus discovered, shows that he began to reign in 315 B.C., and as he reigned twenty-four years, his reign ended in 291 B.C. Chandragupta is a prominent name in both Brahminical and Buddhist writings, ana his accession to the throne is the subject of the drama Mudrarakshasa.

When Alexander was in India, he learned that a king named Xandrames reigned over the Prasa (Prachyas) at the city of Palibothra, situated at the confluence of the Ganges and another river called Erranaboas (the Sone). At this time, Sandracottus was young, but he waged war against Alexander's captains, and he raised bands of robbers, with whose help he succeeded in establishing freedom in India.

Hindu and Buddhist writers are entirely silent as to Alexander's appearance in India, but they show that Chandragupta everthrew the dynasty of the Nandas, which reigned over Magadha, and "established freedom in India by the help of bands of robbers." He established himself at Pataliputra, the capital of the Nandas, which is identical with the Greek Palibothra, and this has been shown to be the modern Patna. That town does not now stand at the confluence of two rivers. but the rivers in the alluvial plains of Bengal frequently change their courses, and a change in the channel of the Sone has been established by direct geographical evidence. There is a difficulty about Xandrames. This is no doubt the Sanskrit Chandramas, which some consider to be only a shorter form of lhe name Chandragupta, while others point out that the Greek references indicate that Xandramcs was the predecessor of Sandracottus, rather than Sandracottus himself.

The dynasty of the Nandas that reigned over Magadha are frequently spoken of as the "nine Nandas," meaning apparently nine descents; but according to some authorities the last Nanda, named Mahapadma, and his eight sons, are intended. Mahapadma Nanda was the son of a Sudra, and so by law he was a Sudra himself. He was powerful and ambitious, cruel and avaricious. His people were disaffected; but his fall is represnted as having been brought about by the Brahmin Chanakya. Chandragupta was then raised to the throne and founded the Mauryan dynasty, the third king of which was the great Asoka, grandson of Chandragupta. The Brahmins and Buddhists are widely at variance as to the origin of the Maurya family. The drama Mudrarakshasa represents Chandragupta as being related to Mahapadma Nanda, and the commentator on the Vishnu Purana says that he was a son of Nanda by a woman of low caste named Mura, wherefore he and his descendants were called Mauryas.

This looks very like an etymological invention, and is inconsistent with the ropresentation that the low caste of Nanda was one cause of his deposition; for were it true, the low-caste king would have been supplanted by one of still lower degree. On the other hand, the Buddhists contend that the Mauryas belonged to the same family as Buddha, who was of the royal family of the Sakyas. The question of the identification of Sandrocotus and Chandragupta has been discussed at length by Wilson in the preface to the Mudrarakshasa in his Hindu Theatre, and in the Vishnu Purana, vol. iv.; also by Max Muller in his History of Ancient Sanskrit Literature.

CHANDRA-VANSA: The Lunar race. The lineage or race which claims deacent from the moon. It is divided into two great branches, the Yadavas and Pauravas, respectively descended from Yadu and Puru. Krishna belonged to the line of Yadu, and Dushyanta with the Kuru and Pandu princes to the line of Puru. The following is a list of the Lunar race as given in the Vishnu Purana, but the authorities vary:

THE LUNAR RACE

Atri, the Rishi. Soma, the Moon.
Buddha, Mercury. Pururavas. Ayu, Ayus

Nahusha (and 3 others).
Yayati (and 5 others).

Yadavas	**Pauravas**	**Kings of Kasi**
Yadu, eldest	Puru, youngest (and	Kshatravriddha
Kroshtu (and 3 others).	3 others).	Suhotra
Vrijinivat	Janamejaya	Kasa
Swahi	Prachinvat	Kasiraja
Rushadgu	Pravira	Dirghatamas
Chitraratha	Manasyu	Dhanwantari
Sasabindu	Abhayada	Ketumat
Prithusravas (one of	Sudyumna	Bhimaratha
a million sons).	Bahugava	Divodasa
Tamas	Samyati	Pratardana
Usanas	Ahamyati	Dyumat
Siteyus	Raudraswa	Satrujit
Rukmakavacha	Riteyu (and 9 others)	Vatsa
or	Rantinara	Ritadhwaja
Ruchaka	Tansu	or
Paravrit	Anila	Kuvalayaswa
Jyamagha	Dushyanta	Alarka
Vidarbha	Bharata	Sannati
Kratha	Bharadwaja	or
Kunti	or } Adopted	Santati
Vrishni	Vitatha	Sunitha
Nirvriti	Bhavanmanyu	Suketu
Dasarha	Brihatkshatra (and	Satyaketu
Vyoman	many others).	Vibhu
Jimuta	Suhotra	Suvibhu
Vikriti	Hastin (of Hastinapur)	Sukumara
Bhimaratha	Ajamidha (and 2 others)	Dhrishtaketu
Navaratha	Riksha (and others)	
Dasaratha	Samvarana	
Sakuni	Kuru	

Karambhi	Jahnu (and many others.)
Devarata	Suratha
Devakshatra	Viduratha
Madhu	Sarvabhauma
Anavaratha	Jayasena
Kuruvatsa	Aravin
Anuratha	
Puruhotra	

Ansu	Ayutayus	Vainahotra
Satwata	Akrodhana	Bharga
Andhaka (and 6 others)	Devatithi	Bharga-bhumi
Bhajamana	Riksha	
Viduratha	Dilipa	
Sura	Pratipa	
Samin	Santanu (and 2 others)	
Pratikshatra	Pandu	
Swayambhoja	Dhritarashtra	
Hridika	Yudhishthira	
Devamidhusha	Parikshit	
Sura	Janamejaya	
Vasudeva (and 9 others)	Satanika	
Krishna and Balarama (Extinct)	Aswamedhadatta	
	Adhisimakrishna	
	Nichakru	
	Ushna	
	Chitraratha	
	Vrishnimat	

Sushena
Sunitha
Rich
Nrichakshush
Sukhabala
Pariplava
Sunaya
Medhavin
Nripanjaya
Mridu
Tigma
Brihadratha
Vasudana
Satanika
Udayana
Ahinara
Khandapani
Niramitra
Kshemaka

CHARAKA: A writer on medicine who lived in Vedic times. According to his own statement, he received the materials of his work from Agnivesa, to whom they were delivered by Atreya. A legend represents him as an incarnation of the serpent Sesha. The work was translated into Arabic before the end of the eighth century. The text has been printed in India.

CHARVAKA: 1. A Rakshasa, and friend of Duryodhana, who disguised himself as a Brahmin and reproached Yudhishthira for his crimes, when he entered Hastinapura in triumph after the great battle. The Brahmins discovered the imposture and reduced Charvaka to ashes with the fire of their eyes.

2. A sceptical philosopher who advocated materialistic doctrines. He probably lived before the composition of the Ramayana, and is perhaps identical with the Charvaka of the Mahabharata. His followers are called by his name.

CHHANDOGYA: Name of an Upanishad of the Samaveda. It has been printed by Dr. Roar, and it has been translated into English by Rajendra Lal, and published in the Bibliotheca Indica. There is also another printed edition of the text. The Chhandogya Upanishad consists of eight out of ten chapters of the Chhandogya Brahmana; the first two chapters are yet wanting. This work is particularly distinguished by its rich store of legends regarding the gradual development of Brahminical theology.

CHYAVANA: A sage, son of the Rishi Bhrigu, and author of some hymns.

In the Rigveda it is said that when "Chyavana had grown old and had been forsaken, the Aswins divested him of his decrepit body, prolonged his life, and restored him to youth, making him acceptable to his wife, and the husband of maidens." This story is thus amplified in the Satapatha Brahmana:—The sage Chyavana assumed a shrivelled form and lay as if abandoned. The sons of Saryata, a descendant of Manu, found this body, and pelted it with clods. Chyavana was greatly incensed, and to appease him Saryata yoked his chariot, and taking with him his daughter Sukanya, presented her to Chyavana. The Aswins endeavoured to seduce her, but she remained faithful to her shrivelled husband, and under his direction she taunted them with being incomplete and imperfect, and consented to tell them in what respect they were deficient, if they would make her husband young again. They directed that he should bathe in a certain pond, and having done so, he came forth with the age that he desired. She then informed them that they were imperfect because they were excluded from a sacrifice the other gods were performing. They departed and succeeded in getting admitted to join the other gods.

According to the Mahabharata, Chyavana besought Indra to allow the Aswins to partake of the libations of soma. Indra replied that the other gods might do as they pleased, but he would not consent. Chyavana then commenced a sacrifice to the Aswins; the other gods were subdued, but Indra, in a rage, rushed with a mountain in one hand and his thunderbolt in another to crush Chyavana. The sage having sprinkled him with water and stopped him, "created a fearful open-mouthed monster called Mada, having teeth and grinders of portentous length, and jaws one of which enclosed the earth, the other the sky; and the gods, including Indra, are said to have been at the root of his tongue like fishes in the mouth of a sea monster." In this predicament "Indra granted the demand of Chyavana, who was thus the cause of the Aswins becoming drinkers of the soma."

In another part of the Mahabharata he is represented as exacting many menial offices from King Kusika and his wife, but he afterwards rewarded them by "creating a magical golden palace," and predicted the birth of "a grandson of great beauty and heroism (Parasurama)."

The Mahabharata, interpreting his name as signifying 'the fallen,' accounts for it by a legend which represents his mother, Pulomi, wife of Bhrigu, as having been carried off by the demon Puloma. She was pregnant, and in her fright the child fell from her womb. The demon was softened, and let the mother depart with her infant.

The version of the story as told in the Mahabharata and Puranas is that Chyavana was so absorbed in penance on the banks of the Narmada that white ants constructed their nests round his body and left only his eyes visible. Sukanya, daughter of King Saryata, seeing two bright eyes in what seemed to be an anthill, poked them with a stick. The sage visited the offence on Saryata, and was appeased only by the promise of the king to give him Sukanya in marriage. Subsequently the Aswins, coming to his hermitage, compassionated her union with so old and ugly a husband as Chyavana, and tried to induce her to take one of them in his place. When their persuasions failed, they told her they were the physicians of the gods, and would restore her husband to youth and beauty, when she could make her choice between him and one of them. Accordingly, the three bathed in a pond and came forth of like celestial beauty. Each one asked her to be his bride, and she recognised and chose her own husband. Chyavana, in gratitude, compelled Indra to admit the Aswins to a participation of the soma ceremonial. Indra at first objected, because the Aswins wandered about among men as physicians and changed their forms at will. But Chyavana was not to be refused; he stayed the arm of Indra as he was about to launch a thunderbolt, and he created a terrific demon who was on the point of devouring the king of the gods when he submitted.

According to the Mahabharata, Chyavana was husband of Arushi or Sukanya and father of Aurva. He is also considered to be the father of Harita.

D

DADHYANCH, DADHICHA: (Dadhicha is a later form.) A Vedic Rishi, son of Atharvan, whose name frequently occurs. The legend about him, as it appears in the Rigveda, is that Indra taught him certain sciences, but threatened to cut off his head if he taught them to anyone else. The Aswins prevailed upon Dadhyanch to communicate his knowledge to them, and, to preserve him from the wrath of Indra, they took off his own head and replaced it with that of a horse. When Indra struck off the sage's equine head the Aswins restored his own to him. A verse of the Rigveda says, "Indra, with the bones of Dadhyanch, slew ninety times nine Vritras;" and the story told by the scholiast in explanation is, that while Dadhyanch was living on earth, the Asuras were controlled and tranquillised by his appearance; but when he had gone to heaven, they overspread the whole earth. Indra inquired for Dadhyanch, or any relic of him. He was told of the horse's head, and when this was found in a lake near Kurukshetra, Indra used the bones as weapons, and with them slew the Asuras, or, as the words of the Vedic verse are explained, he "foiled the nine times ninety Stratagems of the Asuras or Vritras." The story as afterwards told in the Mababharata and Puranas is that the sage devoted himself to death that Indra and the gods might be armed with his bones as more effective weapons than thunderbolts for the destruction of Vritra and the Asuras. According to one account he was instrumental in bringing about the destruction of "Daksha's sacrifice."

DAKSHA: 'Able, competent, intelligent.' This name generally carries with it the idea of a creative power. Daksha is a son of Brahma; he is one of the Prajapatis, and is sometimes regarded as their chisf. There is a great deal of doubt and confusion about him, which of old the sage Parasara could only account for by saying that "in every age Daksha and the rest are born and are again destroyed." In the Rigveda it is said that "Daksha sprang from Aditi, and Aditi from Daksha." Upon this marvellous mutual generation Yaska in the Nirukta remarks, "How can this be possible. They may have had the same origin; or, according to the nature of the gods, they may have been born from each other, and have derived their substance from each other." Roth's view is that Aditi is eternity, and that Daksha (spiritual power) is the male energy which generates the gods in eternity. In the Satapatha Brahmana, Daksha is identified with Prajapati, the creator. As son of Aditi, he is one of the Adityas, and he is also reckoned among the Viswadevas.

Aecording to the Mahabharata, Daksha sprang from the right thumb of Brahma, and his wife from that deity's left thumb. The Puranas adopt this view of his origin, but state that he married Prasuti, daughter of Priyafvrata, and grand-daughter oi Manu. By her he had, according to various statements, twenty-four, fifty, or sixty daughters. The Ramayana and Mahabharata agree in the larger number; and according to Manu and the Mahabharata he gave ten of his daughters to Dharma and thirteen to Kasyapa, who became the mothers of gods and demons, men, birds, serpents, and all living things. Twenty-seven were given in marriage to Soma, the moon, and these became the twenty-seven Nakshatras or lunar mansions. One of the daughters, named Sati, married Siva, and killed herself in consequence of a quarrel between her husband and father. The Kasi Khanda represents that she became a sati and burnt herself.

Another legend of the Mahabharata and Puranas represents Daksha as being born a second time, in another Manvantara, as son of the Prachetasas and Marisha, and that he had seven sons, "the allegorical persons Krodha, Tamas, Dama, Vikrita, Angiras, Kardama, and Aswa." This second birth is said to have happened through his having been cursed to it by his son-in-law Siva. Daksha was in a certain way, by his mother Marisha, an emanation of Soma, the moon; and as twenty-seven of his daughters were married to that luminary, Daksha is sometimes referred to as being both the father and the offspring of the moon, thus reiterating the duality of his nature.

In the Harivansa Daksha appears in another variety of his character. According to this authority, Vishnu himself became Daksha, and formed numerous creatures, or, in other words, he became the creator. Daksha, the first of males, by virtue of yoga, himself took the form of a beautiful woman, by whom he had many fair daughters, whom he disposed of in marriage in the manner related by Manu and above stated.

An important event in the life of Daksha, and very frequently referred to, is "Daksha's sacrifice," which was violently interrupted and broken up by Siva. The germ of this story is found in the Taittiriya Sanhita, where it is related that the gods, having excluded Rudra from a sacrifice, he pierced the sacrifice with an arrow, and that Pushan, attempting to eat a portion of the oblation, broke his teeth. The story is found both in the Ramayana and Mahabharata. According to the latter, Daksha was engaged in sacrifice, when Siva in a rage, and shouting loudly, pierced the offering with an arrow The gods and Asuras were alarmed and the whole universe quaked. The Rishis endeavoured to appease the angry god, but in vain. " He ran up to the gods, and in his rsge knocked out the eyes of Bhaga with a blow, and incensed, assaulted Pyshan with his foot and knocked out his teeth as he was eating the offering." The gods and Rishis humbly propitiated him, and when he was appeased "they apportioned to him a distinguished share in the sacrifice, and through fear resorted to him as their refuge." In another part of the same work the story is again told with considerable variation. Daksha instituted a sacrifice and apportioned no share to Rudra (Siva). Instigated by the sage Dadhichi, the god hurled his blazing trident, which destroyed, the sacrifice of Daksha and fell with great violence on the breast of Narayana (Vishnu). It was hurled back with violence to its owner, and a furious battle ensued between the two gods, which was not intermitted till Brahma prevailed upon

Rudra to propitiate Narayana. That god was gratified, and said to Rudra, "He who knows thee knows me; he who loves thee loves me."

The story is reproduced in the Puranas with many embellishments. Daksha instituted a sacrifice to Vishnu, and many of the gods repaired to it, but Siva was not invited, because the gods had conspired to deprive him of sacrificial offerings. The wife of Siva, the mountain goddess Uma, perceived what was going. Uma was a second birth of Sati, daughter of Daksha, who had deprived herself of life in consequence of her father's quarrel with herself and her husband, Siva. Uma urged her husband to display his power and assert his rights. So he created Vira-bhadra, "a being like the fire of fate," and of most terrific appearance and powers. He also sent with him hundreds and thousands of powerful demigods whom he called into existence. A terrible catastrophe followed; "the mountains tottered, the earth shook, the winds roared, and the depths of the sea were disturbed". The sacrifice is broken up, and, in the words of Wilson, "Indra is knocked down and trampled on, Yama has his staff broken, Saraswati and the Matris have their noses cut off, Mitra or Bhaga has his eyes pulled out, Pushan has his teeth knocked down his throat, Chandra (the moon) is pummelled, Vahni's (fire's) hands are cut off, Bhrigu loses his beard, the Brahmins are pelted with stones, the Prajapatis are beaten, and the gods and demigods are run through with swords or stuck with arrows." Daksha then, in great terror, propitiated the wrathful deity and acknowledged his supremacy. According to some versions, Daksha himself was decapitated and his head thrown into the fire. Siva subsequently restored him and the other dead to life, and as Daksha's head could not be found, it was replaced by that of a goat or ram. The Harivansa, in its glorification of Vishnu, gives a different finish to the story. The sacrifice was destroyed and the gods fled in dismay, till Vishnu intervened, and seizing Siva by the throat, compelled him to desist and acknowledge his master.

"This," says Wilson, "is a legend of some interest, as it is obviously intended to intimate a struggle between the worshippers of Siva and Vishnu, in which at first the latter, but finally tlie former, acquired the ascendancy."

Daksha was a lawgiver, and is reckoned among the eighteen writers of Dharma-sastras.

DARSANA: 'Demonstration.' The Shad-darsanas or six demonstrations, i.e., the six schools of Hindu philosophy. All these schools have one starting-point, *ex nihilo nihil fit*; and all have one and the same final object, the emancipation of the soul from future birth and existence, and its absorption into the supreme soul of the universe. These schools are:—

1. **Nyaya,** founded by the sage Gotama. The word Nyaya means propriety or fitness, the proper method of arriving at a conclusion by analysis. This school has been called the Logical School but the term is applicable to its method rather than to its aims. It is also said to represent "the sensational aspect of Hindu philosophy" because it has "a more pointed regard to the fact of the five senses than the others have, and treats the external more frankly as a solid reality." It is the exoteric school as the Vedanta is the esoteric.

2. **Vaiseshika,** founded by a sage named Kanada, who lived about the same time as Gotama. It is supplementary to the Nyaya, and these two schools are classed together. It is called the Atomic School, because it teaches the existence of a transient world composed of aggregations of eternal atoms.

Both the Nyaya and Vaiseshika recognine a Supreme Being.

3. **Sankhya.** The Sankhya and Yoga are classed together because they have much in common, but the Sankhya is atheistical, while the Yoga is theistical. The Sankhya was

founded by the sage Kapila, and takes its name from its numeral or discriminative tendencies. The Sankhya-Karika, the text-book of this school has been translated by Colebrooke and Wilson, and part of the aphorisms of Kapila were translated for the Biblio-thera Indica by the late Dr. Ballantyne.

4. **Yoga.** This school was founded by Patanjali, and from his name is also called Patanjala. It pursues the method of the Sankhya and holds with many of its dogmas, but it asserts the existence not only of individual souls, but of one all-pervading spirit, which is free from the influences which affect other souls.

5. **Purva-mimansa.**

6. **Uttara-mimansa.** The prior and later Mimansas. These are both included in the general term Vedanta, but the Purva-mimansa is commonly known as the Mimansa and the Uttara-mimansa as the Vedanta, 'the end or object of the Vedas.' The Purva-mimansa was founded by Jaimini, and the Uttara-mimansa is attributed to Vyasa, the arranger of the Vedas. "The object of both these schools is to teach the art of reasoning with the express purpose of aiding the interpretation of the Vedas, not only in the speculative but the practical portion." The principal doctrines of the Vedanta (Uttara) are that "God is the omniscient and omnipotent cause of the existence, continuance, and dissolution of the universe. Creation is an act of his will; he is both the efficient and the material cause of the world." At the consummation of all things all are resolved into him. He is "the sole-existent and universal soul," and besides him there is no second principle; he is Adwaita, 'without o second.' Sankaracharya was the great apostle of this school.

The period of the rise of these schools of philosophy is uncertain, and is entirely a matter of inference, but they are probably later than the fifth century B.C. The Vedanta (Uttara-mimansa) is apparently the latest, and is supposed to have been evoked by the teachings of the Buddhists. This would bring it to within three or four centuries B.C. The other schools are to all appearances older than the Vedanta, but it is considered by some that all the schools show traces of Buddhist influences, and if so, the dates of all must be later. It is a question whether Hindu philosophy is or is not indebted to Greek teaching, and the later the date of the origin of these schools the greater is the possibility of Greek influence. Mr. Colebrooke, the highest authority on the subject, is of opinion that "the Hindus were in this instance the teachers, not the learners."

Besides the six schools, there is yet a later system known as the Pauranik and the Eclectic school. The doctrines of this school are expounded in the Bhagavad-gita.

The merits of the various schools have been thus summed up:—"When we consider the six Darsanas, we shall find that one of them, the Uttara-mimansa, bears no title to be ranked by the side of the others, and is really little more than a mystical explanation of the practical injunctions of the Vedas. We shall also admit that the earlier Vedanta, very different from the school of Nihilists now existing under that name, was chisfly a controversial essay, seeking to support the theology of sacrified writ, but borrowing all its philosophical portions from the Yoga school, the most popular at the time of its composition. Lastly, the Nyaya is little more than a treatise on logic, introducing the doctrines of the theistic Sankhya; while the Vaiseshika is an essay on physics, with, it is true, the theory of atoms as its distinguishing mark, though even to this we feel inclined to refuse the imputation of novelty, since we find some idea of it lurking obscurely in the theory of subtle elements which is brought forward in Kapila's Sankhya. In short, the basis of all Indian philosophy, if indeed we may not say the only system of philosophy really discovered in India is the Sankhya, and this forms the basis of the doctrines expounded in the Bhagavad-gita."—Cockburn Thomson.

Colebrooke's Essays are the great authorities on Hindu philosophy. Ballantyne has translated many of the original aphorisms, and he, Cockburn Thomson, Hall, Banerjea, and others have written on the subject.

DASAKUMARA-CHARITA: 'Tales of the ten princes,' by Dandi. It is one of the few Sanskrit works written in prose, but its style is so studied and elaborate that it is classed as a Kavya or poem. The tales are stories of common life, and display a low condition of morals and a corrupt state of society. The text has been printed with a long analytical introduction by H.H. Wilson, and again in Bombay by Buhler. There is an abridged translation by Jacobs, also a translation in French by Fauche, and a longer analysis in vol. iv. of Wilson's works.

DASARATHA: A prince of the Solar race, son of Aja, a descendant of Ikshwaku, and king of Ayodhya. He had three wives, but bemg childless, he performed the sacrifice of a horse, and, according to the Ramayana, the chisf queen, Kausalya, remained in close contact with the slaughtered horse for a night, and the other two queens beside her. Four sons were then born to him from his three wives. Kausalya bore Rama, Kaikeyi gave birth to Bharata, and Sumitra bore Lakshmana and Satrughna. Rama partook of half the nature of Vishnu, Bharata of a quarter, and the other two shared the remaining fourth. The Ramayana, in explanation of this manifestation of Vishnu, says that he had promised the gods to become incarnate as man for the destruetion of Ravana. He chose Dasaratha for his human parent; and when that king was performing a second sacrifice to obtain progeny, he came to him out of the fire as a glorious being, and gave him a vessel full of nectar to administer to his wives. Dasaratha gave half of it to Kausalya, and a fourth each to Sumitra and Kaikeyi. They all in consequence became pregnant, and their offspring partook of the divine nature according to the portion of the nectar each had drunk.

DEVAYANI: Daughter of Sukra, priest of the Daityas. She fell in love with her father'e pupil Kacha, son of Brihaspati, but he rejected her advances. She cursed him, and in return he cursed her, that she, a Brahmin's daughter, should marry a Kshatriya. Devayani was companion to Sarmistha, daughter of the king of the Daityas. One day they went to bathe, and the god Vayu changed their clothes. When they were dressed, they began to quarrel about the change, and Devayani spoke "with a scowl so bitter that Sarmistha slapped her face, and pushed her into a dry well." She was rescued by King Yayati, who took her home to her father Sukra, and at his daughter's vehement persuasion, demanded satisfaction from Sarmistha's father, the Daitya king.

He conceded Devayani's demand, that upon her marriage Sarmistha should be given to her for a servant. Devayani married King Yayati, a Kshatriya, and Sarmistha became her servant. Subsequently, Yayati became enamoured of Sarmistha, and she bore him a son, the discovery of which so enraged DevayanI that she parted from her husband, and went home to her father, having borne two sons, Yadu and Turvasu. Her father, Sukra, cursed Yayati with the infinity of old age, but afterwards offered to transfer it to any one of Yayati's sons who would submit to receive it. Yadu, the eldest, and progenitor of the Yadavas, refused, and so did all the other sons, with the exception of Sarmistha's youngest son, Puru. Those who refused were cursed by their father, that their posterity should never possess dominion; but Puru, who bore his father's curse for a thousand years, succeeded his father as monarch, and was the ancestor of the Pandavas and Kauravas.

DEVI: 'The goddess,' or Mahadevi, 'the great goddess,' wife of the god Siva, and daughter of Himavat, i.e., the Himalaya mountains. She is mentioned in the Mahabharata under a variety of names, and with several of her peculiar characteristics, but she owes her great distinction to the Puranas and later works. As the Sakti or female energy of Siva she has two characters, one mild, the other fierce; and it is under the latter that she is especially worshipped. She has a great variety of names, referable to her various forms, attributes, and actions, but these names are not always used accurately and distinctively.

In her milder form she is Uma, 'light,' and a type of beauty; Gauri, 'the yellow or brilliant;' Parvati, 'the mountaineer;' and Hemavati, from her parentage; Jaganmata, 'the mother of the world;' and Bhavani. In her terrible form she is Durga, 'the inaccessible;' Kali and Syama, 'the black;' Chandi and Chandika, 'the fierce;' and Bhairavi, 'the terrible.' It is in this character that bloody sacrifices are offered to her, that the barbarities of the Durga-puja and Charak-puja are perpetrated in her honour, and that the indecent orgies of the Tantrikas are held to propitiate her favours and celebrate her powers. She has ten arms, and in most of her hands there are weapons. As Durga she is a beautiful yellow woman, riding on a tiger in a fierce and menacing attitude. As Kali or Kalika, 'the black,' "She is represented with a black skin, a hideous and terrible countenance, dripping with blood, encircled with snakes, hung round with skulls and human heads, and in all respects resembling a fury rather than a goddess." As Vindhyavasini, 'the dweller in the Vindhyas,' she is worshipped at a place of that name where the Vindhyas approach the Ganges, near Mirzapur, and it is said that there the blood before her image is never allowed to get dry. As Mahamaya she is the great illusion.

The Chandi-Mahatmya, which celebrates the victories of this goddess over the Asuras, speaks of her under the following names:—1. Durga, when she received the messengers of the Asuras. 2. Dasabhuja, ' Ten-armed,' when she destroyed part of their army. 3. Sinhavahini, 'Riding on a lion,' when she fought with the Asura general Raktabija. 4. Mahishamardini 'Destroyer of Mahisha,' an Asura in the form of a buffalo. 5. Jagaddhatri. 'Fosterer of the world,' when she again defeated the Asura army. 6. Kali ' The black,' she killed Raktabija. 7. Muktakesi 'With dishevelled hair.' Again defeats the Asuras. 8. Tara. ' Star.' She killed Sumbha. 9. Chhinnamastaka. 'Decapitated' the headless' form in which she killed Nisumbha. 10. Jagadgauri 'World's fair one,' as lauded by the gods for her triumphs.

The names which Devi obtains from her husband are:—Babhravi (Babhru), Bhagavati, Isani, Iswari, Kalanjari, Kapalini, Kausiki, Kirati, Maheswari, Mrida, Mridani, Rudrani, Sarvani, Sivani, Tryambaki. From her origin she is called Adrija and Girija, 'mountain-born;' Kuja, 'earth-born;' Dakshaja, 'sprung from Daksha.' She is Kanya, 'the virgin;' Kanyakumari, 'the youthful virgin;' and Ambika, 'the mother;' Avarn, 'the youngest;' Ananta and Nitya, 'the everlasting;' Arya, 'the revered;' Vijaya, 'victorious;' Riddhi, 'the rich; , Sati, 'virtuous;' Dakshina, 'right-handed;' Pinga, 'tawny, dark;' Karburi, 'spotted;' Bhramari, the bee;' Kotari, 'the naked;' Karnamoti, 'pearl-eared;' Padmalanchhana, 'distinguished by a lotus;' Sarvamangala, 'always auspicious;' Sakambhari, 'nourisher of herbs;' Sivaduti, 'Siva's messenger;' Sinharathi, 'riding on a lion.' As addicted to austerities she is Aparna and Katyayani. As Bhutanayaki she is chisf or leader of the goblins, and as Gana-nayaki, the leader of the Ganas. She is Kamakshi, 'wanton-eyed;' and Kamakhya, 'called by the name of Kama, desire.' Other names, most of them applicable to her terrible forms, are Bhadrakali, Bhimadevi, Chamunda, Maha-kali, Mahamari, Mahasuri. Matangi, Rajasi, 'the fierce;' and Raktadanti, 'red or bloody toothed.'

DHANWANTARI: 1. Name of a Vedic deity to whom offerings at twilight were made in the north-east quarter. 2. The physician of the gods, who was produced at the churning of the ocean. He was a teacher of medical science, and the Ayurveda is attributed to him. In another birth he was son of Dirghatamas, and his "nature was exempt from human infirmities, and in every existence he had been master of universal knowledge." He is called also Sudhapani, 'carrying nectar in his hands,' and Amrita, 'the immortal.' Other physicians seem to have had the name applied to them, as Bhela, Divodasa, and Palakapya. 3. A celebrated physician, who was one of "the nine gems" of the court of Vikrama.

DHARMA-SASTRA: A law-book or code of laws. This term includes the whole body of Hindu law, but it is more especially applicable to the laws otManu, Yajnavalkya, and other inspired sages who first recorded the Smriti or "recolleetions" of what they had received from a divine source. These works are generally in three parts:—(1.) Achara, rules of conduct and practice; (2.) Vyavahara, judicature; and (3.) Prayaschitta, penance.

The inspired lawgivers are spoken of as being eighteen in number, but the names of forty-two old authorities are mentioned. Manu and Yajnavalkya stand apart by themselves at the head of these writers. After them the eighteen other inspired sages are reeognised as the great authorities on law, and the works ascribed to them are still extant, either wholly or partially, or in an abridged form:—(1.) Atri; (2.) Vishnu; (3.) Harita; (4.) Usanas; (5.) Angiras; (6.) Yama; (7.) Apastamba; (8.) Samvarta; (9.) Katyayana; (10.) Brihaspati; (11.) Parasara; (12.) Vyasa; (13, 14.) Sankha and Likhita, whose joint treatise is frequently quoted; (15.) Daksha; (16.) Gotama; (17.) Satatapa; (18.) Vasishtha. But there are others who are more frequently cited than many of these, as Narada, Bhrigu, Marichi, Kasyapa, Viswamitra, and Baudhayana. Other names that are met with are Pulastya, Gargya, Paithinasi, Sumantu, Lokakshi, Kuthumi, and Dhaumya. The writings of some of these lawgivers have appeared in different forms, and are referred to with the descriptive epithets of Vriddha, 'old;' Brihat, 'great;' and Laghu, 'light or small.'

A general collection of the Smritis or Dharma-sastras has been printed in Calcutta under the title of Dharma-sastra-sangraha, by Jivananda.

DHRITARASHTRA: 1. The eldest son of Vichitravirya or Vyasa, and brother of Pandu. His mother was Ambika. He married Gandhari, and by her had a hundred sons, the eldest of whom was Duryodhana. Dhritarashtra was blind, and Pandu was affected with a disease supposed, from his name, "the pale," to be a leprous affection. The two brothers in turn renounced the throne, and the great war recorded in the Mahabharata was fought between their sons, one party being called Kauravas from an ancestor, Kuru, and the other Pandavas, from their father Pandu. Dhritarashtra and his wife were burned in a forest fire. 2. An enormous serpent of many heads and immense strength.

DHRUVA: The polar star. According to the Vishnu Purana, the sons of Manu Swayambhuva were Priyavrata and Uttanapada. The latter had two wives; the favourite, Suruchi, was proud and haughty; the second, Suniti or Sanrita, was humble and gentle. Suruchi had a son named Uttama, and Suniti gave birth to Dhruva. While quite a child Dhruva was contemptuously treated by Suruchi, and she told him that her own son Uttama would alone succeed to the throne. Dhrnva and his mother submitted, and he declared that he wished for no other honours than such as his own actions should acquire. He was a Kshatriya, but he joined a society of Rishis, and becoming a Rishi himself, he went through a rigid course of austerities, notwithstanding the efforts of Indra to distract him. At the end he obtained the favour of Vishnu, who raised him to the skies as the pole-star. He has the patronymic Auttanapadi, and he is called Grahadhara, 'the stay or pivot of the planets.'

DILIPA: Son of Ansumat and father of Bhagiratha. He was of the Solar race and ancestor of Rama. On one occasion he failed to pay due respect to Surabhi, the 'cow of fortune,' and she passed a curse upon him that he should have no offspring until he and his wife Sudakshina had carefully tended Surabhi's daughter Nandini. They obediently waited on this calf Nandini, and Dilipa once offered his own life to save hers from the lion of Siva. In due time the curse was removed, and a son, Raghu, was born to them. This story is told in the Raghuvansa.

DITI: A goddess or personification in the Vedas who is associated with Aditi, and seems to be intended as an antithesis or as a complement to her.

In the Ramayana and in the Puranas she is daughter of Daksha, wife of Kasyapa, and mother of the Daityas. The Vishnu Purana relates that having lost her children, she bagged of Kasyapa a son of irresistible prowess, who should destroy Indra. The boon was granted, but with this condition: "If, with thoughts wholly pious and person entirely pure, you carefully carry the babe in your womb for a hundred years." She assiduously observed the condition; but Indra knew what was preparing for him. So he went to Diti and attended upon her with the utmost humility, watching his opportunity. In the last year of the century, Diti retired one night to reat without washing her feet. Indra then with his thunderbolt divided the embryo in her womb into seven portions. Thus mutilated, the child cried bitterly, and Indra being unable to pacify it, became angry, and divided each of the seven portions into seven, thus forming the swift-moving deities called Maruts, from the words, 'Marodih,' 'Weep not,' which Indra used to quiet them.

DIVODASA: 1. A pious liberal king mentioned in the Rigveda, for whom it is aaid that Indra demolished a hundred stone cities, meaning perhaps the mythological aerial cities of the Asuras. 2. A Brahmin who was the twin-brother of Ahalya.

He is represented in the Veda as a "very liberal sacrificer,' and as being delivered by the gods from the oppressor Sambara. He is also called Atithigwa, 'he to whom guests slould go.' 3. A king of Kasi, son of Bhimaratha and father of Pratardana. He was attacked by the sons of King Vitahavya and all his sons were slain. His son Pratadana was boru to him through a sacrifice performed by Bharadwaja. He was celebrated as a physician and was called Dhanwantari.

DRAUPADI: Daughter of Drupada, king of Panchala, and wife of the five Pandu princes. Draupadi was a damsel of dark complexion but of great beauty, "as radiant and graeeful as if she had descended from the city of the gods." Her hand was sought by many princes, and so her father determined to hold a swayamvara and allow her to exercise her own choice in the selection of a husband. The swayamvara was proclaimed, and princes assembled from all parts to contend in the lists for the hand of the princess; for although in such contests the lady was entitled to exercise her swayamvara or own choice, it generally followed that the champion of the arena became her husband. Most astonishing feats of arms were performed, but Arjuna out-shone all by his marvellous use of the bow, and he became the selected bridegroom.

When the five brothers returned to the house where their mother, Kunti, was staying, they told her that they had made a great acquisition, and she told them to share it among them. These words raised a great difficulty, for if they could not be adroitly evaded, they must be obeyed. The sage Vyasa settled the matter by saying, "The destiny of Draupadi has already been declared by the gods; let her become the wife of all the brethren." So she became their common wife, and it was arranged that she should stay successively two days in the house of each, and that no one of them but the master of the house should enter it while she was there. Arjuna was her favourite, and she showed her jealousy when he married Subhadra. In the great gambling match which the eldest brother, Yudhishthira, played at Hastinapura against his cousins, the Kauvaras, he lost his all—his kingdom, his brothers, himself, and their wife Draupadi. So she became a slave, and Duryodhana called her to come and sweep the room. She refused, and then Duhsasana dragged her by the hair into the pavilion before all the chisftains, and tauntingly told her that she was a slave girl, and had no right to complain of being touched by men. He also abused her and tore off her veil and dress, while Duryodhana invited her to sit on his thigh.

Krishna took compassion upon her, and restored her garments as fast as they were torn. She called vehemently upon her husbands to save her, but they were restrained by Yudhishthira. Bhima was in a rage of passion; he was prevented from action; but he vowed in loud words that he would drink the blood of Duhsasana and smash the thigh of Duryodhana in retaliation of these outrages, which vows he eventually fulfilled. Draupadi vowed that her hair should remain dishevelled until Bhima should tie it up with hands dripping with the blood of Duhsasana. The result of the gambling match was that the Pandavas, with Draupadi, went into exile for twelve years, and were to dwell quite incognito during another year. The period of thirteen years being successfully completed, they were at liberty to return.

Twelve years of exile were passed in the jungle, and in the course of this period Jayadratha, king of Sindhu, came to the house of the Pandavas while they were out hunting. He was courteously received by Draupadi, and was fascinated by her charms. He tried to induce her to elope with him, and when he was scornfully repulsed, he dragged her to his chariot and drove off with her. When the Pandavas returned and heard of the rape, they pursued Jayadratha, and pressed him so close that he put down Draupadi, and endeavoured to escape alone. Bhima resolved to overtake and punish him; and although

Yudhishthira pleaded that Jayadratha was a kinsman, and ought not to be killed, Draupadi called aloud for vengeance, so Bhima and Arjuna continued the pursuit. Bhima dragged Jayadratha from his car, kicked and beat him till he was senseless, but spared his life. He cut off all Jayadratha's hair except five locks, and made him publicly acknowledge that he was a slave. Draupadi's revenge was then slaked, and Jayadratha was reluased at her intercession.

In the thirteenth year, in which her husbands and she were to live undiscovered, they entered the service of the king of Virata, and she, without acknowledging any connection with them, became a waiting-maid to the queen. She stipulated that she should not be required to wash feet or to eat food left by others, and she quieted the jealous fear, which her beauty excited in the queen's mind by representing that she was guarded by five Gandharvas, who would prevent any improper advances. She lived a quiet life for a while, but her beauty excited the passions of Kichaka, the quean's brother, who was commander-in-chisf, and the leading man in the kingdom. His importunities and insults greatly annoyed her, but she met with no protection from the queen, and was rebuked for her complaints and petulance by Yudhishthira. Her spirit of revenge was roused, and she appealed as usual to Bhima, whose fiery passions she well knew how to kindle. She complained of her menial position, of the insults she had received, of the indifference of her husbands, and of the base offices they were content to occupy.

Bhima promised revenge. An assignation was made with Kichaka which Bhima kept, and he so mangled the unfortunate gallant that all his flesh and bones were rolled into a ball, and no one could discover the manner of his death. The murder was attributed to Draupadi's Gandharvas, and she was condemned to be burnt on Kichaka's funeral pile. Then Bhima disguised himself, and tearing up a tree for a club, went to her rescue. He was supposed to be the Gandharva, and every one fled before him. He released Draupadi, and they returned to the city by different ways. After the term of exile was over, and the Pandavas and she were at liberty to return, she was more ambitious than her husbands, and complained to Krishna of the humility and want of resolution shown by Yuddishthira. She had five sons, one by each husband: Prativindhya, son of Yudhishthira; Srutasoma, son of Bhima; Srutakirti, son of Arjuna; Satanika, son of Nakula; and Srutakarman, son of Sahadeva. She with these five sons was present in camp on the eighteenth and last night of the great battle, while her victorious husbands were in the camp of the defeated enemy. Aswatthama with two companions entered the camp of the Pandavas, cut down these five youths, and all whom they found. Draupaui called for vengeance upon Aswatthama. Yudhishthira endeavoured to moderate her anger, but she appealed to Bhima. Arjuna pursued Aswatthama, and overtook him, but he spared his life after taking from him a celebrated jewel which he wore as an amulet. Arjuna gave this jewel to Bhima for presentation to Draupadi. On receiving it she was consoled, and presented the jewel to Yudhishthira as the head of the family. When her husbands retired from the world and went on their journey towards the Himalayas and Indra's heaven, she accompanied them, and was the first to fall on the journey.

Draupadi's real name was Krishna. She was called Draupadi and Yajnaseni, from her father; Parshati, from her grandfather Prishata; Panchali, from her country; Sairandhri, 'the maidservant' of the queen of Virata; Panchami, 'having five husbands;' and Niyayauvani, 'the ever-young.'

DRONA: 'A bucket.' A Brahmin so named from his having been generated by his father, Bharadwaja, in a bucket. He married Kripa, half-sister of Bhishma, and by her was father of Aswatthama. He was acharya, or teacher of the military art, both to the Kaurava and Pandava princes, and so he was called Dronacharya. He had been slighted by Drupada, king of Panchala, and became his enemy. Through the instrumentality of the Pandavas he made Drupada prisoner, and took from him half of his kingdom; but he spared his life and gave him back the other half of his country. But the old animosity rankled, and ended in the death of both. In the great war Drona sided with the Kauravas, and after the death of Bhishma he became their commander-in-chisf. On the fourth day of his command he killed Drupada, and in his turn he was unfairly slain in combat by Dhrishtadyumna, who had swom to avenge his father's death. In the midst of this combat Drona was told that his son was dead, which so unnerved him that he laid down his arms and his opponent decapitated him. But Drona was a Brahmin and an Acharya, and the crime of killing him was enormous, so it is glossed over by the statement that Drona "transported himself to heaven in a glittering state like the sun, and Dhrishtadyumna decapitated merely his lifeless body." Drona was also called Kutaja. The common meaning of Kuta is 'mountain-top,' but one of its many other meanings is ' water-jar.' His patronymic is Bbaradwaja.

DURYODHANA: 'Hard to conquer.' The eldest son of King Dhritarashtra, and leader of the Kaurava princes in the great war of the Mahabharata. His birth was somewhat marvellous. Upon the death of his brother Pandu, Dhritarashtra took his five sons, the Pandava princes, to his own court, and had them educated with his hundred sons. Bickerings and jealousies soon sprang up between the cousins, and Duryodhana took a special dislike to Bhima on account of his skill in the use of the club. Duryodhana had learnt the use of this weapon under Balarama, and was jealous of any rival. He poisoned Bhima and threw his body into the Ganges, but Bhima sank to the regions of the Nagas, where he was restored to health and vigour. When Dhritarashtra proposed to make Yudhishthira heir-apparent, Duryodhana strongly remonstrated, and the result was that the Pandavas went into exile. Even then his animosity pursued them, and he laid a plot to burn them in their house, from which they escaped and retaliated upon his emissaries.

After the return of the Pandavas from exile, and their establishment at Indraprastha, his anger was further excited by Yudhishthira's performance of the Raja-suya sacrifice. He prevailed on his father to invite the Pandavas to Hastinapura to a gambling match, in which, with the help of his confederate Sakuni, he won from Yudhishthira everything he possessed, even to the freedom of himself, his brothers, and his wife Draupadi. Duryodhana exultingly sent for Draupadi to act as a slave and sweep the room. When she refused to come, his brother, Duhsasana, dragged her in by the hair of her head, and Duryodhana insulted her by inviting her to sit upon his knee. This drew from Bhima a vow that he would one day smash Duryodhana's thigh. Dhritarashtra interfered, and the result of the gambling was that the Pandavas again went into exile, and were to remain absent for thirteen years.

While the Pandavas were living in the forest, Duryodhana went out for the purpose of gratifying his hatred with a sight of their poverty. He was attacked and made prisoner by the Gandharvas, probably hill people, and was rescued by the Pandavas. This incident greatly mortified him. The exile of the Pandavas drew to a close. War was inevitable, and both parties prepared for the struggle. Duryodhana sought the aid of Krishna, but made the great mistake of accepting Krishna's army in preference to his personal attendance. He accompanied his army to the field, and on the eighteenth day of the battle, after his party had been utterly defeated, he fled and hid himself in a lake, for he was said to possess the power of remaining under water. He was discovered, and with great difficulty, by taunts and sarcasms, was induced to come out. It was agreed that he and Bhima should fight it out with clubs. The contest was long and furious, and Duryodhana was getting the best of it, when Bhima remembered his vow, and, although it was unfair to strike below the waist, he gave his antagonist such a violent blow on the thigh that the bone was smashed and Duryodhana fell. Then Bhima kicked him on the head and triumphed over him.

Left wounded and alone on the field, he was visited by Aswatthama, son oı Drona, and two other warriors, the only survivors of his army. He thirsted for revenge, and directed them to slay all the Pandavas, and espeeially to bring him the head of Bhima. These men entered the camp of the enemy, and killed the five youthful sons of the Pandavas. The version of the Mahabharata used by Wheeler adds that these warriors brought the heads of the five youths to Duryodhana, representing them to be the heads of the five brothers. Duryodhana was unable in the twilight to distinguish the features, but he exulted greatly, and desired that Bhima's head might be placed in his hands. With dying energy he pressed it with all his might, and when he found that it crushed, he knew that it was not the head of Bhima. Having discovered the deception that had been played upor him, with a redeeming touch of humanity he reproached Aswatthama for his horrid deed in slaying the harmless youths, saying, with his last breath, "My enmity was against the Pandavas, not against these innocents." Duryodhana was called also Su-yodhana, 'good fighter.'

E

EKALAVYA: Grandson of Devasravas, the brother of Vasudeva. He was brother of Satrughna. He was exposed in infancy, and was brought up among the Nishadas, of whom he became king. He assisted in a night attack upon Dwaraka, and was eventually killed by Krishna, who hurled a rock at him.

G

GANDHARI: Princess of Gandhara. The daughter of Subala, king of Gandhara, wife of Dhritarashtra, and mother of his hundred sons. Her husband was blind, so she always wore a bandage over her eyes to be like him. Her husband and she, in their old age, both perished in a forest fire. She is also called by the patronymics Saubali and Saubaleyi. She is said to have owed her hundred sous to the blessing of Vyasa, who, in acknowledgment of her kind hospitality, offered her a boon. She ssked for a hundred sons. Then she became pregnant, and continued so for two years, at the end of which time she was delivered of a lump of flesh. Vyasa took the shapeless mass and divided it into 101 pieces, which he placed in as many jars. In due time Duryodhana was produced, but with such accompanying fearful portents that Dhritarashtra was besought, though in vain, to abandon him. A month afterwards ninetynine other sons came forth, and an only daughter, Duhsala.

GANDHARVA: The 'heavenly Gandharva' of the Veda was a deity who knew and revealed the secrets of heaven and divine truths in general. He is thought by Goldstucker to have been a personification of the fire of the sun. The Gandharvas generally had their dwelling in the sky or atmosphere, and one of their offices was to prepare the heavenly soma juice for the gods. They had a great partiality for women, and had a mystic power over them. The Atharvaveda speaks of "the 6333 Gandharvas." The Gandharvas of later times are similar in claracter; they have charge of the soma, are skilled in medicine, regulate the asterisms, and are fond of women. Those of Indra's heaven are generally intended by the term, and they are singers and musicians who attend the banquets of the gods. The Puranas give contradictory accounts of the origin of the Gandharvas.

The Vishnu Purana says, in one place, that they were born from Brahma, "imbibing melody. Drinking of the goddess of speech, they were born, and thence their appellation." Later on it says that they were the offspring of Kasyapa and his wife Arishta. The Harivansa states that they sprang from Brahma's nose, and also that they were descended from Muni, another of Kasyapa's wives. Chitraratha was chisf of the Gandharvas; and the Apsarases were their wives or mistresses. The "cities of the Gandharvas" are often ıeferred to as being very splendid. The Vishnu Purana has a legend of the Gandharvas fighting with the Nagas in the infernal regions, whose dominions they seized and whose treasures they plundered. The Naga chisfs appealed to Vishnu for relief, and he promised to appear in the person of Purukutsa to help them. Thereupon the Nagas sent their sister Narmada (the river) to this Purukutsa, and she conducted him to the regions below, where he destroyed the Gandharvas. They are sometimes called Gatus and Pulakas. In the Mahabharata, apparently, a race of people dwelling in the hills and wilds is so called.

GANESA (Gana+Isa), GANAPATI: Lord of the Ganas or troops of inferior deities, especially those attendant upon Siva. Son of Siva and Parvati, or of Parvati only. One legend represents that he sprang from the scurf of Parvati's body. He is the god of wisdom and remover of obstacles: hence he is invariably propitiated at the beginning of any important undertaking, and is invoked at the commencement of books. He is said to have written down the Mahabharata from the dictation of Vyasa. He is represented as a short fat man of a yellow colour, with a protuberant belly, four hands, and the head of an elephant, which has only one tusk. In one hand he holds a shell, in another a discus, in the third a club or goad, and in the fourth a water-lily. Sometimes he is depicted riding upon a rat or attended by one; hence his appellation Akhuratha.

His temples are very numerous in the Dakshin. There is a variety of legends accounting for his elephant head. One is that his mother Parvati, proud of her offspring, asked Sani (Saturn) to look at him, forgetful of the effects of Sani's glance. Sani looked and the child's head was burnt to ashes. Brahma told Parvati in her distress to replace the head with the first she could find, and that was an elephant's. Another story is that Parvati went to her bath and told her son to keep the door. Siva wished to enter and was opposed, so he cut off Ganesa's head. To pacify Parvati he replaced it with an elephant's, the first that came to hand. Another version is that his mother formed him so to suit her own fancy, and a further explanation is that Siva slew Aditya the sun, but restored him to life again. For this violence Kasyapa doomed Siva's son to lose his head; and when he did lose it, the head of Indra's elephant was used to replace it.

The loss of one tusk is accounted for by a legend which represents Parasurama as coming to Kailasa on a visit to Siva. The god was asleep and Ganesa opposed the entrance of the visitor to the inner apartments. A wrangle ensued, which ended in a fight. "Ganesa had at first the advantage, seizing Parasuriima with his trunk and giving him a twirl that left him sick and senseless. On recovering, Parsurama threw his axe at Ganesa, who, recognising it as his father's weapon Siva having given it to Parsurama, received it with all humility on one of his tusks, which it immediately severed; hence Ganesa has but one tusk, and is known by the name of Ekadanta or Ekadanshtra the single-tusked. These legends are narrated at length in the Brahma Vaivarta Purana.

Ganesa is also called Gajanana, Gajavadana, and Karimukha, 'elephant-faced;' Heramba 'boastful;' Lambakarna, long-eared;' Lambodara, 'pendant-bellied;' Dwideha, 'double-bodied;' Vighnesa, Yighnahari, 'remover of obstacles.' A peculiar appellation is Dwaimatura, 'having two mothers,' in allusion, it is said, to his birth from the scurf of Parvati's body.

GANGA: The sacred river Ganges. It is said to be mentioned only twice in the Rigveda. The Puranas represent the Viyad. ganga, or heavenly Ganges, to flow from the toe of Vishnu, and to have been brought down from heaven, by the prayers of the king Bhagiratha, to purify the ashes of the sixty thousand sons of King Sagara, who had been burnt by the angry glance of the sage Kapila. From this earthly parent the river is called Bhagirathi. Ganga was angry at being brought down from heaven, and Siva, to save the earth from the shock of her fall, caught the river on his brow, and checked its course with his matted locks. From this action he is called Gangadhara, 'upholder of the Ganges.' The river descended from Siva's brow in several streams, four according to some, and ten according to others, but the number generally accepted is seven, being the Saptasindhava, the seven sindhus or rivers. The Ganges proper is one of the number.

The descent of the Ganges disturbed the sage Jahnu as he was performing a sacrifice, and in his anger he drank up the waters, but he relented and allowed the river to flow from his ear, hence the Ganges has the name of Jahnavi. Personified as a goddess, Ganga is the eldest daughter of Himavat and Mena, and her sister was Uma. She became the wife of King Santanu and bore a son, Bhishma; who is also known by the metronymic Gangeya. Being also, in a peculiar way, the mother of Kartikeya, she is called Kumarasu Gold, according to the Mahabharata, was borne by the goddess Ganga to Agni, by whom she had been impregnated. Other names and titles of the Ganges are Bhadrasoma, Gandini, Kirati, Devabhuti, 'produced in heaven;' Harasekhara, 'crest of Siva;' Khapaga, 'flowing from heaven;' Mandakini, 'gently flowing,' Tripathaga or Trisrotah, 'triple flowing,' running in heaven, earth, and hell.

GARUDA: A mythical bird or vulture, half-man, half-bird, on which Vishnu rides. He is the king of birds, and descended from Kasyapa and Vinata, one of the daughters of Daksha. He is the great enemy of serpents, having inherited his hatred from his mother, who had quarrelled with her co-wife and superior, Kadru, the mother of serpents. His lustre was so brilliant that soon after his birth the gods mistook him for Agni and worshipped him. He is represented as having the head, wings, talons, and beak of an eagle, and the body and limbs of a man. His face is white, his wings red, and his body golden. He had a son named Sampata and his wife was Unnati or Vinayaka. According to the Mahabharata, his parents gave him liberty to devour bad men, but he was not to touch Brahmin. Once, however, he swallowed a Brahmin and his wife, but the Brahmin so burnt his throat that he was glad to disgorge them both.

Garuda is said to have stolen the Amrita from the gods in order to purchase with it the freedom of his mother from Kadru. Indra discovered the theft and fought a fierce battle with Garuda. The Amrita was recovered, but Indra was worsted in the fight, and his thunderbolt was smashed.

Garuda has many names and epithets. From his parents he is called Kasyapi and Vainateya. He is the Suparna and the Garutman, or chisf of birds. He is also called Dakshaya, Salmalia, Tarkshya, and Vinayaka, and among his epithets are the following:—Sitanana, 'white-faced;' Raktapaksha, 'red-winged;' Swetarohita, 'the white and red;' Suvarnakaya, 'golden-bodied;' Gaganeswara, ' lord of the sky;' Khageswara, 'king of birds;' Nagantaka, and Pannaga-nasana, 'destroyer of serpents;' Sarparati, 'enemy of serpents;' Taraswin, 'the swift;' Rasayana, 'who moves like quicksilver;' Kamacharin, 'who goes where he will;' Kamayus, 'who lives at pleasure;' Chirad, 'eating long;' Vishnuratha, 'vehicle of Vishnu;' Amritaharana and Sudhahara, 'stealer of the Amrita;' Surendrajit, 'vanquisher of Indra;' Vajra-jit, 'subduer of the thunderbolt,' etc.

GAYATRI: A most sacred verse of the Rigveda, which it is the duty of every Brahmin to repeat mentally in his morning and evening devotions. It is addressed to the sun as Savitri, the generator, and so it is ealled also Savitri. Personified as a goddess, Savitri is the wife of Brahma, mother of the four Vedas, and also of the twice-born or three superior castes. Colebrooke's translation of the Gayatri is "Earth, sky, heaven. Let us meditate on these, and on the most excellent light and power of that generous, sportive, and resplendent sun, (praying that) it may guide our intellects." Wilson's version is, in his translation of the Rigveda, " We meditate on that desirable light of the divine Savitri who influences our pious rites." In the Vishnu Purana he had before given a somewhat different version, "We meditate on that excellent light of the divine sun: may he illuminate our minds." A later version by Benfey is, "May we receive the glorious brightness of this, the generator, of the god who shall prosper our works."

Wilson observes of it: "The commentators admit some variety of interpretation; but it probably meant, in its original use, a simple invocation of the sun to shed a benignant influence upon the customary offices of worship; and it is still employed by the unphilosophical Hindus with merely that signification. Later notions, and especially those of the Vedanta, have operated to attach to the text an import it did not at first possess, and have converted it into a mystical propitiation of the spiritual origin and essence of existence, or Brahma." It is considered so holy that copyists often refrain from transcribing it.

The name given to Satarupa, Brahma's female half, daughter, and consort, is "the declarer of sacred knowledge." It is also applied to the consort of Siva in the Harivansa.

GHOSHA: It is said in the Veda that the Aswins "bestowed a husband upon Ghosha growing old," and the explanatory legend is that she was a daughter of Kakshivat, but being a leper, was incapable of marriage. When she was advanced in years the Aswins gave her health, youth, and beauty, so that she obtained a husband.

GITA-GOVINDA: A lyrical poem by Jayadeva on the early life of Krishna as Govinda the cowherd. It is an erotic work, and sings the loves of Krishna with Radha, and other of the cowherd damsels, but a mystical interpretation has been put upon it. The poems are supposed to have been written about the twelfth or thirteenth century. There are some translations in the Asiatic Researches by Sir W. Jones, and a small volume of translations has been published by Mr. Edwin Arnold. There is also an edition of the text, with a Latin translation and notes, by Lassen, and there are some others.

GOTAMA: The founder of the Nyaya school of philosophy. He is also called Satananda, and is author of a Dharma-sastra or law-book, which has been edited by Stenzler. He is frequently called Gautama.

GRIHYA SUTRAS: Rules for the conduct of domestic rites and the personal sacraments, extending from the birth to the marriage of a man. The Grihya Sutras of Aswalayana have been printed in the Bibliotheca Indica.

H

HAIHAYA: This name is supposed to be derived from haya, 'a horse.' 1. A prince of the Lunar race, and great-grandson of Yadu. 2. A race or tribe of people to whom a Scythian origin has been ascribed. The Vishnu Purana represents them as decendants of Haihaya of the Yadu race, but they are generally associated with borderers and outlying tribes. In the Vayu and other Puranas, five great divisions of the tribe are named: Talajanghas, Vitihotras, Avantis, Tundikeras, and Jatas, or rather Sujatas. They conquered Bahu or Bahuka, a descendant of King Harischandra and were in their turn conquered, along with many other barbarian tribes, by King Sagara, son of Bahu. According to the Mahabharata, they were descended from Saryati, a son of Manu. They made incursions into the Doab, and they took the city of Kasi (Benares), which had been fortified against them by King Divodasa; but the grandson of this king Pratardana by name, destroyed the Haihayas, and re-established the kingdom of Kasi. Arjuna-Kartavirya, of a thousand arms, was king of the Haihayas, and he was defeated and had his arms cut off by Parsurama.

The Vindhya mountains would seem to have been the home of these tribes; and according to Colonel Todd, a tribe of Haihayas still exists "near the very top of the valley of Sohagpoor, in Baghelkhand, aware of their ancient lineage, and, though few in number, still celebrated for their valour."

HANUMAN, HANUMAT: A celebrated monkey-chief. He was son of Pavana, 'the wind,' by Anjana, wife of a monkey named Kesari. He was able to fly, and is a conspicuous figure in the Ramayana. He and the other monkeys who assisted Rama in his war against Ravana were of divine origin, and their powers were superhuman. Hanuman jumped from India to Lanka in one bound; he tore up trees, carried away the Himalayas, seized the clouds, and performed many other wonderful exploits. His form is "as vast as a mountain and as tall as a gigantic tower. His complexion is yellow and glowing like molten gold. His face is as red as the brightest ruby; while his enormous tail spreads out to an interminable length. He stands on a lofty rock and roars like thunder. He leaps into the air, and flies among the clouds with a rushing noise, whilst the ocean waves are roaring and splashing below."

In one of his fights with Ravana and the Rakshasas, they greased his tail and set it on fire, but to their own great injury, for with it he burnt down their capital city. This exploit obtained for him the name Lankadahi. His services to Rama were great and many. He acted as his spy, and fought most valiantly. He flew to the Himalayas, from whence he brought medicinal herbs with which he restored the wounded, and he killed the monster Kalanemi, and thousands of Gandharvas who assailed him. He accompanied Rama on his return to Ayodhya, and there he received from him the reward of perpetual life and youth. The exploits of Hanuman are favourite topics among Hindus from childhood to old age, and paintings of them are common. He is called Marutputra, and he has the patronymics Anili, Maruti, etc., and the metronymic Anjaneya. He is also Yogachara, from his power in magic or in the healing art, and Rajata-dyuti, 'the brilliant.' Among his othcr accomplishments, Hanumat was a grammarian; and the Ramayana says, "The chisf of monkeys is perfect; no one equals him in the sastras, in learning, and in ascertaining the sense of the scriptures or in moving at will. In all sciences, in the rules of austerity, he rivals the preceptor of the gods. . . . It is well known that Hanumat was the ninth author of grammar."—Muir.

HARIDWAR: 'The gate of Hari.' The modern Hardwar. The place where the Ganges finally breaks through the mountains into the plains of Hindustan. It is a great place of pilgrimage.

HARISCHANDRA: Twenty-eighth king of the Solar race, and son of Trisanku. He was celebrated for his piety and justice. There are several legends about him. The Aitareya Brahmana tells the story of his purchasing Sunahsepha to be offered up as a vicarious sacrifice for his own son. The Mahabharata relates that he was raised to the heaven of Indra for his performance of the Rajasuya sacrifice and for his unbounded liberality. The Markandeya Purana expands the story at considerable length. One day while Harischandra was hunting he heard female lamentations, which pro ceeded "from the Sciences, who were being mastered by the austerely fervid sage Viswamitra, and were crying out in alarm at his superiority." Harischandra, as defender of the distressed, went to the rescue, but Viswamitra was so provoked by his interference that the Sciences instantly perished, and Harischandra was reduced to a state of abject helplessness. Viswamitra demanded the sacrificial gift due to him as a Brahmin, and the king offered him whatever he might choose to ask, "gold, his own son, wife, body, life, kingdom, good fortune," whatever was dearest.

Viswamitra stripped him of wealth and kingdom, leaving him nothing but a garment of bark and his wife and soil. In a state of destitution he left his kingdom and Viswamitra struck Saibya, the queen, with his staff to haste her reluctant departure. To escape from his oppressor he proceeded to the holy city of Benares, but the relentless sage was waiting for him and demanded the completion of the gift. With bitter grief wife and child were sold, and there remained only himself. Dharma, the god of justice, appeared in the form of a hideous and offensive Chandala, and offered to buy him. Notwithstanding the exile's repugnance and horror, Viswamitra insisted upon the sale, and Harischandra was carried off "bound, beaten, confused, and afflicted," to the abode of the Chandala. He was sent by his master to steal grave-clothes from a cemetery. In this horrid place and degrading work he spent twelve months. His wife then came to the cemetery to perform the obsequies of her son, who had died from the bite of a serpent. They recognised each other, and Harischandra and his wife resolved to die upon the funeral pyre of their son, though he hesitated to take away his own life without the consent of his master.

After all was prepared, he gave himself up to meditation on Vishnu. The gods then arrived, headed by Dharma and accompanied by Viswamitra. Dharma entreated him to refrain from his intention, and Indra informed him "that he, his wife, and son, had conquered heaven by their good works." Harischandra declared that he could not go to heaven without the permission of his master the Chandala. Dharma then revealed himself. When this difficulty was removed, Harischandra objected to go to heaven without his faithful subjects. "This request was granted by Indra, and after Viswamitra had inaugurated Rohitaswa, the king's son, to be his successor, Harischandra, his friends, and followers, all ascended in company to heaven." There he was induced by the sage Narada to boast of his merits, and this led to his expulsion from heaven. As he was falling he repented of his fault and was forgiven. His downward course was arrested, and he and his followers dwell in an aerial city, which, aecording to popular belief, is still visible occasionally in mid-air.

HARIVANSA: The genealogy of Hari or Vishnu, a long poem of 16,375 verses. It purports to be a part of the Mahabharata, but it is of much later date, and "may more accurately be ranked with the Pauranik compilations of least authenticity and latest date." It is in three parts: the first is introductory, and gives particulars of the creation and of the patriarchal and regal dynasties; the second contains the life and adventures of Krishna; and the last and the third treats of the future of the world and the corruptions of the Kali age. It contains many indications of its having been written in the south of India.

HASTINAPURA: The capital city of the Kauravas, for which the great war of the Mahabharata was waged. It was founded by Hastin, son of the first Bharata, and hence, as some say, its name; but the Mahabharata and the Vishnu Purana call it the "elephant city," from hastin, an elephant. The ruins are traceable near an old bed of the Ganges, about 57 miles N.E. of Delhi, and local tradition has preserved the name. It is said to have been washed away by the Ganges.

HIDIMBA (mas), HIDIMBAA (fem.): A powerful Asura, who had yellow eyes and a horrible aspect. He was a cannibal and dwelt in the forest to which the Pandavas retired after the burning of their house. He had a sister named Hidimbaa, whom he sent to lure the Pandavas to him; but on meeting with Bhima, she fell in love with him, and offered to carry him away to safety on her back. Bhima refused, and while they were parleying, Hidimbaa came up, and a terrible fight ensued, in which Bhima killed the monster. Hidimbia was at first much terrified and fled, but she returned and claimed Bhima for her husband. By his mother's desire Bhima married her, and by her had a son named Ghatotkacha.

HIRANYAGARBHA: 'Golden egg' or 'golden womb.' In the Rigveda Hiranyagarbha "is said to have arisen in the beginning, the one lord of all beings, who upholds heaven and earth, who gives life and breath, whose command even the gods obey, who is the god over all gods, and the one animating principle of their being." According to Manu, Hiranyagarbha was Brahma, the first male, formed by the undiscernible eternal First Cause in a golden egg resplendent as the sun. " Having continued a year in the egg, Brahma divided it into two parts by his mere thought, and with these two shells he formed the heavens and the earth; and in the middle he placed the sky, the eight regions, and the eternal abode of the waters."

HIRANYAKSHA: 'Golden eye.' A Daitya who dragged the earth to the depths of the ocean. He was twin-brother of Hiranyakasipu, and was killed by Vishnu in the Boar incarnation.

I

IDA: In the Rigveda Ida is primarily food, refreshment, or a libation of milk; thence a stream of praise, personified as the goddeas of speech. She is called the instructress of Manu, and frequent passages ascribe to her the first institution of the rules of performing sacrifices. According to Sayana, she is the goddess presiding over the earth. A legend in the Satapatha Brahmana represents her as springing from a sacrifice which Manu performed for the purpose of obtaining offspring. She was claimed by MitraVaruna, but remained faithful to him who had produced her. Manu lived with her, and praying and fasting to obtain offspring, he begat upon her the race of Manu. In the Puranas she is daughter of the Manu Vaivaswata, wife of Budha (Mercury), and mother of Puraravas.

The Manu Vaivaswata, before he had sons, instituted a sacrifice to Mitra and Varuna for the purpose of obtaining one; but the officiating priest mismanaged the performance, and the result was the birth of a daughter, Ida or Ila. Through the favour of the two deities her sex was changed, and she became a man, Sudyumna. Under the malediction of Siva, Sudyumna was again turned into woman, and, as Ida, married Budha or Mercury. After she had given birth to Puraravas, she, under the favour of Vishnu, once more became Sudyumna, and was the father of three sons. According to another version of the legend, Manu's eldest son was named Ila. He having trespassed on a grove sacred to Parvati, was changed into a female, Ila. Upon the supplications and prayers of Ila's friends, Siva and his consort conceded that the offender should be a male one month and a female another. There are other variations in the story which is apparently ancient.

INDRA: The god of the firmament, the personified atmosphere. In the Vedas he stands in the first rank among the gods, but he is not uncreated, and is represented as having a father and mother: "a vigorous god begot him; a heroic female brought him forth." He is described as being of a ruddy or golden colour, and as having arms of enormous length; "but his forms are endless, and he can assume any shape at will." He rides in a bright golden car, drawn by two tawny or ruddy horses with flowing manes and tails. His weapon is the thunderbolt, which he carries in his right hand; he also uses arrows a great hook, and a net, in which he is said to entangle his foes. The soma juice is his especial delight; he takes enormous draughts of it, and, stimulated by its exhilarating qualities, be goes forth to war against his foes, and to perform his other duties.

As deity of the atmosphere, he governs the weather and dispenses the rain; he sends forth his lightnings and thunder, and he is continually at war with Vritra or Ahi, the demon of drought and inclement weather, whom he overcomes with his thunderbolts, and compels to pour down the rain. Strabo describes the Indians as worshipping Jupiter Pluvias, no doubt meaning Indra, and he has also been compared to Jupiter Tonans. One myth is that of his discovering and rescuing the cows of the priests or of the gods, which had been stolen by an Asura named Pani or Vala, whom he killed, and he is hence called Valabhid. He is frequently represented as destroying the "stone-built cities" of the Asuras or atmospheric demons, and of the Dasyus or aborigines of India. In his warfare he is sometimes represented as escorted by troops of Maruts, and attended by his comrade Vishnu.

More hymns are addressed to Indra than to any other deity in the Vedas, with the exception of Agni. For he was reverenced in his beneficent character as the bestower of rain and the cause of fertility, and he was feared as the awful ruler of the storm and director of the lightning and thunder. In many places of the Rigveda the highest divine functions and attributes are ascribed to him. There was a triad of gods—Agni, Vayu, and Surya which held a pre-eminence above tbe rest, and Indra frequently took the place of Vayu. In some parts of the Veda, as Dr. Muir remarks, the ideas expressed of Indra are grand and lofty; at other times he is treated with familiarity, and his devotion to the soma juice is dilated upon, though nothing debasing is perceived in his sensuality. Indra is mentioned and having a wife, and the name of Indrani oı Aindri is invoked among the goddesses. In the Satapatha Brahmana she is called Indra's beloved wife.

In the later mythology Indra has fallen into the second rank. He is inferior to the triad, but he is the chisf of all the other gods. He is the regent of the atmosphere and of the east quarter of the compass, and he reigns over Swarga, the heaven of the gods and of beatified spirits, which is a region of great magnificence and splendour. He retains many of his Vedic characteristics, and some of them are intensified. He sends the lightning and hurls the thunderbolt, and the rainbow is his bow. He is frequently at war with the Asuras, of whom he lives in constant dread, and by whom he is often worsted. But he slew the demon Vritra, who, being regarded as a Brahmin, Indra had to conceal himself and make sacrifice until his guilt was purged away. His continued love for the soma juice is shown by a legend in the Mahabharata, which represents him as being compelled by the sage Chyavana to allow the Aswins to partake of the soma libations, and his sensuality has now developed into an extreme lasciviousness.

Many instances are recorded of his incontinence and adultery, and his example is frequently referred to as an excuse in cases of gallantry, as by King Nahusha when he tried to obtain Indra's wife while the latter was hiding in fear for having killed the Brahmin in the person of the demon Vritra. According to the Mahabharata, he seduced, or endeavoured to seduce, Ahalya, the wife of the sage Gautama, and that sage's curse impressed upon him a thousand marks resembling the female organ, so he was called Sayoni; but these marks were afterwards changed to eyes, and he is hence called Netrayoni, and Sahasraksha 'the thousand-eyed.' In the Ramayana it is related that Ravana, the Rakshasa king of Lanka or Ceylon, warred against Indra in his own heaven, and that Indra was defeated and carried off to Lanka by Ravana's son Meghanada, who for this exploit received the title of Indrajit, 'conqueror of Indra.' Brahma and the gods had to sue for the release of Indra, and to purchase it with the boon of immortality to the victor. Brahma then told the humiliated god that his defeat was a punishment for the seduction of Ahalya. The Taittiriya Brahmana states that he chose Indrani to be his wife in preference to other goddesses because of her voluptuous attractions, and later authorities say that he ravished her, and slew her father, the Daitya Puloman, to escape his curse. Mythologically he was father of Arjuna, and for him he cheated Kama of his divine coat of mail, but gave Kama in recompense a javelin of deadly effect. His libertine character is also shown by his frequently sending celestial nymphs to excite the passions of holy men, and to beguile them from the potent penances which he dreaded.

In the Puranas many stories are told of him, and he appears especially in rivalry with Krishna. He incurred the wrath of the choleric sage Durvasa by slighting a garland of flowers which that sage presented to him, and so brought upon himself the curse that his whole dominion should be whelmed in rain. He was utterly defeated by the Daityas, or rather by their ally, Raja, son of Ayus, and grandson of Puraravas, and he was reduced to such a forlorn condition that he, "the god of a hundred sacrifices," was compelled to beg for a little sacrificial butter. Puffed up by their victory, his conquerors neglected their duties, and so they became the easy prey of Indra, who recovered his dominion. The Bhagavata Purana represents him as having killed a Brahmin, and of being haunted by that crime, personified as a Chandali.

Indra had been an object of worship among the pastoral people of Vraja, but Krishna persuaded them to cease this worship. Indra was greatly enraged at this, and sent a deluge of rain to overwhelm them; but Krishna lifted up the mountain Govardhana on his finger to shelter them, and so held it for seven days, till Indra was baffled and rendered homage to Krishna. Again, when Krishna went to visit Swarga, and was about to carry off the Parijata tree, Indra resented its removal, and a fierce fight ensued, in which Indra was worsted, and the tree was carried off. Among the deeds of Indra recorded in the Puranas is that of the destruction of the offspring of Diti to her womb, and the production therefrom of the Maruts; and there is a story of his cutting off the wings of the mountains with his thunderbolts, because they were refractory and troublesome. Indrs is represented as a fair man riding on white horse or an elephant, and bearing the vajra or thunderbolt in his hand. His son is named Jayanta. Indra is not the object of direct worship, but he receives incidental adoration, and there is a festival kept in his honour called Sakra-dhwajotthana, 'the raising of the standard of Indra.'

Indra's names are many, as Mahendra, Sakra, Maghavan, Ribhuksha., Vasava, Arha, Datteya. His epithets or titles also are numerous. He is Vritrahan, 'the destroyer of Vritra;' Vajra-pani, 'of the thunderbolt hand;' Meghavahana, 'borne upon the clouds;' Pakasasana., 'the subduer of Pika;' Satakratu, 'of a hundred sacrifices;' Devapati and Suradhipa, 'chisf of the gods;' Divaspati, 'ruler of the atmosphere;' Marutwan, Lord of the winds;' Swargapati, 'lord of paradise;' Jishnu, 'leader of the celestial host;' Purandara, 'destroyer of cities;' Uluka, 'the owl;' Ugradhanwan, 'of the terrible bow,' and many others. The heaven of Indra is Swarga; its capital is Amaravati; his palace, Vaijayanta; his garden, Nandana, Kandasara, or Pirushya; his elephant is Airavata; his horse, Uchchahsravas; his chariot, Vimana; his charioteer, Matali; his bow, the rainbow, Sakradhanus; and his sword, Paranja.

INDRA-DYUMNA: Son of Sumati and grandson of Bharata. There were several of the name, among them a king of Avanti, by whom the temple of Vishnu was built, and the image of Jagannatha was set up in Orissa.

INDRAJIT: Meghanada, son of Ravana. When Ravana went against Indra's forces in Swarga., his son Meghanada accompanied him, and fought most valiantly. Indra himself was obliged to interfere, when Meghanada, availing himself of the magical power of becoming invisible, which he had obtained from Siva, bound Indra and carried him off to Lanka. The gods, headed by Brahma, went thither to obtain the release of Indra, and Brahma gave to Meghanada the name Indrajit, conqueror of Indra. Still the victor refused to release his prisoner for anything less than the boon of immortality. Brahma refused, but Indrajit persisted in his demand and achisved his object. One version of the Ramayana states that Indrajit was killed and had his head cut off by Lakshmana, who surprised him while he was engaged in a sacrifice.

INDRANI: Wife of Indra, and mother of Jayanta and Jayanti. She is also called Sachi and Aindri. She is mentioned a few times in the Rigveda, and is said to be the most fortunate of females, "for her husband shall never die of old age." The Taittiriya Brahmana states that Indra chose her for his wife from a number of competing goddesses, because she surpassed them all in voluptuous attractions. In the Ramayana and Puranas she appears as the daughter of the Daitya Puloman, from whom she has the patronymic Paulomi. She was ravished by Indra, who killed her father to escape his curse. According to the Mahabharata, King Nahusha became enamoured of her, and she escaped from him with difficulty. Indrani has never been held in very high esteem as a goddess.

J

JABALI, JAVALI: A Brahmin who was priest of King Dasaratha, and held sceptical philosophical opinions. He is represented in the Ramayana as enforcing his views upon Rama, who decidedly repudiated them. Thereupon he asserted that his atheistical arguments had been used only for a purpose, and that he was really imbued with sentiments of piety and religion. He is said to have been a logician, so probably he belonged to the Nyaya school.

JAGANNATHA: 'Lord of the world.' A particular form or Vishnu, or rather of Krishna. He is worshipped in Bengal and other parts of India, but Puri, near the town of Cuttack, in Orissa, is the great seat of his worship, and multitudes of pilgrims resort thither from all parts, especially to the two great festivals of the Snanayatra and Rathayatra, in the months of Jyaishtha and Ashadha. The first of these is when the image is bathed, and in the second, or car festival, the image is brought out upon a car with the images of his brother Balarama and sister Subhadra, and is drawn by the devotees. The legend of the origin of Jagannatha is peculiar. Krishna was killed by a hunter, and his body was left to rot under a tree, but some pious persons found the bones and placed them in a box. A devout king named Indradyumna was directed by Vishnu to form an image of Jagannatha and to place the bones of Krishna inside it. Viswakarma, the architect of the gods, undertook to make the image, on condition of being left quite undisturbed till the work was complete. After fifteen days the king was impatient and went to Viswakarma, who was angry, and left off work before he had made either hands or feet, so that the image has only stumps. Indradyumna prayed to Brahma, who promised to make the image famous, and he did so by giving to it eyes and a soul, and by acting as high priest at its consecration.

JAHNU: A sage descended from Pururavas. He was disturbed in his devotions by the passage of the river Ganga, and consequently drank up its waters. He afterwards relented, and allowed the stream to issue from his ear, hence Ganga is called Jahnavi, daughter of Jahnu.

JAIMINI: A celebrated sage, a disciple of Vyasa. He is said to have received the Samaveda from his master, and to have been its publisher or teacher. He was also the founder of the Purvamimansa philosophy. The text of Jaimini is printed in the Bibliotheca Indica.

JAMADAGNI: A Brahmin and a descendant of Bhrigu. He was the son of Richika and Satyavati, and was the father of five sons, the youngest and most renowned of whom was Parsurama. Jamadagni's mother, Satyavati, was daughter of King Gadhi, a Kshatriya. The Vishnu Purana relates that when Satya-vati was pregnant, her Brahmin husband, Richika, prepared a mess for her to eat for the purpose of securing that her son should be born with the qualities of a Brahmin. He also gave another mess to her mother that she might bear a son with the character of a warrior. The women changed the messes, and so Jamadagni, the son of Richika, was born as a warrior-Brahmin, and Viswamitra, son of the Kshatriya Gadhi, was born as a priest.

The Mahabharata relates that Jamadagni engaged deeply in study and "obtained entire possession of the Vedas." He went to King Renu or Prasenajit of the solar race and demanded of him his daughter Renuka. The king gave her to him, and he retired with her to his hermitage, where the princess shared in his ascetic life. She bore him five sons, Rumanwat, Sushena, Vasu, Viswavasu, and Parsurama, and she was exact in the performance of all her duties. One day she went out to bathe and beheld a loving pair sporting and dallying in the water. Their pleasure made her feel envious, so she was "defiled by unworthy thoughts, and returned wetted but not purified by the stream." Her husband beheld her "fallen from perfection and shorn of the lustre of her sanctity." So he reproved her and was exceedingly wroth. His sons came into the hermitage in the order of their birth, and he commanded each of them in succession to kill his mother. Influenced by natural affection, four of them held their peace and did nothing. Their father cursed them and they became idiots bereft of all understanding. When Parsurama entered, he obeyed his father's order and struck off his mother's head with his axe. The deed assuaged the father's anger, and he desired his son to make request. Parsurama begged that his mother might be restored to life in purity, and that his brothers might regain their natural condition. All this the father granted.

The mighty Kartavirya, king of the Haihayas, who had a thousand arms, paid a visit to the hermitage of Jamadagni. The sage and his sons were out, but his wife treated her guest with all proper respect. Unmindful of the hospitality he had received, Kartavirya threw down the trees round the hermitage, and carried the calf of the sacred cow, Surabhi, which Jamadagni had acquired by penance. Parsurama returned and discovered what had happened, he then pursued Kartavirya, cut off his thousand arms with arrows, and killed him. The sons of Kartavirya went in revenge to the hermitage of Jamadagni, and in the absence of Parsurama slew the pious sage without pity. When Parsurama found the lifeless body of his father, he laid it on a funeral pile, and vowed that he would extirpate the whole Kshatriya race. He slew all the sons of Karta-virya, and "thrice seven times" he cleared the earth of the Kshatriya caste.

JAMBUDWIPA: One of the seven islands or continents of which the world is made up. The great mountain, Meru, stands in its centre, and Bharatavarsha or India is its best part. Its varshas or divisions are nine in number:—(1.) Bharata, south of the Himalayas and southernmost of all, (2.) Kimpurusha, (3.) Harivarsha, (4.) Ilavrita, containing Meru, (5.) Ramyaka, (6.) Hiranmaya, (7.) Uttarakuru, each to the north of the preceding one, (8.) Bhadraswa and (9.) Ketumala lie respectively in the east and west of Ilavrita, the central region.

JANAKA: 1. King of Mithila, of the Solar race. When Nimi, his predecessor, died without leaving a successor, the sages subjected the body of Nimi to attrition, and produced from it a prince "who was called Janaka, from being born without a progenitor." He was the first Janaka, and twenty generations earlier than Janaka the father of Sita.

2. King of Videha and father of Sita, remarkable for his great knowledge and good works and sanctity. He is called Sita-dhwaja, 'he of the plough banner,' because his daughter Sita sprang up ready formed from the furrow when he was ploughing the ground and preparing for a sacrifice to obtain offspring. The sage Yajnawalkya was his priest and adviser. The Brahmanas relate that he "refused to submit to the hierarchical pretensions of the Brahmins, and asserted his right of performing sacrifices without the intervention of priests." He succeeded in his contention, for it is said that through his pure and righteous life he became a Brahmin and one of the Rajarshis. He and his priest Yajnawalkya are thought to have prepared the way for Buddha.

JANAMEJAYA: A great king, who was son of Parikshit, and grest-grandson of Arjuna. It was to this king that the Mahabharata was recited by Vaisampayana, and the king listened to it in expiation of the sin of killing a Brahmin. His father, Parikshit, died from the bite of a serpent, and Janamijaya is said to have performed a great sacrifice of serpents (Nagas) and to have conquered the Naga people of Takshsila. Hence he is called Sarpasatri, 'serpent-sacrificer.' There were several others of the same name.

JARASANDHA: Son of Brihadratha, and king of Magadha. Brihadratha had two wives, who after being long barren brought forth two halves of a boy. These abortions were regarded with horror and thrown away. A female maneating demon named Jara picked them up and put them together to carry them off. On their coming in contact a boy was formed, who cried out so lustily that he brought out the king and his two queens. The Rakshasi explained what had happened, resigned the child, and retired. The father gave the boy the name of Jarasandha, because he had been put together by Jara. Future greatness was prophesied for the boy, and he became an ardent worshipper of Siva. Through the favour of this god he prevailed over many kings, and he especially fought against Krishna, who had killed Kansa, the husband of two of Jara sandha's daughters. He besieged Mathura, and attacked Krishna eighteen times, and was as often defeated; but Krishna was so weakened that he retired to Dwaraka. Jarasandha had many kings in captivity, and when Krishna returned from Dwaraka, he, with Bhima and Arjuna, went to Jarasandha's capital for the purpose of slaying their enemy and liberating the kings. Jarasandha refused to release the kings, and accepted the alternative of a combat, in which he was killed by Bhima.

JATAVEDAS: A Vedic epithet for fire. "The meaning is explained in five ways:—(1.) Knowing all created beings; (2.) Possessing all creatures or everything existent; (3.) Known by crested beings; (4.) Possessing riches; (5.) Possessing Vedas, wisdom. Other derivations and explanations are found in the Brahmanas, but the exact sense of the word seems to have been very early lost, and of the five explanations given, only the first two would seem to be admissible for the Vedic texts. In one passage a form, Jataveda, seems to occur."—Williams. This form of the term, and the statement of Manu that the Vedas wers milked out from fire, air, and the sun, may perhaps justify the explanation, producer of the Vedas.'

JATAYU: According to the Ramayana, a bird who was son of Vishnu's bird Garuda, and king of the vultures. Others say he was a son of Aruna. He became an ally of Rama's, and he fought furiously against Ravana to prevent the carrying away of Sita. Ravana overpowered him and left him mortally wounded. Rama found him in time to hear his dying words, and to learn what had become of Sita. Rama and Lakshmana performed his funeral rites to "secure his soul in the enjoyment of heaven," whither he ascended in a chariot of fire. In the Puranas he is the friend of Dasaratha. When that king went to the ecliptic to recover Sita from Sani (Saturn), his carriage was consumed by a glance from the eye of the latter, but Jatayu caught the falling king and saved him. The Padma Purana says Dasaratha assailed Saturn because of a dearth, and when he and his car were hurled from heaven, Jatayu caught him.

JAYADRATHA: A prince of the Lunar race, son of Brihanmana. He was king of Sindhu, and was "indifferently termed Raja of the Sindhus or Saindhavas, and Raja of the Sauviras, or sometimes in concert Sindhusauviras," the Saindhavas and Sauviras both being tribes living along the Indus. Jayadratha married Duhsala, daughter of Dhritarashtra, and was an ally of the Kauravas. When the Pandavas were in exile he called at their forest abode while they were out hunting, and Draupadi was at home alone. He had with him six brothers and a large retinue, but the resources of the Pandavas were equal to the occasion, and Draupadi was able to supply five hundred deer with accompaniments for breakfast. This is explained by the statement that Yudhishthira, having worshipped the sun, obtained from that luminary an inexhaustible cauldron which was to supply all and every viand that might be required by the Pandavas in their exile.

Jayadratha was captivated by the charms of Draupadi, and tried to induce her to elope with him. When he was indignantly repulsed he carried her off by force. On the return of the

Pandavas they pursued the ravisher, defeated his forces, and made him prisoner. His life was spared by command of Yudhishthira, but Bhima kicked and beat him terribly, cut off his hair, and made him go before the assembled Pandavas and acknowledge himself to be their slave. At the intercession of Draupadi he was allowed to depart. He was killed, after a desperate conflict, by Arjuna on the fourteenth day of the great battle.

K

KABANDHA: 1. A disciple of Sumantu, the earliest teacher of the Atharvaveda. 2. A monstrous Rakshasa slain by Rama. He is asid to have been a son of the goddess Sri. He is described as "covered with hair vast as a mountain, without head or neck, having a mouth armed with immense teeth in the middle of his belly, arms a league long, and one enormous eye in his breast." He was originally a Gandharva, and his hideous deformity arose, according to one account, from a quarrel with Indra, whom he challenged, and who struck him with his thunderbolt, and drove his head and thighs into his body. According to another statement, his deformity arose from the curse of a sage. When mortally wounded, he requested Rama to burn his body, and when that was done he came out of the fire in his real shape as a Gandharva, and counselled Rama as to the conduct of the war against Ravana. He was also called Danu.

KACHA: A son of Brihaspati. According to the Mahabharata, he became a disciple of Sukra or Usanas, the priest of the Asuras, with the object of obtaining from him the mystic power of restoring the dead to life, a charm which Sukra alone possessed. "To prevent this the Asuras killed Kacha again and again, but on both occasions he was restored to life by the sage at the intercession of Devayani, his daughter, who had fallen in love with Kacha. They killed him a third time, burnt his body, and mixed his ashes with Sukra's wine, but Devayani again implored her father to bring back the young man. Unable to resist his daughter's importunity, Sukra once more performed the charm, and to his surprise heard the voice of Kacha come out from his own belly.

To save his own life, Sukra taught his pupil the great charm. He then allowed himself to be ripped open, and Kacha, upon coming out, performed the charm, and restored his master to life. This incident is said to have caused Sukra to prohibit the use of wine to Brahmins. Kacha resisted the proposals of Devayani, and refused to make her his wife. She then cursed him, that the charms he had learnt from her father should be powerless, and he in return condemned her to be sought by no Brahmin, and to become the wife of a Kshatriya.

KADRU: A daughter of Daksha, and one of the thirteen that were married to Kasyapa. She was mother of "a thousand powerful manyheaded serpents, the chief amongst whom were Sesha, Vasuki, and many other fierce and venomous serpents." The Vishnu Purana, from which this is taken, names twelve, the Vayu Purana forty. Her offspring bear tho metronymic Kadraveya.

KAIKEYI: A princess of Kaikeya, wife of King Dasaratha, and mother of Bharata, his third son. She carefully tended Dasaratha when he was wounded in battle, and in gratitude he promised to grant any two requests she might make. Urged by the malignant counsels of Manthara, a female attendant, she made use of this promise to procure the exile of Rama, and to promote the advancement of her own son, Bharata, to his place.

KAILASA: A mountain in the Himalayas, north of the Manasa lake. Siva's paradise is said to be on Mount Kailasa, so also is Kuvera's abode. It is called also Ganaparvata and Rajatadri, 'silver mountain.'

KAKSHIVAT, KAKSHIVAN: A Vedic sage, particularly connected with the worship of the Aswins. He was the son of Dirghatamas and Usij, and is author of several hymns in the Rigveda. He was also called Pajriya, because he was or the race of Pajra. In one of his hymns he lauds the liberality of King Swanaya. The following legend, in explanation, is given by the commentator Sayana and the Nitimanjari:—Kakshivat, having finished his course of study, took leave of his preceptor and departed homewards. As he journeyed night came on, and he fell asleep by the roadside. In the morning he was aroused by Raja Swanaya, who, being pleased with his appearance, treated him cordially and took him home. After ascertaining his worthiness, he married him to his ten daughters, presenting him at the same time with a hundred nishkas of gold, a hundred horses, a hundred bulls, a thousand and sixty cows, and eleven chariots, one for each of his ten wives, and one for himself, each drawn by four horses. With these he returned home to his father, and recited the hymn in praise of the munificence of Swanaya.

KALANEMI: 1. In the Ramayana a Rakshasa, uncle of Ravana. At the solicitation of Ravana, and with the promise of half his kingdom, he endeavoured to kill Hanuman. Assuming the form of a hermitdevotee, he went to the Gandhamadana mountain, and when Hanuman proceeded thither in search of medicinal herbs, the disguised Rakshasa invited him to his hermitage and offered him food. Hanuman refused, but went to bathe in a neighbouring pond. Upon his placing his foot in the water it was seized by a crocodile, but he dragged the creature out and killed it. From the dead body there arose a lovely Apsara, who had been cursed by Daksha to live as a crocodile till she should be released by Hanuman. She told her deliverer to be beware of Kalanemi so Hanuman went back to that deceiver, told him that he knew him, and, taking him by the feet, sent him whirling through the air to Lanka, where he fell before the throne of Ravana in the councilroom. 2. In the Puranas a great Asura, son of Virochana, the grandson of Hiranyakasipu. He was killed by Vishnu, but was said to live again in Kansa and in Kaliya.

KALAYAVANA: Lit. 'Black Yavana,' Yavana meaning a Greek or foreigner. A Yavana or foreign king who led an army of barbarians to Mathura against Krishna. That hero lured him into the cave of the mighty Muchukunda, who being disturbed from sleep by a kick from Kalayavana, cast a fiery glance upon him and reduced him to ashes. This legend appears to indicate an invasion from the Himalayas. According to the Vishnu Purana and Harivansa, Kalayavana was the son of a Brahmin named Garga, who had an especial spite against the Yadavas, and was begotten by him on the wife of a childless Yavana king.

KALIKA PURANA: One of the eighteen Upa Puranas. "It contains about 9000 stanzas in 98 chapters, and is the only work of the series dedicated to recommend the worship of the bride of Siva, in one or other of her manifold forms as Girija, Devi, Bhadrakali, Kali, Mahamaya. It belongs, therefore, to the Sakta modification of Hindu belief, or the worship of the female powers of the deities. The influence of this worship shows itself in the very first pages of the work, which relate the incestuous passion of Brahma for his daughter, Sandhya, in a strain that has nothing analogous to it in the Vayu, Linga, or Siva Puranas. The marriage of Siva and Parvati is a subject early described, with the sacrifice of Daksha and the death of Sati And this work is authority for Siva's carrying the dead body about the world, and the origin of the Pithasthanas, or places where the different members of it were scattered, and where Lingas were consequently erected.

A legend follows of the births of Bhairava and Vetala, whose devotion to the different forms of Devi furnishes occasion to describe, in great detail, the rites and formulae of which her worship consists, including the chapters on sanguinary sacrifices translated in the Asiatic Researches. Another peculiarity in this work is afforded by very prolix descriptions of a number of rivers and mountains at Kamarwpa Tirtha, in Assam, and rendered holy ground by the celebrated temple of Durga in that country, as Kamakshi or Kamakhya. It is a singular and yet uninvestigated circumstance, that Assam, or at least the northeast of Bengal, seems to have been, in a great degree, the source from which the Tantrika and Sakta corruptions of the religion of the Vedas and Puranas proceeded."—Wilson.

KALIYA: A serpent king who had five heads, and dwelt in a deep pool of the Yamuna, with numerous attendant serpents. His mouths vomited fire and smoke, and he laid waste all the country round. Krishna, while yet a child, jumped into his pool, when he was quickly laced and entwined in the coils of the snakes. His companions and friends were horrified, but Balarama called upon him to exercise his divine power. He did so, and the serpents were soon overcome. Placing his foot on the middle head of Kaliya, he compelled him and his followers to implore mercy. He spared them, but bade Kaliya and his followers to free the earth from their presence, and to remove to the ocean. The Asura Kalanemi is said to have been animate in him.

KALIYUGA: The fourth or present age of the world, which is to endure for 432,000 years. It commenced in 3102 B.C.

KALMASHAPADA: A king of the Solar race, son of Sudasa (hence he is called Saudasa), and a descendant of Ikshwaku. His legend, as told in the Mahabharata, relates that while hunting in the forest he encountered Saktri, the eldest son of Vasishtha, and as this sage refused to get out of his way, he struck him with his whip. The incensed sage cursed him to become a cannibal This curse was heard by Viswamitra, the rival of Vasishtha, and he so contrived that the body of the king became possessed by a maneating Rakshasa. In this condition he caused human flesh to be served up to a Brahmin named Mitrasaha, who discovered what it was, and intensified the curse of Saktri by a new imprecation. One of Kalmashapada's first victims was Saktri himself, and all the hundred sons of Vasishtha fell a prey to his disordered appetite. After remaining twelve years in this state, he was restored to his natural condition by Vasishtha.

The Vishnu Purana tells the story differently. The king went out to hunt and found two destructive tigers. He killed one of them, but as it expired it was changed into a Rakshasa. The other tiger disappeared threatening vengeance. Kalmashapada celebrated a sacrifice at which Vasishtha officiated. When it was over and Vasishtha went out, the Rakshasa assumed his appearance, and proposed that food should be served. Then the Rakshasa transformed himself into a cook and, preparing human flesh, he served it to Vasishtha on his return. The indignant sage cursed the king that henceforth his appetite should be excited only by similar food. A wrangle ensued, and Vasishtha having found out the truth, limited the duration of his curse to twelve years. The angry king took water in his hands to pronounce, in his turn, a curse upon Vasishtha, but was dissuaded from his purpose by his wife, Madayanti. "Unwilling to cast the water on the ground, lest it should wither up the grain, and equally reluctant to throw it up into the air, lest it should blast the clouds and dry up their contents, he threw it upon his own feet," and they were so scalded by it that they became black and white, and so gained for him the name of Kalmashapada, 'spotted feet.' Every day for twelve years, at the sixth watch of the day, he gave way to his cannibal appetite, " and devoured multitudes of men." On one occasion he devoured a Brahmin in the midst of his connubial happiness, and the Brahmin's wife passed upon him a curse that he should die whenever he aasociated with his wife. At the expiration of Vasishtha's curse, the king returned home, but, mindful of the Brahmini's imprecation, he abstained from conjugal intercourse. By the interposition of Vasishtha, his wife, Madayanti, became pregnant, and bore a child in her womb for seven years, when she performed the Cesarean operation with a sharp stone, and a child came forth who was called Asmaka (from Asman, 'a stone').

KAMA, KAMADEVA: The god of love. Eros, Cupid. In the Rigveda (x. 129) desire is said to have been the first movement that arose in the one after it had come into life through the power of fervour or abstraction. "Desire first arose in it, which was the primal germ of mind; (and which) sages, searching with their intellect, have discovered in their heart to be the bond which connects entity with nonentity." "It is well known," observes Dr. Muir, "that Greek mythology connected Eros, the god of love, with the creation of the universe somewhat in the same way." "This Kama or desire, not of sexual enjoyment, but of good in general, is celebrated in a curious 'hymn of the Atharvaveda," which exalts Kama into a supreme God and Creator: "Kama was born the first. Him neither gods, nor fathers, nor men have equalled. Thou art superior to these and for ever great." In another part of the same Veda Kama appears to be first desire, then the power which gratifies the desire. Kama is also in "the same Veda often identified with Agni, and when" distinguished from each other, Kama may be looked upon as a superior form of the other deity."

According to the Taittiriya Brahmana, he is the son of Dharma, the god of justice, by Sraddhi, the goddess of faith; but according to the Harivansa he is son of Lakshmi. Another account represents him as springing from the heart of Brahma. A fourth view is that he was born from water, wherefore he is called Iraja, 'the waterborn;' a fifth is that he is Atmabhu, 'self-existent,' and therefore he is called, like other of the gods, Aja, 'unborn,' or Ananyaja, 'born of no other.' In the Puranas his wife is Rati or Reva, the goddess of desire. He inspired Siva with amorous thoughts of Parvati while he was engaged in penitential devotion, and for this offence the angry god reduced him to ashes by fire from his central eye. Siva afterwards relented and allowed Kama to be born again as Pradyumna, son of Krishna and Rukmini or Maya, 'delusion.' He has a son named Aniruddha, and a daughter, Trisha. He is lord of the Apsarases or heavenly nymphs. He is armed with a bow and arrows: the bow is of sugarcane, the bowstring a line of bees, and each arrow is tipped with a distinct flower. He is usually represented as a handsome youth riding on a parrot and attended by nymphs, one of whom bears his banner displaying the Makara, or a fish on a red ground.

The mysterious origin of Kama and the universal operation of the passion he inspires have accumulated upon him a great variety of names and epithets. Among his Dames are Ishma, Kanjana and Kinkira, Mada, Rama or Ramana, and Smara. As produced in the mind or heart he is Bhavaja and Manoja. As Pradyumna, son of Krishna, he is Karshni, and as son of Lakshmi he is Mayi or Mayasuta and Srinandana. As reduced to ashes by Siva he is Ananga, 'the bodiless.' He is Abhirapa, 'the beautiful;' Darpaka and Dipaka, 'the inflamer;' Gadayitnu, Gridhu, and Gritsa, 'lustful or sharp;' Kamana and Kharu, 'desirous;' Kandarpa, , the inflamer of Brahma;' Kantu, 'the happy;' Kalakeli, 'the gay or wanton;' Mara, 'destroyer;' Mayi, 'deluder;' Madhudipa, 'the lamp of honey or of spring;' Muhira, 'the bewilderer;' Murmura, 'the crackling fire;' Ragavrinta, 'the stalk of passion;' Rupastra, 'the weapon of beauty;' Ratanaricha, 'the voluptuary;' Samantaka, 'destroyer of peace;' Sansaraguru, 'teacher of the world;' Smara, 'remembrance;' Sringarayoni, 'source of love;' Titha, 'fire;' Vama, 'the handsome.' From his bow and arrows he is called Kusumayudha, 'armed with flowera;' Pushpadhanus, 'whose bow is flowers;' and Pushpasara, 'whose arrows are flowers.' From his banner he is known as Makaraketu; and from the flower be carries in his hand he is Pushpaketana.

KAMADHENU: The cow which grants desires, belonging to the sage Vasishtha. She was produced at the churning of the ocean. Among the examples of her supernatural powers was the creation of a host of warriors who aided Vasishtha against Kartavirya. She is called also Kamaduh, Savala, and Surabhi.

KANISHKA: "Hushka, Jushka, Kanishka." These are the names recorded in the Raja-Tarangini of three great Turushka, that is Turk or Tatar, kings, who were of the Buddhist religion. It may, perhaps, be taken for granted that Hushka and Jushka come in their natural succession, for the names might be transposed without detriment to the metre; but the short syllable of the name Kanishka is required where it stands by the rule of prosody, so that the position of the name in the verse is not decisive of his place in the succession of kings. Nothing is known of Jushka beyond the simple recital of his name as above quoted, but the names of Kanishka and Hushka (or Huvishka) have been found in inscriptions and upon coins, showing that their dominions were of considerable extent in Northern India, and that they were, as the Raja-Tarangini represents, great supporters of the Buddhist religion. The name of Kanishka has been found in inscriptions at Mathura, Manikyala, Bhawalpur, and Zeds, while his name appears on the corrupt Greek coins as Kaneski. Huvishka's name has been found at Mathura and on a metal vase from Wardak in Afghanistan; on the coins his name is represented as Oerki, Kanishka preceded Huvishka, and it is certain that their reigns covered a period of fiftyone years, and probably more. The time at which they reigned seems to have been just before the

Christian era. A Roman coin of the date 33 B.C. was found in the tope of Manikyala, which was built by Kanishka.

KANSA: A tyrannical king of Mathura, son of Ugrasena and cousin of Devakl the mother of Krishna. He married two daughters of Jarasandha, king of Magadha. He deposed his father. It was foretold that a son born of Devaki should kill him, so he endeavoured to destroy all her children. But Balarama, her seventh son, was smuggled away to Gokula, and was brought up by Rohini. When Krishna the eighth was born his parents fled with him. The tyrant then gave orders for a general massacre of all vigorous male infants. Kansa became the great persecutor of Krishna, but was eventually killed by him. Kansa is also called Kalankura, 'crane.' He is looked upon as an Asura, and is in some way identified with the Asura Kalanemi.

KANWA: Name of a Rishi to whom some hymns of the Rigveda are ascribed; he is sometimes counted as one of the seven great Rishis. The sage who brought up Sakuntala as his daughter. There are several others of the same name.

KARNA: Son of Pritha or Kunti by Surya, the sun, before her marriage to Pandu. Karna was thus halfbrother of the Pandavas, but this relationship was not known to them till after his death. Kunti, on one occasion, paid such attention to the sage Durvasas, that he gave her a charm by virtue of which she might have a child by any god she preferred to invoke. She chose the sun, and the result was Karna, who was born equipped with arms and armour. Afraid of censure and disgrace, Kunti exposed the child on the banks of the Yamuna, where it was found by Nandana or Adhiratha, the suta or charioteer of Dhritarashtra. The charioteer and his wife, Radha, brought him up as their own, and the child passed as such. When he grew up, Indra disguised himself as a Brahmin, and cajoled him out of his divine cuirass. He gave him in return great strength and a javelin charged with certain death to whomsoever it was hurled against. Karna became king of Anga or Bengal. Some authorities represent his foster father as having been ruler of that country, but others say that Karna was made king of Anga by Duryodhana, in order to qualify him to fight in the passage of arms at the swayamvara of Draupadi. This princess haughtily rejected him, saying, "I wed not with the baseborn." Karna knew that he was halfbrother of the Pandavas, but he took the side of their cousins, the Kauravas, and he had especial rivalry and animosity against Arjuna, whom he vowed to kill. In the great battle he killed Ghatotkacha, the son of Bhima, with Indra's javelin. Afterwards there was a terrific combat between him and Arjuna, in which the latter was nearly overpowered, but he killed Karna with a crescent shaped arrow. After Karna's death his relationship to the Pandavas became known to them, and they showed their regret for his loss by great kindness to his widows, children, and dependants. From his father, Vikartana (the sun), Karna was called Vaikartana; from his foster parents, Vasusena; from his foster father's profession, Adhirathi and Suta; and from his foster mother, Radheya. He was also called Angaraja, king of Anga; Champadhipa, 'king of Champa;' and Kanina, 'the bastard.'

KARTAVIRYA: Son of Kritavirya, king of the Haihayas. This is his patronymic by which he is best known; his real name was Arjuna. " Having worshipped a portion of the divine being called Dattatreya, sprung from the race of Atri, he sought and obtained these boons, a thousand arms and a golden chariot that went wheresoever he willed it to go; the power of restraining wrong by justice; the conquest of the earth and the disposition to rule it righteously; invincibility by enemies, and death at the hands of a man renowned over the whole world. By him this earth was perfectly governed," and of him it is said:—"No other king shall ever equal Kartavirya in regard is sacrifices, liberality, austerities, courtesy, and selfrestraint. "Thus he ruled for 85,000 years with unbroken health, prosperity, strength, and valour."—V.P. He visited the hermitage of Jamadagni, and was received by that sage's wife with all respect; but he made an ill return for her hospitality, and carried off by violence "the calf of the milchcow of the sacred oblation." For this outrage Parasurama cut off his thousand arms and killed him.

In another place a different character is given to him, and more in accordance with his behaviour at Jamadagni's hut. "He oppressed both men and gods," so that the latter appealed to Vishnu for succour. That god then came down to the earth as Parasurama or the especial purpose of killing him. Kartavirya was the contemporary of Ravana, and when that demon monarch came "in the course of his campaign of conquest to Mahishmati the capital of Kartavirya, he was captured without difficulty, and was confined like a wild beast in a corner of his city." The statement of the Vayu Purana is that Kartavirya invaded Lanka, and there took Ravana prisoner.

KARTIKEYA: The god of war and the planet Mars, also called Skanda. He is said in the Mahabharata and Ramayana to be the son of Siva or Rudra, and to have been produred without the intervention of a woman. Siva cast his seed into fire, and it was afterwards received by the Ganges: Kartikeya was the result; hence he is called Agnibhu and Gangaja. He was fostered by the Pleiades (Krittika), and hence he has six heads and the name Kartikeya. His paternity is sometimes assigned to Agni (fire); Ganga (the Ganges) and Parvati are variously represented to be his mother. He was born for the purpose of destroying Taraka, a Daitya whose austerities had made him formidable to the gods. He is represented riding on a peacock called Paravani, holding a bow in one hand and an arrow in the other. His wife is Kaumari or Sena. He has many titles: as a warrior he is called Mahasena, Senapati; Siddhasena, 'leader of the Siddhas;' and Yudharanga; also Kumara, the boy; Guha, 'the mysterious one;' Saktidhara, spearholder;' and in the south he is called Subrahmarya. He is Gangaputra, 'son of the Ganges;' Sarabhu, 'born in the thicket; Tarakajit, 'vanquisher of Taraka;' Dwadasakara and Dwadasaksha, 'twelvehanded' and' twelveeyed;' Rijukaya, 'straightbodied.'

KASYAPA: A Vedic sage to whom some hymns are attributed. All authorities agree in assigning to him a large part in the work of creation. According to the Mahabharata, the Ramayana, and the Puranas, he was the son of Marichi, the son of Brahma, and he was father of Vivaswat, the father of Manu, the progenitor of mankind. The Satapatha Brahmana gives a different and not very intelligible account of his origin thus:—"Having assumed the form of a tortoise, Prajapati created offspring. That which he created he made (akarot); hence the word kurma (tortoise). Kasyapa means tortoise; hence men say, 'All creatures are descendants of Kasyapa.' This tortoise is the same as Aditya." The Atharvaveda says, "The selfborn Kasyapa sprang from Time," and Time is often identical with Vishnu. The Mahabharata and later authorities agree in representing that Kasyapa married Aditi and twelve other daughters of Daksha. Upon Aditi he begat the Adityas, headed by Indra, and also Vivaswat, and "to Vivaswat was born the wise and mighty Manu." The Ramayana and Vishnu Purana also state that "Vishnu was born as a dwarf, the son of Aditi and Kasyapa." By his other twelve wives he had a numerous and very diversified offspring: demons, nagas, reptiles, birds, and all kinds of living things. He was thus the father of all, and as such is sometimes called Prajapati. He is one of the seven great Rishis, and he appears as the priest of Parasurama and Ramachandra.

KATHAKA: A school or recension of the Yajurveda, occupying a position between the Black and the White. It is supposed to be lost.

KATHA-SARITSAGARA: 'The ocean of the rivers of stories.' A collection of popular stories by Somadeva Bhatta of Kashmir, made about the beginning of the twelfth century A.D. It is drawn from a larger work called Brihatkatha. They text has been printed and in part translated by Brockhaus.

KATYAYANA: An ancient writer of great celebrity, who came after Panini, whose grammar he completed and corrected in what he called Vartikas, 'supplementary rules and annotations.' He is generally identified with Vararuchi, the author of the Prakrita Prakasa. Max Muller places him in the second half of the fourth century B.C.; Goldstucker in the first half of the second century B.C.; Weber about twentyfive years B.C. Besides his additions to Panini's Grammar, he was the author of the Srauta Sutras. which bear his name, and of the Yajurveda Pratisakhya. His Sutras have been edited by Weber. A story in the Kathasarit sagara makes him the incarnation of a demigod named Pushpadanta. A Katyayana was author also of a Dharmasastra.

KAUSALYA (mas), KAUSALYA (fem): Belonging to the Kosala nation. There are several women known by this name. The wife of Puru and mother of Janamejaya. The wife of Dasaratha and mother of Rama. The mother of Dhritarashtra and the mother of Pandu both were known by this name, being daughters of a king of Kasi.

KAUSHITAKI: 1. A sakha of the Rigveda. 2. The name of a Brahmana, an Aranyaka, and an Upanishad. The Brahmana has been published with a translation by Professor Cowell in the Bibliotheca Indica.

KAUTSA: A rationalistic philosopher, who lived before the days of Yaska, the author of the Nirukta. He regarded "the a Vedas as devoid of meaning, and the Brahmanas as false interpretations." Yaska replied to his objections.

KAVASHA, KAVASHA AILUSHA: Son of Ilusha by a slave girl. He was author of several hymns in the tenth book of the Rigveda. The Aitareya Brahmana relates that the Rishis were performing a sacrifice on the banks of the Saraswati, and that Kavasha was with them; but they drove him from among them because he was the son of a slave, and therefore unworthy to drink the water of the of the Saraswati. When he was alone in the desert, a hymn was revealed to him by which he prevailed over the Saraswati, and its waters came and surrounded him. The Rishis saw this, and knowing that it was by the special favour of the gods, they admitted him to their society.

KHANDAVA, KHANDAVAPRASTHA: A forest and country on the banks of the Yamuna, which the Pandavas received as their moiety when Dhritarashtra divided his kingdom. In it they built the city of Indraprastha and made it their capital. The forest was consumed with fire by the god Agni assisted by Krishna and Arjuna.

KICHAKA: Brother-in-law of the king of Virata, who was commander of the forces and general director of the affairs of the kingdom. He tried to make love to Draupadi, and was slain by Bhima, who rolled his bones and flesh into a ball, so that no one could tell how he was killed.

KIRATARJUNIYA: A poem descriptive of the combat between Siva in the guise of a Kirata or mountaineer and the Pandu prince Arjuna. The story is first told in the Mahabharata, and has been worked up in this artificial poem of eighteen cantos by Bharavi. Part of it has been translated into German by Schutz. There are several editions of the text.

KIRATAS: Foresters and mountaineera living in the mountains east of Hindustan. (There is a tribe in the Central Himalayas called Kirantis.) They are described in the Ramayana as "islanders, who eat raw fish, live in the waters, and are men-tigers" (men below and tigers above, according to the commentator). Their females are described as "goldcoloured and pleasant to behold," and as having "sharp pointed hair knots." They are perhaps the Cirrhadae placed on the Coromandel coast by classic writers.

KISHKINDHA: A country in the peninsula, thought to be in Mysore, which was taken by Rama from the monkey king Bali, and given back to his brother Sugriva, the friend and ally of Rama. The capital city was Kishkindha.

KOSALA: A country on the Sarayu river, having Ayodhya for its capital. The name is variously applied to other countries in the east, and in the south, and in the Vindhya mountains. It probably widened with the dominions of its rulers, and part of Vidarbha is called Dakshina Kosala, the Southern Kosala.

KRAUNCHA: 1. A pass situated somewhere in the Himalayas, said to have boen opened by Parasurama with his arrows to make a passage from Kailasa to the southwards. The Vayu Purana attributes the splitting of the mountain to Kartikeya. Indra and Kartikeya had a dispute about their respective powers, and agreed to decide it by running a race round the mountain. They disagreed as to the result, and therefore appealed to the mountain, who untruly decided in favour of Indra. "Kartikeya hurled his lance at the mountain and pierced at once it and the demon Mahisha." 2. A. confederate of the demon Taraka, against whom Kartikeya led the gods and triumpbed. 3. One of the seven Dwipas.

KRISHNA: 'Black.' This name occurs in the Rigveda, but without any relation to the great deity of later times. The earliest mention of Krishna, the son of Devaki, is in the Chhandogya Upanishad, where he appears as a scholar. There was a Rishi of the name who was a son of Viswaka. There was also a great Asura so named, who with 10,000 followers committed fearful devastation, until he was defeated and skinned by Indra. In another Vedic hymn, 50,000 Krishnas are said to have been slain, and it is added in another that his pregnant wives were slain with him that he might leave no posterity. This is supposed to have reference to the Rukshasas or to the darkcoloured aborigines of India.

The modern deity Krishna is the most celebrated hero of Indian mythology, and the most popular of all the deities. He is said to be the eighth Avatara or incarnation of Vishnu, or rather a direct manifestation of Vishnu himself. This hero, around whom a vast mass of legend and fable has been gathered, probably lived in the Epic age, when the Hindus had not advaneed far beyond their early settlements in the northwest. He appears prominently in the Mahabharata, where his character is invested with a certain degree of mysticism. Additions and interpolations have raised him to divinity, and it is in the character of the "Divine One" that he delivered the celebrated song, Bhagavadgita, a production of comparatively late date, now held. to be part of the great epic. In this work he distinctly declares himself to be the Supreme Being. He says:— "All this universe has been created by me; all things exist in me;" and Arjuna addresses him as "the supreme universal spirit, the supreme dwelling, the eternal person, divine, prior to the gods, unborn, omnipresent."

The divine character of Krishna having thus been established, it was still further developed in the Harivansa, a later addition to the Mahabharata ; and in the Puranas, especially in the Bhagavata Purana, it attained full expansion. There the story of the life of Krishna, from his earliest days, is related with minute details, and it is upon this portion of his life that the popular mind delights to dwell. The mischievous pranks of the child, the follies of the boy, and the amours of the youth, are the subjects of boundless wonder and delight. All these stories, as told in the Bhagavata Purana, have been made accessible and popular by the Hindi translation known by the name Prem Sagar, 'ocean of love,' and by other versions. Much of the story of the early days of Krishna is thus of comparatively modern invention, while the incidents of his relations with the Pandava princes are among the most ancient.

Krishna was of the Yadava race, being descended from Yadu, one of the sons of Yayati The Yadavas of old were a pastoral race, and dwelt on the river Yamuna, in Vrindavans, on the western side, and in Gokula on the other. In those days, Kansa, Raja of the Bhojas, having deposed his father, Ugrasena, ruled in the city of Mathura, near Vrindavana. Ugrasena had a brother named Devaka, and Devaka had a daughter named Devaki, who married Vasudeva, son of Sura, also a descendant ofYadu. rhe history of Krishna's birth, as given in the Mahabharata, and followed by the Vishnu Purana, is that Vishnu plucked out two of is own hairs, one white, the other black. These two hairs entered the wombs of Rohini and Devaki; the white hair became Balarama and the black (krishna) hair (kesa) became Krishna or Kesan. His reputed father, Vasudeva, was brother of Kunti, the wife of Pandu, and so Krishna was cousin of the three elder Pandava princes.

The Mahabharata gives two summaries of his exploits, of which the following are abridgments:—"While Krishna was growing up as a highsouled boy in the tribe of cowherds, the force of his arms was rendered famous by him in the three worlds." He slew the king of the Hayas (horses), dwelling in the woods of the Yamuna. He slew the direful Danava, who bore the form of a bull. He also slew Pralamba, Naraka, Jambha, and Pitha, the great Asura, and Muru. He overthrew and slew Kansa, who was supported by Jarasandha. With the help of Balarama he defeated and destroyed Sunaman, brother of Kansa and king of the Surasenas. He carried off the daughter of the king of the Gandharas at a swayamvara, and princes were yoked to his car. He secured the death of Jarasandha and slew Sisupala. He overthrew Saubha, the selfsupporting or flying city of the Daityas, on the shore of the ocean. He conquered the Angas and Bangas, and numerous other tribes. Entering the ocean filled with marine monsters, he overcame Varuna. In Patala he slew Panchajana, and obtained the divine shell Panchajanya. With Arjuna he propitiated Agni in the Khandava forest, and obtained the fiery weapon the discus. Mounted on Garuda, he alarmed Amaravati, the city of Indra, and brought away the Parijata tree from thence.

In another passage, Arjuna rehearses some of Krishna's exploits. He destroyed the Bhoja kings in battle, and carried off Rukmini for his bride. He destroyed the Gandharas, vanquished the sons of Nagnajit, and released King Sudarsana, whom they had bound. He slew Pandya with the fragment of a door, and crushed the Kalingas in Dantakura. Through him the burnt city of Benares was restored. He killed Ekalàvya, king of the Nishadas, and the demon Jambha. With the aid of Balarama he killed Sunaman, the wicked son of Ugrasena, and restored the kingdom to the latter. He conquered the flying city of Saubha and the king of the Salwas, and there hs obtained the fiery weapon Sataghni. Naraka, son of the earth, had carried off the beautiful jewelled earrings of Aditi to Pragjyotisha, the impregnable castle of the Asuras. The gods, headed by Indra, were unable to prevail against Naraka, so they appointed Krishna to slay him. Accordingly he killed Muru and the Rakshasa Ogha; and finally he slew Naraka and brought back the earrings.

It further appears in different parts of the Mahabharata that Krishna, prince of Dwaraka, was present at the swayamvara of Draupadi, and gave his judgment that she had been fairly won by Arjuna. While the Pandavas were reigning at Indraprastha, he paid them a visit, and went out hunting with them in the Khandava forest. There he and Arjuna allied themselves with Agni, who was desirous of burning the Khandava forest, but was prevented by Indra. Agni having secured the help of Krishna and Arjuna, he gave the former the celebrated Chakra (discus) Vajranabha, and the club

Kaumodaki. Then Indra was defeated and Agni burnt the forest. Arjuna afterwards visited Krishna at Dwaraka, and was received with greaı demonstrations of joy. Arjuna, with the connivance of Krishna, eloped with Subhadra, Krishna's sister, much to the annoyance of Balarama, her elder brother.

When Yudhishthira was desirous of performing the Rajasuya sacrifice, Krishna told him that he must first conquer Jarasandha, king of Magadha. Jarasandha was attacked and slain, and Krishna was thus revenged upon the enemy who had forced him to leave Mathura and emigrate to Dwaraka. Krishna attended the Rajasaya sacrifice performed by Yudhishthira, and there he met Sisupala, whose betrothed wife he had carried off. Sisupala reviled him and acted very violently, so Krishna cast his discus and cut off his enemy's head. He was present at the gambling match between Yudhishthira and the Kauravas. When Draupadi had been staked and lost, she was dragged into the public hall by Duhsasana, who tore off her clothes, but Krishna pitied her, and renewed her clothes as fast as they were torn away.

After the close of the exile of the Pandavas, Krishna was present, and took part in the council which preceded the great war, and strongly advised a peaceful settlement. Then he returned to Dwaraka. Thither Arjuna and Duryodhana followed him with the object of enlisting his services in the coming war, but he refused to take any active part because he was related to both parties. He gave them the choice of his personal attendance or of the use of his army. Arjuna, who had arrived first, and therefore had the first choice, asked for Krishna himself, and Duryodhana joyfully accepted the army; Krishna then became the charioteer of Arjuna. After this, at the request of the Pandavas, he went in splendid state to Hastinapura as a mediator, but his efforts were unavailing, and he returned. Preparations for action were then made and the forces drawn out. On the eve of the battle, while acting as

Arjuna's charioteer, he is represented as relating to Arjuna the Bhagavadgita or divine song. He rendered valuable services to Arjuna throughout the battle, but on two occasions he suggested unfair dealing. He prompted the lie by which Yudhishthira broke down the prowess of Drona, and suggested the foul blow by which Bhima shattered the thigh of Duryodhana. He afterwards went to Hastinapura with the conquerors, and he also attended their Aswamedha sacrifice.

On returning to Dwaraka he issued a proclamation forbidding the use of wine. Portents and fearful signs appeared, and a general feeling of alarm spread among all in Dwaraka. Krishna gave directions that the inhabitants should go out to Prabhasa on the seashore and endeavour to propitiate the deity. He gave permission also that wine might be drunk for one day. A drunken brawl followed, in which his son Pradyumna was killed in his presence, and nearly all the chiefs of the Yadavas were slain. Balarama went out from the fray and died peacefully under a tree, and Krishna himself was killed unintentionally by a hunter named Jaras, who shot him with an arrow, mistaking him at a distance for a deer. Arjuna proceeded to Dwaraka and performed the obsequies of Krishna. A few days afterwards the city was swallowed up by the sea. Five of Krishna's widows were subsequently burnt upon a funeral pile in the plain of Kurukshetra.

"Among the texts of the Mahabharata," says Dr. Muir, "there are some in which Krishna is distinctly subordinated to Mahadeva (Siva), of whom he is exhibited as a worshipper, and from whom, as well as from his wife Uma, he is stated to have received a variety of boons. Even in these passages, however, a superhuman character is ascribed to Krishna."

The popular history of Krishna, especially of his childhood and youth, is given in the Puranas, and is the subject of many a story. The Bhagavata Purana is the great authority, and from that the following account is condensed:—

The sage Narada had foretold to Kansa that a son of Devaki, his brother's daughter, should destroy him and overthrow his kingdom. To obviate this danger, Kansa kept his cousin Devaki confined in his own palace, and six children that she bore he caused to be put to death. She conceived a seventh time, but the child was an incarnation of Vishnu, and was miraculously preserved by being transferred from the womb of Devaki to that of Rohinl, who was Vasudeva's second wife. This child was Balarama. Devaki again conceived, and her eighth child was born at midnight with a very dark skin, whence he was called Krishna. He had a peculiar curl of hair, called Srivatsa, upon his breast. The gods interposed to preserve the life of this divinely begotten child. The guards of the palace were over powered with sleep, and bolts and barriers were removed. Vasudeva took up the child and escaped with him from Mathura. He repaired to the bank of the Yamuna, and, crossing the river, went to the house of Nanda, a cowherd, whose wife, Yasoda, had on that very night been delivered of a female child. Vasudeva secretly changed the infants, and carried back the daughter of Yasoda to his wife Devaki.

Kansa discovered that he had been cheated, and in his wrath he ordered that every male infant that gave signs of vigour should be put to death. Vasudeva and Devaki, being no longer dangerous, were set at liberty. Nanda, alarmed by the order for the massacre, took the young child and removed with Yasoda and with Rohini and Balarama to Gokula. Here Krishna was brought up, and wandered about in company of his elder brother Balarama. They played many pranks and passed many practical jokes; but they exhibited such marvellous strength and such godlike powers that they soon became famous. Kansa was continually forming schemes for the death of Krishna. The female demon Putana assumed a lovely form, and tried to kill him by suckling him, but the child sucked away her life. Another demon tried to drive a cart over him, but he dashed the cart to pieces. A demon named Trinavarta took the form of a whirlwind and flew off with him, but the child brought the demon to the ground with such violence that he died. One day Krishna broke the vessels of milk and curds and ate the butter, which made Yasoda angry. She fastened a rope round his body, and tied him to a large bowl, but he dragged the bowl away till it caught between two trees and uprooted them. From this feat he got the name of Damodara (rope-belly). He had a terrible conflict with the great serpent Kaliya, who lived in the Yamuna. and he compelled him to go away. On one occasion, when the gopis or milkmaids were bathing, he took away all their clothes and climbed up a tree, and there he remained till the damsels came to him naked to recover them. He persuaded Nanda and the cowherds to give up the worship of Indra, and to worship the mountain Govardhana, which sheltered them and their cattle. Incensed at the loss of his offerings, Indra poured down a heavy rain, which would have deluged them, but Krishna lifted up the mountain Govardhana, and held it upon his finger as a shelter for seven days and nights, till Indra felt that he was foiled. From this feat he obtained the name of Govardhanadhara and Tungisa. As he had protected the kine, Indra expressed his satisfaction, and gave him the title of Upendra.

He was now approaching manhood, and was very handsome. The gopis were all enamoured of him, and he dispensed his favours very freely. He married seven or eight of them, but his first and favourite wife was Radha. At this period of his life he is represented with flowing hair and with a flute in his hand. One of his favourite pastimes was a round dance, called Mandala-nritya or Rasa-mandala, in which he and Radha formed the centre whilst the gopis danced round them. But his happiness was interrupted by the machinations of Kansa, who sent formidable demons to destroy him—Arishta in the form of a bull, and Kesin in the form of a horse. These attempts having failed, Kansa sent his messenger, Akrura, to invite Krishna and Balarama to Mathura to attend some games, and he formed severa! plans for their destruction. They accepted the invitation, and went to Mathura. Near the city they found Kansa's washerman engaged in his calling. They threw down some of his clothes, and he addressed them insolently, upon which they killed him, and took such clothes as they liked. In his progress he met Kubja, a crooked damsel, who gave him some unguent, and he repaid her gift by making her straight. In the games he killed Chanura, the king's boxer. Afterwards he killed Kansa himself, and replaced Ugrasena on the throne.

He remained in Mathura and studied the science of arms under Sandipani. He went down to the infernal regions and brought back his six brothers, whom Kansa had killed, and these, having tasted the milk of their mother ascended to heaven. During this period he killed a demon named Panchajana, who had attacked the son of his teacher. This demon lived in the sea in the form of a conchshell, and Krishna afterwards used this shell, called Panchajanya, as a trumpet. Kansa's two wives were daughters of Jarasandha, king of Magadha. This king assembled his forces and marched against Mathura to chastise Krishna, but he was defeated. He renewed his attacks eighteen times, and was as often defeated. A new enemy then threatened Krishna, a Yavana or foreigner named Kalayavana, and Krishna had been so weakened that he knew he must succumb either to him or to his old enemy the king of Magadha, so he and all his people migrated to the coast of Gujerat, where he built and fortified the city of Dwaraka. [The Mahabharata makes no mention of this foreign king, and says that Krishna retired before the eighteenth attack of Jarasandha. The foreign king would, therefore, seem to be an invention of the Puranas for saving Krishna's reputation.]

After his settlement at Dwaraka, Krishna carried off and married Rukmini, daughter of the Raja of Vidarbha, and the betrothed of Sisupala. An incident now occurred which brought him two more wives. A Yadava chief named Satrajit had a beautiful gem called Syamantaka, which Krishna wished to possess. Satrajit, for the sake of security, gave the gem into the charge of his brother Prasena, and Prasena was killed in the forest by a lion, who carried off the jewel in his mouth. This lion was killed by Jambavat, the king of the bears. Satrajit suspected Krishna of taking the jewel, and he, to clear himself, went out into the forest, ascertained the manner of Prasena's death, fought with Jambavat, and recovered the jewel. Krishna then married Jambavati, the daughter of Jambavat, and Satyabhama, the daughter of Satrajit. But the number of his wives was practically unlimited, for he had 16,000 and a hundred or so besides, and he had 180,000 sons. By Rukmini he had a son Pradyumna and a daughter Charumati. His son by Jambavati was Samba, and by Satyabhama he had ten sons.

Indra came to visit Krishna at Dwaraka, and implored him to suppress the evil deeds of the demon Naraka. Krishna accordingly went to the city of Naraka, killed the demon Muru, who guarded the city, and then destroyed Naraka himself Krishna next went to pay a visit to Indra in Swarga, taking with him his wife Satyabhama. At her request he requited the hospitality shown him by carrying off the famed Parijata tree, which was produced at the churning of the ocean. The tree belonged to Sachi, wife of Indra, and she complained to her husband. Indra drew out his forces and tried to recover it, but was defeated by Krishna. Pradyumna, son of Krishna, had a son named Aniruddha, with whom a female Daitya, Usha, daughter of Bana, fell in love. She induced a companion to carry off the young man, and Krishna, Balarama, and Pradyumna went to rescue him. Bana, with the whole Daitya host, and assisted by Siva and Skanda, the god of war, encountered them. Krishna, "with the weapon of yawning, set Siva agape," and so overpowered him. Skanda was wounded. Bana maintained a fierce combat with Krishna, and was severely wounded, but Krishna spared his life at the intercession of Siva, and Aniruddha was released.

There was a man named Paundraka, who was a Vasudeva, or descendant of one Vasudeva. Upon the strength of the identity of this name with that of Vasudeva, the father of Krishna, this man Paundraka assumed the insignia and title of Krishna, and he had the king of Kasi or Benares for an ally. Krishna slew Paundraka, and he hurled his flaming discus at Benares and destroyed that city. Such are the principal incidents of the life of Krishna as given in the Harivansa, the Puranas, and the Prem Sagar.

Similarity in the sound of the name, and some incidents in the life of Krishna, have led some to believe that the legend of Krishna had its origin in the life of Christ, but this is not the general opinion.

Krishna has many appellations derived from his family relations, his exploits, and personal characteristics; and there are many which apply both to the full deity, Vishnu, and his incarnation, Krishna.

KUMARASAMBHAVA: 'The birth of the war god (Kumara).' A poem by Kalidasa. The complete work consists of sixteen cantos, but only seven are usually given, and these have been translated into Latin by Stenzler. Parts have been rendered into English verse by Griffith. There are several editions of the text.

KUMARILA BHATTA, KUMARILASWAMI: A celebrated teacher of the Mimansa philosophy and opponent of the Buddhists, whom he is said to have extirpated by argument and by force. He was prior to Sankaracharya, in whose presence he is recorded to have burnt himself.

KUNTI (also called Pritha and Prashni): 1. Daughter of the Yadava prince Sura, king of the Surasenas, whose capital was Mathura on the Yamuna. She was sister of Vasudeva, and was given by her father to his childless cousin Kuntibhoja, by whom he was brought up. In her maidenhood she showed such respectful devotion to the sage Durvasa, that he gave her a charm by means of which she might have a child by any god she pleased to invoke. She called upon the sun, and by him had a son named Karna, but without any detriment to her virginity; still, to keep the affair secret, the child was exposed on the banks of the Yamuna. Subsequently, she married Pandu, whom she chose at a swayamvara, and bore three sons, Yudhishthira, Bhima, and Arjuna, who were called Pandavas although they were said to be the sons of the gods Dharma, Vayu, and Indra respectively. This may have happened, as is stated, from the potency of the old charm, but if so, it is strange that Madri, the second wife of Pandu, should have enjoyed the same privilege, and have borne twin children to the Aswins. This difficulty, however, is got over by a statement that Kunti imparted to her the charm. Kunti was a discreet and devoted mother, and although rather jealous of Madri, she was a kind mother to her children, after Madri was burnt on her husband's pyre. After the end of the great war she retired into the forest with Dhritarashtra and his wife Gandhari, and there they all perished in forest fire. 2. Name of a people and country in Upper India.

KURMA PURANA: "That in which Janardana (Vishnu), in the form of a tortoise, in the regions under the earth, explained the objects of lifeduty, wealth, pleasure, and liberation—in communication with Indradyumna and the Rishis in the proximity of Sakra, which refers to the Lakshmi Kalpa, and contains 17,000 stanzas, is the Kurma Purana." The account which the Purana gives of itself and its actual contents do not agree with this description. "The name being that of an

Avatara of Vishnu, might lead us to expect a Vaishnava work; but it is always and correctly classed with the Saiva Puranas, the greater portion of it inculcating the worship of Siva and Durga. The date of this Purana cannot be very remote."— Wilson.

KURU: A prince of the Lunar race, son of Samvarana by Tapati, a daughter of the sun. He ruled in the northwest of India over the country about Delhi. A people called Kurus, and dwelling about Kurukshetra in that part of India, are connected with him. He was ancestor both of Dhritarashtra and Pandu, but the patronymic Kaurava is generally applied to the sons of the former.

KURUKSHETRA: 'The field of the Kurus.' A plain near Delhi where the great battle between the Kauravas and Pandavas was fought. It lies southeast of Thanesar, not far from Panipat, the scene of many battles in later days.

KUVERA: In the Vedas, a chief of the evil beings or spirits living in the shades: a sort of Pluto, and called by his patronymic Vaisravana. Later he is Pluto in another sense, as god of wealth and chief of the Yakshas and Guhyakas. He was son of Visravas by Idavida, but he is sometimes called son of Pulastya, who was father of Visravas. This is explained by the Mahabharata, according to which Kuvera was son of Pulastya, but that sage being offended with Kuvera for his adulation of Brahma, "reproduced the half of himself in the form of Visravas," and had Ravana and other children. Kuvera's city is Alaka—also called Prabha, Vasudhara and Vasusthali in the Himalayas, and his garden Chaitraratha on Mandara, one of the Spur of Mount Meru, where he is waited upon by the Kinnaras. Some authoritiee place his abode on Mount Kailasa in a palace built by Viswakarma.

He was halfbrother of Ravana and, according to the Ramayana and Mahabharata, he once had possession of the city of Lanka, which was also built by Viswakarma, and from which he was expelled by Ravana. The same authority states that he performed austerities for thousands of years, and obtained the boon from Brahma that he should be immortal, one of the guardian deities of the world, and the god of wealth. So he is regent of the north, and the keeper of gold and silver, jewels and pearls, and all the treasures of the earth, besides nine particulsr Nidhis, or treasures, the nature of which is not well understood. Brahma also gave him the great selfmoving aerial car Pushpaka. His wife is Yaksha, Charvi, or Kauveri, daughter of the Danava Mura. His sons are Manigriva or Varnakavi and Nalakubara or Mayuraja, and his daughter Minakshi (fisheyed).

He is represented as a white man deformed in body, and having three legs and only eight teeth. His body is covered with ornaments. He receives no worship. The name Kuvera, as also the variant Kutanu, signifies 'vile body,' referring to his ugliness. He is also called Dhanapati, 'lord of wealth;' Ichchhavasa, 'who has wealth at will;' Yaksharaja, 'chief of the Yakshas;' Mayuraja, 'king of the Kinnaras;' Rakshasendra, 'chief of the Rakshasas;' Ratnagarbha, 'belly of jewels;' Rajaraja, 'king oi kings;' and Nararaja, 'king of men' (in allusion to the power of riches). From his parentage he is called Vaisravana, Paulastya, and Aidavida or Ailavila. As an especial friend of Siva he is called Isasakhs, etc.

L

LAKSHMANA: 1. Son of King Dasaratha by his wife Sumitra. He was the twin brother of Satrughna, and the half brother and special friend of Ramachandra. Under the peculiar circumstances of his birth, oneeighth part of the divinity of Vishnu became manifest in him. But according to the Adhyatma Ramayana, he was an incarnation of Sesha. When

Rama left his father's home to go to the hermitage of Viswamitra, Lakshmana accompanied him, and afterwards attended him in his exile and in all his wanderings. He was also very attached to Rama's wife, Sita. His own wife was Urmila, the sister of Sita, and he had two sons, Angada and Chandraketu. While Rama and Lakshmana were living in the wilderness, a Rakshasi named Surpanakha, sister of Ravana, fell in love with Rama and made advances to him. He jestingly referred her to Lakshmana, who in like manner sent her back to Rama. When she was again repulsed she attacked Sita, whom Rama was obliged to defend. Rama then called upon Lakshmana to disfigure the Rakshasi, and accordingly he cut off her nose and ears. The mutilated female called upon her brother to avenge her, and a fierce war ensued.

When Sita was carried off by Ravana, Lakshmana accompanied Rama in his search, and he ably and bravely supported him in his war against Ravana. Rama's earthly career was drawing to a close, and Time (Kala) was sent to inform him that he must elect whether to stay longer on earth, or to return to the place from whence he had come. While they were in conference, the irascible sage Durvasa, came and demanded to see Rama instantly, threatening him with the most direful curses if any delay were allowed to occur. To save his brother Rama from the threatened curse, but aware of the consequences that would ensue to himself from breaking in upon Rama's interview with Time, he went in and brought Rama out. Lakshmana knowing his fate, retired to the river Sarayu and resigned himself. The gods then showered down flowers upon him and conveyed him bodily to heaven. 2. A son of Duryodhana, killed by Abhimanyu.

LAKSHMI: The word occurs in the Rigveda with the sense of good fortune, and in the Atharvaveda the idea has become personified in females both of a lucky and unlucky character.

The Taittiriya Sanhita, as explained by the commentator, makes Lakshmi and Sri to be two wives of Aditya, and the Satapatha Brahmana describes Sri as issuing forth from Prajapati.

Lakshmi or Sri in later times is the goddess of fortune, wife of Vishnu, and mother of Kama. The origin ascribed to her by the Ramayana is the one commonly received. According to this legend, she sprang, like Aphrodite, from the froth of the ocean, in full beauty with a lotus in her hand, when it was churned by the gods and the Asuras. Another legend represents her as floating on the flower of a lotus at the creation. With reference to this origin, one of her names is Kshirabdhi-tanaya, 'daughter of the sea of milk.' From her connection with the lotus she is called Padma. According to the Puranas, she was the daughter of Bhrigu and Khyati. The Vishnu Purana says, "Her first birth was the daughter of Bhrigu by Khyati. It was at a subsequent period that, she was produced from the sea at the churning of the ocean. When Hari was born as a dwarf, Lakshmi appeared from a lotus as Padma or Kamala. When he was born as Rama of the race of Bhrigu (or Parasurama), she was Dharani. When he was Raghava (Ramachandra), she was Sita. And when he was Krishna, she became Rukmini In the other descents of Vishnu she is his associate." One version of the Ramayana also affirms that "Lakshmi, the mistress of the worlds, was born by her own will, in a beautiful field opened up by the plough," and received from Janaka the name of Sita.

Lakshmi is said to have four arms, but she is the ideal of beauty, and is generally depicted as having only two. In one hand she holds a lotus. "She has no temples, but being goddess of abundance and fortune, she continues to be assiduously courted, and is not likely to fall into neglect." Other names of Lakshmi are Hira, Indira, Jaladhija, 'ocean-born;' Chanchala or Lola, 'the fickle,' as goddess of fortune; Lokamata, 'mother, of the world.'

LANKA: The island of Srilanka or its capital city. The city is described in the Ramayana as of vast extent and of great magnificence, with seven broad moats and seven stupendous walls of stone and metal. It is said to have been built of gold by Viswakarma for the residence of Kuvera, from whom it was taken by Ravana. The Bhagavata Purana represents that the island was originally the summit of Mount Meru, which was broken off by the god of the wind and hurled into the sea. 2. Name of one of the Sakinis or evil spirits attendant on Siva and Devi.

LINGA, LINGAM: The male organ. The phallus. The symbol under which Siva is universally worshipped. It is of comparatively modern introduction and is unknown to the Vedas, but it receives distinct notice in the Mahabharata. "The emblem—a plain column of stone or sometimes a cone of plastic mud—auggests no offensive ideas. The people call it Siva or Mahadeva, and there's an end." In the Siva Purana, and in the Nandi Upapurana, Siva is made to say, "I am omnipresent, but I am especially in twelve forms and placea.' These are the twelve great Lingas, which are as follows:—

1. Somanatha: 'Lord of the moon.' At Somanath Pattan, a city which still remains in Gujerat. This was the celebrated "idol" destroyed by Mahmud of Ghazni.

2. Mallikarjuna or Sri Saila: 'The mountain of Sri.' On a mountain near the river Krishna.

3. Mahakala, Maha-Kaleswara: At Ujjain. Upon the capture of Ujjain in the reign of Altamsh, 1231 A.D., this deity of stone was carried to Delhi and there broken up.

4. Omkara: This is also said to have been at Ujjain, but it is probably the shrine of Mahadeva at Omkara Mandhatta, on the Narmada.

5. Amareswara: 'God of gods.' This is also placed at Ujjain.

6. Vaidya Natha: 'Lord of physicians.' At Deogarh in Bengal. The temple is still in being, and is a celebrated place of pilgrimage.

7. Ramesa or Rameswara: 'Lord of Rama.' On the island of Rameswaram, between the continent and Srilanka. This Lingam, whose name signifies 'Rama's lord,' is fabled to have been set up by Rama. The temple is still in tolerable repair, and is one of the most magnificent in India.

8. Bhima Sankara: This is in all probability the same with Bhimesvara, a Lingam worshipped at Dracharam, in the Rajamahendri (Rajamundry) district, and there venerated as one of the twelve.

9. Visweswara: 'Lord of all.' At Benares. It has been for many oenturies the chief object of worship at Benares. Also called Jyotirlinga.

10. *Tryambaka, Tryakska*: 'Triocular.' On the banks of the Gomati.

11. Gautamesa: 'Lord of Gautama.'

12. Kedaresa, Kedaranathesa: In the Himalaya. The deity is represented as a shapeless mass of rock.

Naganatha or Naganathesa and Vameswara are other names, probably of No. 6 and No. 11.

LINGA PURANA: "Where Maheswara (Siva), present in the Agni Linga, explained the objects of life, virtue, wealth, pleasure, and final liberation, at the end of the Agni Kalpa, that Purana, consisting of 11,000 stanzas, was called the Linga by Brahma himself." The work conforms accurately enough to this description. "Although the Linga holds a prominent place in this Purana, the spirit of the worship is as little influenced by the character of the type as can well be imagined. There is nothing like the phallic orgies of antiquity: it is all mystical and spiritual. The work has preserved, apparently, some Saiva legends of an early date, but the greater part is ritual and mysticism of comparatively recent introduction."—Wllson. It is not likely that this Purana is earlier than the eighth or ninth century. This Purana has been lithographed in Bombay.

LOPAMUDRA: A girl whom the sage Agastya formed from the most graceful parts of different animals and secretly introduced into the palace of the king of Vidarbha, where the child was believed to be the daughter of the king. Agastya had made this girl with the object of having a wife after his own heart, and when she was marriageable he demanded her hand. The king was loath to consent, but was obliged to yield, and she became the wife of Agastya. Her name is explained as signifying that the animals suffered loss (lopa) by her engrossing their distinctive beauties (mudra), as the eyes of the deer, etc. She is also called Kaushitaki and Varaprada. A hymn in tha Rigveda is attributed to her.

M

MADHAVA, MADHAVACHARYA: A celebrated scholar and religious teacher. He was a native of Tuluva, and became prime minister of Vira Bukka Raya, king of the great Hindu state of Vijayanagara, who lived in the fourteenth century. He was brother of Sayana, the author of the great commentary on the Veda, in which work Madhava himself is believed to have shared. Wilson observes: "Both the brothers are celebrated as scholars, and many important works are attributed to them; not only scholia on the Sanhitas and Brahmanas of the Vedas, but original works on grammar and law; the fact no doubt being, that they availed themselves of those means which their situation and influence secured them, and employed the most learned Brahmins they could attract to Vijayanagara upon the works which bear their names, and to which they contributed their own labour and learning; their works were therefore compiled under peculiar advantages, and are deservedly held in the highest estimation." Among the works of Madhava are the Sarvadarsana and the Sankshepa Sankaravijaya. Madhava was a worshipper of Vishnu, and as a religious philosopher he held the doctrine of dwaita or dualism, according to which the supreme soul of the universe and the human soul are distinct. Thus he was opposed to the teaching of Sankaracharya, who was a follower of Siva, and upheld the Vedanta doctrine of adwaita, "no duality," according to which God and soul, spirit and matter, are all one.

MADHYANDINA: A Vedic school, a subdivision of the Vajasaneyi school, and connected with the Satapatha Brahmana. It had also its own system of astronomy, and obtained its name from making noon (madhyadina) the startingpoint of the planetary movement.

MADRI: A sister of the king of the Madra, and second wife of Pandu, to whom she bore twinsons, Nakula and Sahadeva; but the Aswins are alleged to have been their real father. She became a sati on the funeral pyre of her husband.

MAHABHARATA: 'The great (war of the) Bharatas.' The great epic poem of the Hindus, probably the longest in the world. It is divided into eighteen parvas or books, and contains about 220,000 lines. The poem has been subjected to much modification and has received numerous comparatively modern additions, but many of its legends and stories are of Vedic character and of great antiquity. They seem to have long existed in a scattered state, and to have been brought together at different times. Upon them have been founded many of the poems and dramas of later days, and among them is the story of Rama upon which the Ramayana itself may have been based. According to Hindu authorities, they were finally arranged and reduced to writing by a Brahmin or Brahmins. There is a good deal of mystery about this, for the poem is attributed to a divine source. The reputed author was Krishna Dwaipayana, the Vyasa, or arranger, of the Vedas. He is said to have taught the poem to his pupil Vaishampayana, who afterwards recited it at a festival to King Janamejaya. The leading subject of the poem is the great war between the Kauravas and Pandavas, who were descendants, through Bharata, from Puru, the great ancestor of one branch of the Lunar race. The object of the great struggle was the kingdom whose capital was Hastinapura (elephant city), the ruins of which are traceable fiftyseven miles northeast of Delhi, on an old bed of the Ganges.

Krishna Dwaipayana Vyasa is not only the author of the poem, but the source from whom the chief actors sprung. He was the son of the Rishi Parasara by a nymph named Satyavati, who, although she had given birth to a son, remained a virgin. There was a king, a descendant of Bharata, named Santanu, who had a son called Santavana, better known as Bhishma. In his old age Santanu wished to marry again, but the hereditary rights of Bhishma were an obstacle to his obtaining a desirable match. To gratify his father's desire, Bhishma divested himself of all rights of succession, and Santanu then married Satyavati. She bore him two sons, the elder of whom, Chitravirya, succeeded to the throne, but was soon killed in battle by a Gandharva king who bore the same name. Vichitravirya, the younger, succeeded, but died childless, leaving two widows, named Ambika and Ambalika, daughters of a king of Kasi.

Satyavati then called on Krishna Dwaipayana Vyasa to fulfil the law, and raise up seed to his halfbrother. Vyasa had lived the life of an anchorite in the woods, and his severe austerities had made him terrible in appearance. The two widows were so frightened at him that the elder one closed her eyes, and so gave birth to a blind son, who received the name of Dhritarashtra; and the younger turned so pale that her son was called Pandu, 'the pale.' Satyavati wished for a child without blemish, but the elder widow shrank from a second association with Vyasa, and made a slave girl take her place. From this girl was born a son who was named Vidura. These children were brought up by their uncle Bhishma, who acted as regent. When they came of age, Dhritarashtra was deemed incapable of reigning in consequence of his blindness, and Pandu came to the throne. The name Pandu has suggested a suspicion of leprosy, and either through that, or in consequence of a curse, as the poem states, he retired to the forest, and Dhritarashtra then became king.

Pandu had two wives, Kunti or Pritha, daughter of Sura, king of the Surasenas, and Madri, sister of the king of the Madra; but either through disease or the curse passed upon him, he did not consort with his wives. He retired into solitude in the Himalaya mountains, and there he died; his wives, who accompanied him having borne him five sons. The paternity of these children is attributed to different gods, but Pandu acknowledged them, and they received the patronymic of Pandava. Kunti was the mother of the three elder sons, and Madri of the two younger. Yudhishthira (firm in fight), the eldest, was son of Dharma, the judge of the dead, and is considered a pattern of manly firmness, justice, and integrity. Bhima or Bhimasena (the terrible), the second, was son of Vayu, the god of the wind. He was noted for his strength, daring, and brute courage; but he was coarse, choleric, and given to vaunting. He was such a great eater that he was called Vrikodara, 'wolf's belly.' Arjuna (the bright or silvery), the third, was son of Indra, the god of the sky. He is the most prominent character, if not the hero, of the poem. He was brave as the bravest, highminded, generous, tenderhearted, and chivalric in his notions of honour. Nakula and Sahadeva, the fourth and fifth sons, were the twin children of Madri by the Aswini Kumaras, the twin sons of Surya, the sun. They were brave, spirited, and amiable, but they do not occupy such prominent positions as their elder brothers.

Dhritarashtra, who reigned at Hastinapura, was blind. By his wife Gandhari he had a hundred sons, and one daughter named Duhsala. This numerous offspring was owing to a blessing from Vyasa, and was produced in a marvellous way. From their ancestor Kuru these princes were known as the Kauravas. The eldest of them, Duryodhana (hard to subdue), was their leader, and was a bold, crafty, malicious man, an embodiment of all that is bad in a prince. While the Hindu princes were yet children, they, on the death of their father, were brought to Dhritarashtra, and presented to him as his nephews. He took charge of them, showed them great kindness, and had them educated with his own sons. Differences and dislikes soon arose, and the juvenile emulation and rivalry of the princes ripened into bitter hatred on the part of the Kauravas. This broke into an open flame when Dhritarashtra nominated Yudhishthira as his Yuvaraja or heir apparent. The jealousy and the opposition of his sons to this act was so great that Dhritarishtra sent the Pandavas away to Varanavata, where they dwelt in retirement. While they were living there Duryodhana plotted to destroy his cousins by setting fire to their house, which he had caused to be made very combustible. All the five brothers were for a time supposed to have perished in the fire, but they had received timely warning from Vidura, and they escaped to the forest, where they dressed and lived in disguise as Brahmins upon alms.

While the Pandavas were living in the forest they heard that Drupada, king of the Panchalas, had proclaimed a swayamvara, at which his daughter Draupadi was to select her husband from among the princely and warlike suitors. They went there, still disguised as Brahmins, Arjuna bent the mighty bow which had defied the strength of the Kauravas and all other competitors, and the Pandavas were victorious over every opponent. They threw off their disguise, and Draupadi was won by Arjuna. The brothers then conducted Draupadi to their home. On their arrival they told their mother Kunti that they had made a great acquisition, and she unwittingly directed them to share it among them. The mother's command could not be evaded, and Vyasa confirmed her direction; so Draupadi became the wife in common of the five brothers, and it was arranged that she should dwell for two days in the house of each of the five brothers in succession. This marriage has been justified by a piece of special pleading, which contends that the five princes were all portions of one deity, and therefore only one distinct person, to whom a woman might lawfully be married.

This public appearance made known the existence of the Pandavas. Their uncle Dhritarashtra recalled them to his court and divided his kingdom between his own sons and them. His sons received Hastinapura, and the chief city given to his nephews was Indraprastha on the river Yamuna, close to the modem Delhi, where the name still survives. The close proximity of Hastinapura and Indraprastha shows that the territory of Dhritarashtra must have been of very moderate extent. The reign of Yudhishthra was a pattern of justice and wisdom. Having conquered many countries, he announced his intention of performing the Rajasuya sacrifice, thus setting up a claim to universal dominion, or at least to be a king over kings. This excited still more the hatred and envy of the sons of Dhrita-rashtra, who induced their father to invite the Pandavas to Hastinapura. The Kauravas had laid their plot, and insidiously prevailed upon Yudhishthira to gamble. His opponent was Sakuni, uncle of the Kaurava princes, a great gambler and a cheat. Yudhishthira lost his all: his wealth, his palace, his kingdom, his brothers, himself, and, last of all, their wife. Draupadi was brought into the assembly as a slave, and when she rushed out she was dragged back again by her hair by Duhsasana, an insult for which Bhima vowed to drink his blood. Duryodhana also insulted her by seating her upon his thigh, and Bhima vowed that he would amash that thigh. Both these vows he afterwards performed.

Through the interference and commands of Dhritarishtra the possessiona of Yudhishthira were restored to him. But he was once more tempted to play, upon the condition that if he lost he and his brothers should pass twelve years in the forest, and should remain incognito during the thirteenth year. He was again the loser, and retired with his brothers and wife into exile. In the thirteenth year they entered the service of the king of Virata in disguise—Yudhishthira as a Brahmin skilful as a gamester; Bhima as a cook; Arjuna as an eunuch and teacher of music and dancing; Nakula as a horsetrainer; and Sahadeva as a herdsman. Draupadi also took service as attendant and needlewoman of the queen, Sudeshni. The five princes each assumed two names, one for use among themselves and one for public use. Yudhishthira was Jaya in private Kanka' in public; Bhima was Jayanta and Ballava; Arjuna was Vijaya and Brihannala; Nakula was Jayasena and Granthika; Sahadeva was Jayadbala and Arishtanemi, a Vaisya. The beauty of DraupadI attracted Kichaka, brother of the queen, and the chief man in the kingdom. He endeavoured to seduce her, and Bhima killed him. The relatives of Kichaka were about to burn Draupadi on his funeral pyre, but Bhima appeared as a wild Gandharva and rescued her. The brothers grew in favour, and rendered great resistance to the king in repelling the attacks of the king of Trigarta and the Kauravas. The time of exile being expired, the princes made themselves known, and Abhimanyu, son of Arjuna, received Uttara, the king's daughter, in marriage.

The Pandavas now determined to attempt the recovery of their kingdom. The king of Virata became their firm ally, and preparations for the war began. Allies were sought on all sides. Krishna and Balarama, being relatives of both parties, were reluctant to fight. Krishna conceded to Arjuna and Duryodhana the choice of himself unarmed or of a large army. Arjuna chose Krishna and Duryodhana joyfully accepted the army. Krishna agreed to act as charioteer of his especial friend Arjuna. It was in this capacity that he is represented to have spoken the divine song Bhagavadgita, when the rival armies were drawn up for battle at Kurukshetra, a plain north of Delhi. Many battles follow. The army of Duryodhana is commanded in succession by his greatuncle Bhishma, Drona his military preceptor, Karna, king of Anga, and Salya, king of Madra and brother of Madri. Bhishma was wounded by Arjuna, but survived for a time. All the others fell in succession, and at length only three of the Kuru warriors Kripa, Aswatthama, and Kritavarma—were left alive with Duryodhana. Bhima and Duryodhana fought in single combat with maces, and Duryodhana had his thigh broken and was mortally wounded. The three surviving Kauravas fell by night upon the camp of the Pandavas and destroyed five children of the Pandavas, and all the army except the five brothers themselves. These five boys were sons of Draupadi, one by each of the five brothers. Yudhishthira's son was Prativindhya, Bhima's was Srutasoma, Arjuna's was Srutakirtti, Nakula's was Satanika, and Sabadeva's was Srutakarma. Yudhishthira and his brothers then went to Hastinapura, and after a reconciliation with Dhritarashtra, Yudhishthira was crowned there. But he was greatly depressed and troubled at the loss of kindred and friends. Soon after he was seated on the throne, the Aswamedha sacrifice was performed with great ceremony, and the Pandavas lived in peace and prosperity.

The old blind king Dhritarashtra could not forget or forgive the loss of his sons, and mourned especially for Duryodhana. Bitter reproaches and taunts passed between him and Bhima; at length he, with his wife Gandhari, with Kunti, mother of the Pandavas, and with some of his ministers, retired to a hermitage in the woods, where, after two years' residence, they perished in a forest fire. Deep sorrow and remorse seized upon the Pandavas, and after a while Yudhishthira abdicated his throne and departed with his brothers to the Himalayas, in order to reach the heaven of Indra on Mount Meru. A dog followed them from Hastinapura. The story of this journey is full of grandeur and tenderness, and has been most effectively rendered into English by Professor Goldstucker. Sins and moral defects now prove fatal to the pilgrims. First fell Draupadi: "Too great was her love for Arjuna." Next Sahadeva: He esteemed none equal to himself." Then Nakula: "ever was the thought in his heart, "There is none equal in beauty to me." Arjuna's turn came next: "In one day I could destroy all my enemies." "Such was Arjuna's boast, and he falls, for he fulfilled it not." When Bhima fell he inquired the reason of his fall, and he was told, "When thou gazedst on thy foe, thou hast cursed him with thy breath; therefore thou fallest today." Yudhishthira went on alone with the dog until he reached the gate of heaven. He was invited by Indra to enter, but he refused unless his brothers and Draupadi were also received. "Not even into thy heaven would I enter if they were not there." He is assured that they are already there, and is again told to enter "wearing his body of flesh." He again refuses unless, in the words of Pope, "admitted to that equal sky, his faithful dog shall bear him company." Indra expostulates in vain. " Never, come weal or come woe, will I abandon your faithful dog." He is at length admitted, but to his dismay he finds there Duryodhana and his enemies, but not his brothers or Draupadi. He refuses to remain in heaven without them, and is conducted to the jaws of hell, where he beholds terrific sights and hears wailings of grief and anguish. He recoils, but wellknown voices implore him to remain and assuage their suffering. He triumphs in this crowning trial, and resolves to share the fate of his friends in hell rather than abide with their foes in heaven. Having endured this supreme test, the whole scene is shown to be the effect of maya or illusion, and he and his brothers and friends dwell with Indra in full content of heart for ever.

Such is the leading story of the Mahabharata, which no doubt had a basis of fact in the old Hindu traditions. Different poets of different ages have added to it and embellished it by the powers of their imagination. Great additions have been made in later times. The Bhagavadgita and the episode of Nala, with some others, are the productions of later writers; the Harivansa, which affects to be a part of the Mahabharata, is of still later date, and besides these, it cannot be doubted that numerous interpolations, from single verses to long passages, have been made to uphold and further the religious opinions of sects and individuals. To use the words of Max Muller, "The epic character of the story has throughout been changed and almost obliterated by the didactic tendencies of the latest editors, who were clearly Brahmins brought up in the strict school of the laws of Manu."

The date of the Mahabharata is very uncertain, and is at best a matter of conjecture and deduction. As a compiled work it is generally considered to be about a century later in date than the Ramayana, though there can be no doubt that the general thread of the story, and the incidents directly connected with it, belong to a period of time anterior to the story and scenes of that epic. The fact that the scene of the Mahabharata is in Upper India, while that of the Ramayana is in the Dakhin and Srilanka, is of itself sufficient to raise a strong presumption in favour of the superior antiquity of the former. Weber shows that the Mahabharata was known to Dion Chrysostom in the second half of the first century A.D.; and as Megasthenes, who was in India about 315 B.C., says nothing about the epic, Weber's hypothesis is that the date of the. Mahabharata is between the two. Professor Williams believes that "the earliest or pre-brahminical composition of both epics took place at a period not later than the fifth century B.C.," but that "the first orderly completion of the two poems in their Brahminised form may have taken place in the case of the Ramayana about the beginning of the third century B.C., and in the case of the Mahabharata still later."

Lassen thinks that three distinct arrangements of the Mahabharata are distinctly traceable. The varied contents of the Mahabharata and their disjointed arrangement afford some warrant for these opinions, and although the Ramayana is a compact, continuous, and complete poem, the professed work of one author, there are several recensions extant which differ considerably from each other. Taking a wide interval, but none too wide for a matter of such great uncertainty, the two poems may be considered as having assumed a complete form at some period in the six centuries preceding the Christian era, and that the Ramayana had the priority. The complete text of the Mahabharata has been twice printed in India, and a complete translation in French by Fauche has been interrupted by his death. But M. Fauche's translations are not in much repute. This particular one, says Weber, "can only pass for a translation in a very qualified sense." Many episodes and portions of the poem have been printed and translated. The following is a short epitome of the eighteen books of the Mahabharata:—

1. Adi-parva, 'Introductory book.' Describes the genealogy of the two families, the birth and nurture of Dhritarashtra and Pandu, their marriages, the births of the hundred sons of the former and the five of the latter, the enmity and rivalry between the young princes of the two branches, and the winning of Draupadi at the swayamvara.

2. Sabha-parva, 'Assembly book.' The assembly of the princes at Hastinapura when Yudhishthira lost his kingdom and the Pandavas had to retire into exile.

3. Vana-parva, 'Forest chapter.' The life of the Pandavas in the Kamyaka forest. This book is one of the longest and contains many episodes: among them the story of Nala, and an outline of the story of the Ramayana.

4. Virata-parva, 'Virata chapter.' Adventures of the Pandvas in the thirteenth year of their exile, while they were in the service of King Virata.

5. Udyoga-parva, 'Effort book.' The preparations of both sides for war.

6. Bhishma-parva, 'Book of Bhishma.' The battles fought while Bhishma commanded the Kaurava army.

7. Drona-parva, 'The Book of Drona.' Drona's command of the Kaurava army.

8. Karna-parva, 'Book of Karna.' Karna's command and his death at the hands of Arjuna.

9. Salya-parva, 'Book of Salya.' Salya's command, in which Duryodhana is mortally wounded and only three Kauravas are left alive.

10. Sauptika-parva, 'Nocturnal book.' The night attack of the three surviving Kauravas on the Pandava camp.

11. Stri-parva, 'Book of the women.' The lamentations of Queen Gandhari and the women over the slain.

12. Santi-parva, 'Book of consolation.' A long and diffuse didactic discourse by Bhishma on the morals and duties of kings, tntended to assuage the grief of Yudhishthira.

13. Anusasana-parva, 'Book of precepts.' A continuation of Bhishma's discourses and his death.

14. Aswamedhika-parva, 'Book of the Aswamadha.' Yudhishthira's performance of the horse sacrifice.

15. Asrama-parva, 'Book of the hermitage.' The retirement of Dhritarashtra, Gandhari, and Kunti to a hermitage in the woods, and their death in a forest fire.

16. Mausala-parva, 'Book of the clubs.' The death of Krishna and Balarama, the submersion of Dwaraka by the sea, and the mutual destruction of the Yadavas in a fight with clubs (musala) of miraculous origin.

17. Mahaprasthanika-parva, 'Book of the great journey.' Yudhishthira's abdication of the throne, and his departure with his brothers towards the Himalayas on their way to Indra's heaven on Mount Meru.

18. Swargarohan-parva, 'Book of the ascent to heaven.' Entrance into heaven of Yudhishthira and his brothers, and of their wife Draupadi.

The Harivansa, detailing the genealogy, birth, and life of Krishna at great length, is a supplement of much later date.

Genealogy of the Kauravas and Pandavas

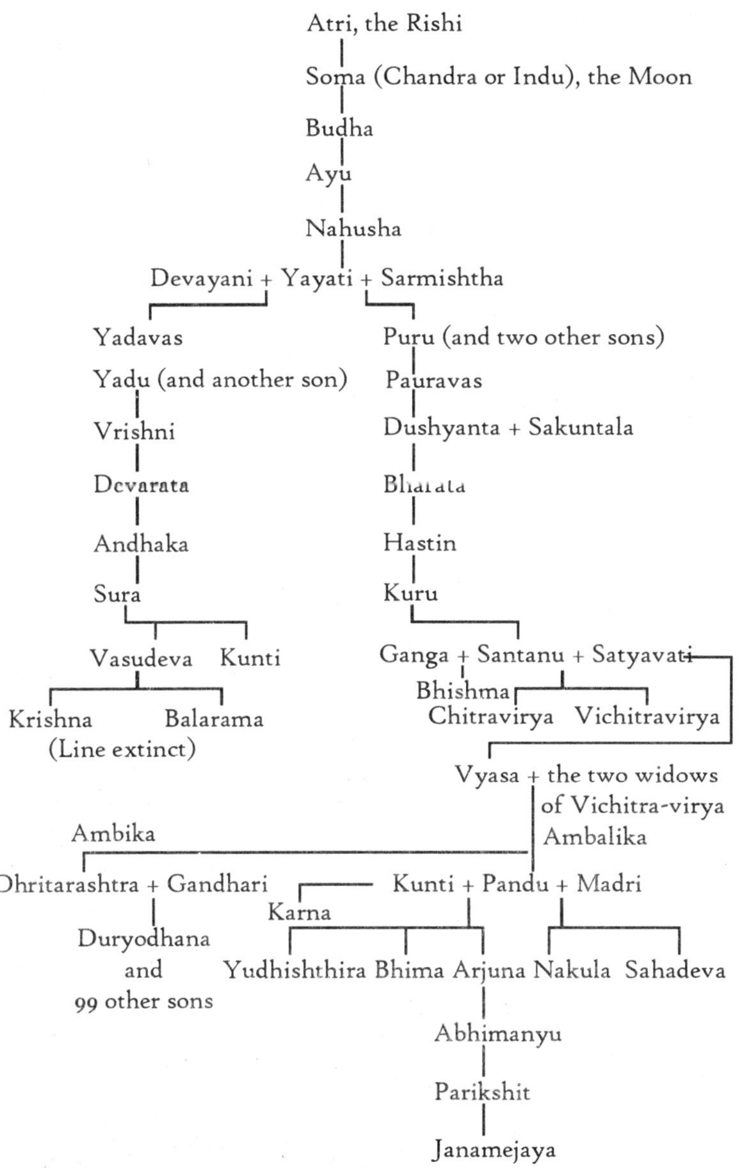

MAHABHASHYA: A commentary by Patanjali on the Grammar of Panini, in answer to the criticisms of Katyayana. A fine photolithographed edition has been produced, under the superintendence of Professor Goldstucker, at the expense of the Indian Government. The work has received a long notice in Weber's Indische Studien. vol. xiii, and has been the subject of much discussion in the Indian Antiquary. Other editions have appeared in India.

MAHISHMATI: The capital of Kartavirya, king of the Talajanghaa, who had a thousand arms. It has been identified by Colonel Tod with the village of Chuli Maheswar, which, according to him, is still called "the village of the thousand-armed."

MAINAKA: A mountain stated in the Mahabharata to the north of Kailasa; so called as being the son of Himavat and Menaka. When, as the poets sing, Indra clipped the wings of the mountains, this is said to have been the only one which escaped. This mountain, according to some, stands in Central India, and according to others, near the extremity of the Peninsula.

MAITREYI: Wife of the Rishi Yajnawalkya, who was indoctrinated by her husband in the mysteries of religion and philosophy.

MALATIMADHAVA: (Malati and Madhava). A drama by Bhavabhuti, translated by Wilson. "This drama," says the translator, "offers nothing to offend the most fastidious delicacy, and may be compared in this respect advantageously with many of the dramas of modern Europe which treat of the passion (of love) that constitutes its subject."

MALAVIKAGṄIMITRA (Malavika and Agnimitra): A drama ascribed to Kalidasa, and although inferior to his other productions, it is probably his work. The text, with a translation, has been published by Tullberg. There is a German translation by Weber, an English one by Tawney, and a French one by Foucaux. The text has been printed at Bombay and Calcutta.

MALLINATHA: A poet, and author of commentaries of great repute on several of the great poems, as the Raghuvansa, Meghaduta; Sisupalavadha, etc.

MANASA, MANASASAROVARA: The lake Manasa in the Himalayas. In the Vayu Purana it is stated that when the ocean fell from heaven upon Mount Meru, it ran four times round the mountain, then it divided into four rivers which ran down the mountain and formed four great lakes, Arunoda on the east, Sitoda on the west, Mahabhadra on the north, and Manasa on the south. According to the mythological account, the river Ganges flows out of it, but in reality no river issues from this lake, though the river Satluj flows from another and larger lake called Ravanahriida, which lies close to the west of Manasa.

MANDARA: The great mountain which the gods used for the churning of the ocean. It is supposed to be the mountain so named in Bhagalpur, which is held sacred.

MANDHATRI: A king, son of Yuvanaswa, of the race of Ikshwaku, and author of a hymn in tbe Rigveda. The Harivansa and some of the Puranas make Mandhatri to have been born in a natural way from his mother Gauri, but the Vishnu and Bhagavata Puranas tell an extraordinary story about his birth, which is probably based upon a forced derivation of his name. Yuvanaswa had no son, which grieved him much. Some holy sages near whom he lived instituted a religious rite to procure progeny for him. One night they placed a consecrated vessel of water upon an altar as part of their ceremony, and the water became endowed with prolific energy. Yuvanaswa woke up in the night thirsty, and finding the water, he drank it. So he conceived, and in due time a child came forth from his right side. The sages then asked who would suckle the child, whereupon Indra appeared, gave his finger for the child to suck, and said, "He shall suck me," *mam ayam dhasyati.* These words were contracted, and the boy was named Mandhatri. When he grew up, he had three sons and fifty daughters. An old sage named Saubhari came to Mandhatri and asked that one might be given him to wife. Unwilling to give one to so old and emaciated a man, but yet afraid to refuse, the king temporised, but at length yielded to the sage's request that the matter might be left to the choice of the girls. Saubhari then assumed a handsome form, and there was such a contention for him that he had to marry the whole fifty, and he provided for them a row of crystal palaces in a most beautiful garden.

MANDODARI: Ravana's favourite wife and the mother of Indrajit.

MANTHARA: An ugly deformed slave, nurse of Queen Kaikeyi, who stirred up her mistress' jealousy against Ramachandra, and led her to persuade King Dasaratha to banish Rama from court. Satrughna beat her and threatened to kill her, but she was saved by his brother Bharata.

MANU: (From the root *man*, to think.) 'The man.' This name belongs to fourteen mythological progenitors of mankind and rulers of the earth, each of whom holds sway for the period called a Manwantara (manuantara), the age of a Manu, i.e., a period of no less than 4,320,000 years. The first of these Manus was Swayambhuva, who sprang from Swayambhu, the selfexistent. The selfexistent, as identified with Brahma the creator, divided himself into two persons, male and female. From this pair was produced the male Viraj, and from him sprang the Manu Swayambhuva.

As the acting creator, this Manu produced the ten Prajapatis or progenitors of mankind, called also Maharshis. According to another account, this Manu sprang from the incestuous intercourse of Brahma with his daughter and wife, Satarupa. Brahma created himself Manu, "born of and identical with his original self, and the female portion of himself he constituted Satarupa," whom Manu took to wife. The lawbook commonly known as Manu Sanhita is ascribed to this Manu, and so also is a Sutra work on ritual bearing the same name. The Manu of the present age is the seventh, named Vaivaswata, 'sunborn,' who was the son of Vivaswat, the sun, and he is a Kshatriya by race. He is also called Satyavrata. There are various legends about his having been saved from a great flood by Vishnu or Brahma. The names of the fourteen Manus are—(1.) Swayambhuva, (2.) Swarochisha, (3.) Auttami, (4.) Tamasa, (5.) Raivata, (6.) Chakshusha, (7.) Vaivaswata or Satyavrata, (8.) Savarna, (9.) Dakshasavarna, (10.) Brahmasavarna, (11.) Dharmasavarna, (12.) Rudrasavarna, (13.) Rauchya, and (14.) Bhautya.

The sons of Manu Vaivaswata were—Ikshwaku, Nabhaga or Nriga, Dhrishta, Saryati, Narishyanta, Pransu, Nabhaganedishta or Nabhanedishta, Karasha, and Prishadhra. But there is some variety in the names.

With the seventh Manu, Vaivaswata, is connected the curious and intereating legend of the deluge. The first account of this is found in the Satapatha Brahmana, of which the following is a summary:—One morning, in the water which was brought to Manu for washing his hands, he caught a fish which spake, and said, "Take care of me and I will preserve thee." Manu asked, "From what wilt thou preserve me?" The fish answered, "A flood will carry away all living beings; I will save thee from that." The fish desired Manu to keep him alive in an earthen vessel, to remove him to a dyke as he grew larger, and eventually to the ocean, "so that he might be beyond the risk of destruction." The fish grew rapidly, and again addressed Manu, saying, "After so many years the deluge will take place; then construct a ship and pay me homage, and when the waters rise, go into the ship and I will rescue thee." Manu did as he was desired, he built the ship, conveyed the fish to the ocean, and did him homage. The flood rose, and Manu fastened the cable of the ship to the fish's horn. Thus he passed over the northern mountain (the Himalaya, as the commentator explains). The fish then desired Manu to fasten the ship to a tree, and to go down with the subsiding waters. He did so, and found that the flood had swept away all living creatures. He alone was left. Desirous of offspring, he offered sacrifice and engaged in devotion. A woman was produced, who came to Manu and declared herself his daughter. "With her he lived, worshipping and toiling in arduous religious rites, desirous of offspring. With her he begat the offspring which is the offspring of Manu."

The story, as told in the Mahabharata, represents Manu as engaged in devotion by the side of a river, and the fish craving his protection from the bigger fish. Manu placed the fish in a glass vase, but it grew larger and larger till the ocean alone could contain it. Then it warned Manu of the coming flood, and directed him to build a ship and to embark with the seven Rishis. He did so, and fastened his ship to the horn of the fish. Then, according to the rendering of Professor Williams-

'Along the ocean in that stately ship was borne the lord of men, and through

Its dancing, tumbling billows and its roaring waters; and the bark,

Tossed to and fro by violent winds, reeled on the surface of the deep,

Staggering and trembling like a drunken woman: land was seen no more,

Nor far horizon, nor the space between; for everywhere around spread the wild waste of waters, reeking atmosphere, and boundless sky.

And now, when all the world was deluged, nought appeared above the waves.

But Manu and the seven sages, and the fish that drew the bark. Unwearied thus for years on years that fish pulled on the ship across.

"The heapedup waters, till at length it bore the vessel to the peak of Himavan; then, softly smiling, thus the fish addressed the sage:

"Haste now to bind thy ship to this high crag. Know me, the lord of all,

The great creator Brahma, mightier than all might, omnipotent. By me, in fishlike shape, have you been saved in dire emergency. From Manu all creation, gods, Asuras, men, must be produced; By him the world must be created, that which moves and moveth not."

The commentators on this legend of the Mahabharata give a metaphysical turn to the legend, and endeavour to illustrate it by philosophical and allegorical interpretations. The same story is reproduced with variations in the Matsya, Bhagavata, and Agni Puranas, and Muir has given translations of the passages in vol. i. of his Sanskrit Texts.

In the Ramayana mention is made of a female Manu, and it appears that the word is sometimes used for "the wife of Manu."

MANU-SANHITA: The wellknown lawbook, the Code of Manu, or Institutes of Manu. It is attributed to the first Manu, Swayambhuva, who existed nearly thirty millions of years ago, but it bears the marks of being the production of more than one mind. This is the first and chief of the works classified as Smriti, and is a collection or digest of current laws and creeds rather than a planned systematic code. It is the foundation of Hindu law, and is held in the highest reverence. The work belongs to a period later than that of the Vedas, when the Brahmins had obtained the ascendancy, but its deities are those of the vedic rather than the Epic or Puranic age. It is apparently anterior to the philosophical schools. The fifth century B.C. is supposed to be about the time when it was composed, but the rules and precepts it contains had probably existed as traditions long before. It is commonly called the Code of Manu, and was current among the Manavas, a class or school of Brahmins who were followers of the Black Yajurveda; but its deals with many subjects besides law, and is a most important record of old Hindu society. It is said to have consisted originally of 100,000 verses, arranged in twentyfour chapters; that Narada shortened the work to 12,000 verses; and that Sumati made a second abridgment, reducing it to 4000, but only 2685 are extant. It is evident that there was more than one redaction of the laws of the Manavas, for a Brihan or Vrihan Manu, 'great Manu,' and Vriddha Manu, 'old Manu,' are often referred to. Sir W. Jones's translation, edited by Haughton, is excellent, and is the basis of all others in French, German, etc. The text has often been printed.

MANWANTARA (**Manuantara**): The life or period of a Manu, 4,320,000 years.

MARKANDEYA: A sage, the son of Mrikanda, and reputed author of the Markandeya Purana. He was remarkable for his austerities and great age, and is called Dirghayus, 'the longlived.'

MARKANDEYA PURANA: "That Purana in which, commencing with the story of the birds that were acquainted with right and wrong, everything is narrated fully by Markandeya as it was explained by holy sages in reply to the question of the Muni, is called the Markandeya, containing 9000 verses." This Purana is narrated in the first place by Markandeya, and in the second by certain fabulous birds profoundly versed in the Vedas, who relate their knowledge in answer to the questions of the sage Jaimini. "It has a character different from all the other Puranas. It has nothing of a sectarial spirit, little of a religious tone; rarely inserting prayers and invocations to any deity, and such as are inserted are brief and moderate. It deals little in precepts, ceremonial or moral. Its leading feature is narrative, and it presents an uninterrupted succession of legends, most of which, when ancient, are embellished with new circumstances, and, when new, partake so far of the spirit of the old, that they are disinterested creations of the imagination, having no particular motive, being designed to recommend no special doctrine or observance. Whether they are derived from any other source, or whether they are original inventions, it is not possible to ascertain. They are most probably, for the greater part at least, original; and the whole has been narrated in the compiler's own manner, a manner superior to that of the Puranas in general, with exception of the Bhagavata." The popular Durga Mahatmya or Chandipatha is an episode of this Purana. In the absence of any guide to a positive conclusion as to the date, it may conjecturally be placed in the ninth or tenth century. Professor Banerjea places it in the eighth century. This Purana has been published in the Bibliotheca Indica, and translated by the Rev. Professor K.M. Banerjea.

MATHURA: An ancient and celebrated city on the right bank of the Yamuna. It was the birthplace of Krishna and one of the seven sacred cities. The Vishnu Purana states that it was originally called Madhu or Madhuvana, from the demon Madhu, who reigned there, but when Lavana, his son and successor, was killed by Satrughna, the conqueror set up his own rule there and built a city which he called Madhura or Mathura.

MATSYA: 'A fish.' 1. The Fish Incarnation. 2. Name of a country. Wilson says, "Dinajpoor, Rungpoor, and Cooch

Behar;" but there was more than one country of this name, and one would appear to have been situated in Northern India. Manu places Matsya in Brahmarshi. According to the Mahabharata, King Virata's capital was called Matsya, his people also were called Matsyas, and he himself was styled Matsya. General Cunningham finds it in the neighbourhood of Jaypur, and says that the town of Virat or Bairat, 105 miles south of Delhi, was its capital.

MATSYA PURANA: This Purana is so called from its contents having been narrated to Manu by Vishnu in the form of a fish (matsya). It consists of between 14,000 and 15,000 stanzas. This work is a miscellaneous compilation, but includes in its contents the elemcnts of a genuine Purana. At the same time, it is of too mixed a character to be considered as a genuine work of the Pauranik class. Many of its chapters are the same as parts of the Vishnu and Padma Puranas. It has also drawn largely from the Mahabharata. "Although a Saiva work, it is not cxclusively so, and it has no such sectarial absurdities as the Kurma and Linga."

MAURYA: The dynasty founded by Chandragupta at Palaliputra (Patna) in Magadha. According to the Vishnu Purana, the Maurya kings were ten in number and reigned 137 years. Their names were—(1.) Chandragupta, (2.) Bindusara, (3.) Asokavardhana, (4.) Suyasaas, (5.) Dasaratha, (6.) Sangata, (7.) Salisaka, (8.) Somasarman, (9.) Sasadharman, (10.) Brihadratha. The names vary in other Puranas.

MAYA: A Daitya who was the architect and artificer of the Asuras, as Viswakarma was the artificer of the Suras or gods. He was son of Viprachitti and father of Vajrakama and Mandodari, wife of Ravana. He dwelt in the Devagiri mountains not very far from Delhi, and his chief works were in the neighbourhood of that city, where he worked for men as well as Daityas. The Mahabharata speaks of a palace he built for the Pandavas. In tho Harivansa he appears frequently both as victor and vanquished in contests with the gods.

MAYA: 'Illusion, deception.' Illusion personified as a female form of celestial origin, created for the purpose of beguiling some individual. Sometimes identified with Durga as the source of spells, or as a personification of the unreality of worldly things. In this character she is called Mayadevi or Mahamaya. 2. A name of Gaya, one of the seven sacred cities.

MEDHATITHI: Name of a Kanwa who was a Vedic Rishi. There is a legend in one of the Upanishads that he was carried up to heaven by Indra in the form of a ram, because the god had been pleased with his austerities.

MEGHADUTA: 'Cloud messenger.' A celebrated poem by Kalidasa, in which a banished Yaksha implores a cloud to convey tidings of him to his wife. It has been translated into English verse by Wilson, and there are versions in French and German. The text has been printed with a vocabulary by Johnson.

MENA, MENAKA: 1. In the Rigveda, a daughter of Vrishanaswa. A Brahmana tells a strange story of Indra having assumed the form of Mena and then fallen in love with her. In the Puranas, wife of Himavat and mother of Uma and Ganga, and of a son named Mainaka. 2. An Apsaras sent to Seduce the sage Viswamitra from his devotions, and succeeding in this object, she became the mother of the nymph Sakuntala.

MERU: A fabulous mountain in the navel or centre of the earth, on which is situated Swarga, the heaven of Indra, containing the cities of the gods and the habitations of celestial spirits. The Olympus of the Hindus. Regarded as a terrestrial object, it would seem to be some mountain north of the Himalayas. It is also Sumeru, Hemadri, ' golden mountain;' Ratnasanu, 'jewel peak;' Karnikachala, 'lotus mountain;' and Amaradri and Devaparvata, 'mountain of the gods.'

MIMANSA DARSANA: A work on the Mimansa philosophy. Printed in the Bibliotheca Indica.

MITAKSHARA: A commentary by Vijnaneswara on the Smriti or textbook of Yajnawalkya. The authority of this book is admitted all over India, with the exception of Bengal proper. The portion on inheritance has been translated by Colebrooke, and into French by Orianne. The text has been printed in India.

MITHILA: A city, the capital of Videha or North Bihar, which corresponds to the modern Tirhut and Puraniya, between the Gandaki and Kosi rivers. It has given its name to one of the five northern nations of Brahmins, and to a school of law. It was the country of King Janaka, and the name of his capitol, Janakapura, still survives in "Janakpur," on the northern frontier.

MITRA: Probably connected with the Persian Mithra. A form of the sun. In the Vedas he is generally associated with Varuna, he being the ruler of the day and Varuna the ruler of the night. They together uphold and rule the earth and sky, guard the world, encourage religion, and chastise sin. He is one of the Adityas or sons of Aditi.

MRICHCHHA-KATIKA: 'The toycart.' A drama in ten acts by King Sudraka, supposed to be the oldest Sanskrit drama extant, and to have been written in the first or second century A.D. The country over which Sudraka reigned is not known. This play, says Wilson, its translator, "is a curious and interesting picture of national manners... free from all exterior influence or adulteration. It is a portrait purely Indian. It represents a state of society sufficiently advanced in civilisation to be luxurious and corrupt, and is certainly very far from offering a flattering similitude, although not without some attractive features." Williams observes, "The dexterity with which the plot is arranged, the ingenuity with which the incidents are connected, the skill with which the characters are delineated and contrasted, the boldness and felicity of the diction, are scarcely unworthy of our own great dramatists." There are translations in French and several editions of the text.

MUCHUKUNDA: In the Puranas, son of Mandhatri, and called 'king of men.' He rendered assistance to the gods in their wars with the Asuras or demons, and he asked and obtained as a reward the boon of a long uninterrupted sleep. Whosoever disturbed him was to be burnt to ashes by fire issuing from his body. Kalayavana was lured into his cave by Krishna and woke the sleeper, who cast a fiery glance upon the intruder which destroyed him. Muchukunda then paid laud and honour to Krishna, who gave him power to go to whatever celestial region he wished, and to enjoy all heavenly pleasures. Muchukunda left his cave and went to Gandhamadana to perform penance. The Mahabharata says he was reproved by Kuvera for trusting to his priest more than to his own prowess for success in war, but he replied that the religious aid of Brahmins was as necessary as the warlike powers of Kshatriyas.

MUDGALA: A Vedic Rishi from whom the Maudgalya Brahmins sprang. There were several other Brahmins named Mudgala. A sage of this name is recorded in the Mahabharata to have lived a life of poverty, piety, and selfrestraint, offering hospitality to thousands of Brahmins, according to his humble means, with the grain which he gleaned like a pigeon, and which never underwent diminution, or rather increased again, when it was required." The choleric sage Durvasa went to test the patience of Mudgala, and six times devoured all the food which his host possessed without ruffling his temper. Durvasa in his admiration declared that Mudgala would go bodily to heaven, and the messenger of the gods arrived with his heavenly car. The sage, before accepting the invitation, desired to be informed of the joys and ills of heaven. After hearing a full explanation, he found that the enjoyments of heaven must come to a close, so he declared that he "had no desire for heaven, and would seek only that eternal abode where there is no sorrow, nor distress, nor change." He dismissed the messenger of the gods, and began to practise ascetic virtues, becoming indifferent to praise and blame, regarding clods, gold, stones, and gold as alike. Pure knowledge led to fixed contemplation; and that again imparted strength and complete comprehension, whereby he obtained supreme eternal perfection in the nature of quietude (nirvana).

MUDRA-RAKSHASA: 'The signet of the minister.' A drama by Visakhadatta. This play has an historical interest, for Chandragupta, the Sandracottus of Greek writers, is a leading character in it. The date of its production is apparently the eleventh or twelfth century A.D. It is one of the dramas translated by Wilson, who says, "The author was not a poet of the sphere of Bhavabhati or Kalidasa. His imagination rises not to their level, and there is scarcely a brilliant or beautiful thought in the play. As some equivalent for the want of imagination, he has a vigorous perception of character and a manly strain of sentiment, that are inferior only to elevated conception and delicate feeling. He is the Massinger of the Hindus. The language of the original partakes of the general character of the play; it is rarely beautiful or delicate, but always vigorous, and occasionally splendid."

MUNDAKA: Name of an Upanishad translated by Dr. Roer in the Bibliotheca Indica and by Rammohun Roy. There are several editions of the text.

N

NACHIKETA: The story of Nachiketa is told in the a Taittiriya Brahmana and Kath Upanishad. Vajasravasa or Aruni, the father of Nachiketa, desirous of attaining heaven, performed great sacrifices, and was profuse in his gifts to the priests. The son told him that he had not given all, for that he, his son, was left, and said, "To whom shall I be given?" On repeating the question, the father angrily replied, "To death." So the son departed to the abode of death, and, after staying there three nights, Yama was constrained to offer him a boon. He prayed to see his father again and be reconciled. This boon was granted and another offered. All kinds of blessings were proposed, but the youth refused to be contented with anything but a true knowledge of the soul. Yama then proceeded to instruct him. The story has been done into verse by Muir.

NAGA: A snake, especially the cobracapella. A mythical semidivine being, having a human face with the tail of a serpent, and the expanded neck of the cobra. The race of Nagas is said to be a thousand in number, and to have sprung from Kadru, the wife of Kasyapa, for the purpose of peopling Patala, or the regions below the earth, where they reign in great splendour. From the name of their mother they are called Kadraveya. Their mother is sometimes called Surasi. This dominion was taken from them by the Gandharvas, but they recovered it through their sister, the Narmada river, who induced Vishnu to send Pratardana to their assistance. Their females were handsome, and some of them intermarried with men, as ulupi with Arjuna.

The Nagas, or a people bearing the same name, are historical, and have left many traces behind them. There were mountains so called, and Nagadwipa was one of the seven divisions of Bharatavaraha. Kings of this race reigned at Mathura, Padmavati, etc., and the name survives in the modem Nagpur. There are various speculations as to who and what they were, but it seems clear they were a race distinct from the Hindus. The mythological accounts are probably based upon the historical, but they have been mixed up together and confused. The favourite theory is that they were a Scythic race, and probably obtained their name from worshipping serpents or holding them in awe and reverence.

NAHUSHA: Son of Ayus, the eldest son of Puraravas, and father of Yayati. This king is mentioned by Manu as having come into conflict with the Brahmins, and his story is repeated several times with variations in different parts of the Mahabharata as well as in the Puranas, the aim and object of it evidently being to exhibit the retribution awaiting any man who derogates from the power of Brahmins and the respect due to them. "By sacrifices, austere fervour, sacred study, selfrestraint, and valour, Nahusha acquired the undisturbed sovereignty of the three worlds. Through want of virtuous humility the great king Nahusha was utterly ruined."—Manu. One version of the story says that he aspired to the possession of Indrani, wife of Indra, when that god had concealed himself for having killed a Brahmin. A thousand great Rishis bore the car of Nahusha through the air, and on one occasion he touched with his foot the great Agastya, who was carrying him. The sage in his anger cried out, "Fall, thou serpent," and Nahusha fell from his glorious car and became a serpent. Agastya, at the supplication of Nahusha, put a limit to the curse; and according to one version, the doomed man was released from it by the instrumentality of Yudhishthira, when he threw off "his huge reptile form, became clothed in a celestial body, and ascended to heaven."

NAIMISHA, NAIMISHARANYA: A forest (aranya) near the Gomati river, in which the Mahabharata was rehearsed by Sauti to the assembled Rishis.

NAISHADHA-CHARITA, NAISHADHIYA: A poem on tho life of Nala, king of Nishadha, by Sri Harsha, a great sceptical philosopher who lived in the eleventh or twelfth century A.D. It is one of the six Mahakavyas. There are several printed editions.

NAKULA: The fourth of the Pandu princes. He was the twin son of Madri, the second wife of Pandu, but mythologically he was the son of the Aswins, or more specifically of the Aswin Nasatya. He was taught the art of training and managing horses by Drona, and when he entered the service of the king of Virata, he was master of the horses. He had a son named Niramitra by his wife Karenumati, a princess of Chedi.

NALA: 1. King of Nishadha and husband of Damayanti. The story of Nala and Damayanti is one of the episodes of the Mahabharata, and is well known from having been translated into Latin by Bopp and into English verse by Dean Milman. Damayanti was the only daughter of Bhima, king of Vidarbha, and was very lovely and accomplished. Nala was brave and handsome, virtuous, and learned in the Vedas, skilled in arms and in the management of horses, but addicted to the vice of gambling. They loved each other upon the mere fame of their respective virtues and beauty, and Damayanti pined for the presence of her unknown lover. Bhima determined that his daughter should hold a swayamvara. Rajas flocked to it in crowds, and among them Nala. Four gods, Indra, Agni, Varuna, and Yama, also attended. Nala met them on the way, and reverently promised to do their will. They bade him enter the palace and inform Damayanti that they would present themselves among the candidates, and that she must choose one of them.

Nala reluctantly performed his task, but his presence perfected his conquest, and the maiden announced her resolve to pay due homage to the gods, but to choose him for her lord. Each of the four gods assumed the form of Nala, but the lover's eye distinguished the real one, and she made her choice. They married and lived for some time in great happiness, a son and a daughter, named Indrasen and Indrasena, being born to them. Kali, a personification of the Kali or iron age, arrived too late for the swayamvara. He resolved to be revenged, and he employed his peculiar powers to ruin Nala through his love of gambling. At his instigation, Pushkara, Nala's younger brother, proposed a game of dice. Kali charmed the dice, and Nala went on losing; but he was infatuated; the entreaties of friends and ministers, wife and children, were of no avail; he went on till he had lost his all, even to his clothes. His rival Pushkara became king, and proclaimed that no one was to give food or shelter to Nala, so the ruined monarch wandered forth into the forest with his wife, and suffered great privations. Some birds flew away with his only garment.

He resolved to abandon his wife in the hope that she would return to her father's court, so he divided her sole remaining garment while she slept and left her. Thus left alone, Damayanti wandered about in great distress. She did not go home, but she at length found service and protection with the princess of Chedi. Nala fell in with the king of serpents, who was under a curse from which Nala was to deliver him. The serpent bit Nala, and told him that the poison should work upon him till the evil spirit was gone out of him, and that he should then be restored to all he loved. Through the effects of the bite he was transformed into a misshapen dwarf. In this form he entered the service of Rituparna, king of Ayodhya, as a trainer of horses and an accomplished cook, under the name of Bahuka. Damayanti was discovered and conducted to her father's home, where she found her children. Great search was made for Nala, but in vain, for no one knew him in his altered form. One Brahmin, however, suspected him, and infonned Damayanti She resolved to test his feelings by announcing her intention of holding a second swayamvara.

King Rituparna determined to attend, and took Nala with him as driver of his chariot. Rituparna was skilled in numbers and the rules of chances. On their journey he gave a wonderful proof of this, and he instructed Nala in the science. When Nala had acquired this knowledge the evil spirit went out of him, but still he retained his deformity. Damayanti half penetrated his disguise, and was at length convinced that he was her husband by the flavour of a dish which he had cooked. They met and, after some loving reproaches and the interference of the gods, they became reconciled, and Nala resumed his form. He again played with Pushkara, and staked his wife against the kingdom. Profiting by the knowledge he had obtained from Rituparna, he won back all and again became king. Pushkara then humbled himself, and Nala not only forgave him, but sent him home to his own city enriched with many gifts. The text of this poem has been often printed, and there are translations in various languages.

2. A monkey chief, said to be a son of Viswakanna. According to the Ramayana, he had the power of making stones float in water. He was in Rama's army and built the bridge of stone called Ramasetu, or Nalasetu, from the continent to Lanka, over which Rama passed with his army.

NAMUCHI: A demon slain by Indra with the form of water. The legend of Namuchi first appears in the Rigveda, where it is said that Indra ground "the head of the slave Namuchi like a sounding and rolling cloud," but it is amplified by the commentator and also in the Satapatha Brahmana and Mahabharata. When Indra conquered the Asuras there was one Namuchi who resisted so strongly that he overpowered Indra and held him. Namuchi offered to let Indra go on promise not to kill him by day or by night, with wet or with dry. Indra gave the promise and was released, but he cut off Namuchi's head at twilight, between day and night, and with foam of water, which was, according to the authorities, neither wet nor dry. The Mahabharata adds that the severed head followed Indra calling out "O wicked slayer of thy friend."

NANDA: 1. The cowherd by whom Krishna was brought up. 2. A king, or dynasty of kings, of Magadha, that reigned at Pataliputra, and was overthrown by Chandragupta Maurya about 315 B.C.

NANDI: The bull of Siva. The Vayu Purana makes him the son of Kasyapa and Surabhi. His image, of a milky white colour, is always conspicuous before the temples of Siva. He is the chamberlain of Siva, chief of his personal attendants (ganas), and carries a staff of office. He is guardian of all quadrupeds. He is also called Salankayana, and he has the appellations of Nadideha and Tandavatalika, because he accompanies with music the tandava dance of his master.

NARADA: A Rishi to whom some hymns of the Rigveda are ascribed. He is one of the Prajapatis, and also one of the seven great Rishis. The various notices of him are somewhat inconsistent. The Rigveda describes him as "of the Kanwa family." Another authority states that he sprang from the forehead of Brahma, and the Vishnu Purana makes him a son of Kasyapa and one of Daksha's daughters. The Mahabharata and some Puranas state that he frustrated the scheme which Daksha had formed for peopling the earth, and consequently incurred that patriarch's curse to enter again the womb of a woman and be born Dakha, however, relented at the solicitation of Brahma, and consented that Narada should be born again of Brahma and one of Daksha's daughters; he was hence talled Brahma and Devabrahma. In some respects he bears a resemblance to Orpheus. He is the inventor of the vina (lute), and was chief of the Gandharvas or heavenly musicians. He also went down to the infernal regions (Patala), and was delighted with what he saw there. In later times he is connected with the legend of Krishna. He warned Kansa of the imminent incarnation of Vishnu, and he afterwards became the friend and associate of Krishna.

The Narada-pancharatra relates that Brahma advised his son Narada to marry, but Narada censured his father as a false teacher, because devotion to Krishna was the only true means of felicity. Brahma then cursed Narada to lead a life of sensuality, in subjection to women, and Narada retorted the curse, condemning Brahma to lust after his own daughter, and to be an object unworthy of adoration. Narada has the appellations, Kalikaraka, 'strifemaker;' Kapivaktra, 'monkeyfaced;' Pisuna, 'messenger or spy.'

Narada was also one of the great writers upon law. His textbook, called Naradiya Dharmasastra, has been translated into English by Dr. Jolly.

NARAKA: Hell; a place of torture to which the souls of the wicked are sent. Manu enumerates twentyone hells:—Tamisra, Andhatamisra, Maharaurava, Raurava, Naraka, Kalasutra, Mahanaraka, Sanjivana, Mahavichi, Tapana, Sampratapana, Sanhata, Sakakola, Kudmala, Putimrittika, Lohasanku, Rijisha, Panthana, Salmali, Asipatravana, and Lohadaraka. Other authorities vary greatly as to the numbers and names of the hells.

NARAKA: An Asura, son of the Earth. In the Mahabharata and Vishnu Purana he is said to have carried off the earrings of Aditi to the impregnable castle of Pragjyotisha, but Krishna, at the request of the gods, went there and killed him and recovered the jewels. In the Harivansa the legend differs. According to this, Naraka, king of Pragjyotisha, was an implacable enemy of the gods. He assumed the form of an elephant, and having carried off the daughter of Viswakarma, he subjected her to violation. He seized the daughters of the Gandharvas, and of gods and of men, as well as the Apsarasas themselves, and had more than 16,000 women, for whom he built a splendid residence. He also appropriated to himself jewels, garments, and valuables of all sorts, and no Asura before him had ever been so horrible in his actions.

NARA-NARAYANA: Two ancient Rishis, sons of Dharma and Ahinsa. The names are sometimes applied to Krishna and to Krishna and Arjuna. The Vamana Purana has a legend about them which is alluded to in the drama of

Vikramorvasi. Their penances and austerities alarmed the gods, so Indra sent nymphs to inspire them with passion and disturb their devotions. Narayana took a flower and placed it on his thigh. Immediately there spring from it a beautiful nymph whose eharms far excelled those of the celestial nymphs, and made them return to heaven filled with shame and vexation. Narayana sent this nymph to Indra with them, and from her having been produced from the thigh (uru) of the sage, she was called Urvasi.

NARAYANA: 1. The son of Nara, the original man, and often identified or coupled with Nara. 2. The creator Brahma, who, according to Manu, was so called because the waters (nara) were his first ayana or place of motion. The name as commonly used is applied for vishnu, and is that under which he was first worshipped.

NARMADA: The river which is esteemed holy. The personified river is variously represented as being daughter of a Rishi named Mekala (from whom she if called Mekala and Mekalakanya), as a daughter of the moon, as a 'mindborn daughter' of the Somapas, and as sister of the Nagas. It was she who brought Purukutsa to the aid of the Nagas against the Gandharvas, and the grateful snakegods made her name a charm against the venom of snakes. According to the Vishnu Purana, she had a son by Purukutsa who was named Trasadasyu. The Matsya Purana gives Duhsaha as the name of her husband. The Harivansa is inconsistent with itself. In one place it makes her wife of Purukutsa and mother of Trasadasyu; in another it makes her the wife of Trasadasyu. She is also called Reva and Purvaganga, and, as a daughter of the moon, Induja and Somodbhava.

NIGHANTU, NIGHANTUKA: A glossary, especially of synonyms and obsolete and obscure Vedic terms. There was at least one work of this kind before the days of Yaska.

NIKUMBHA: A Rakshasa who fought against Rama. He was son of Kumbhakarna. 2. An Asura who, according to the Harivansa, received the boon from Brahma that he should die only by the hands of Vishnu. He was king of Shatpura and had great magical powers, so that he could multiply himself into many forms, though he commonly assumed only three. He carried off the daughters of Brahmadatta, the friend of Krishna, and that hero attacked him and killed him under different forms more than once, but he was eventually slain outright by Krishna, and his city of Shatpura was given to Brahmadatta.

NIMI: Son of Ikshwaku, and founder of the dynasty of Mithila. He was cursed by the sage Vasishtha to lose his corporeal form, and he retorted the imprecation upon the sage. Both abandoned the bodily condition. Vasishtha was born again as the issue of Mitra and Varuna, but "the corpse of Nimi was preserved from decay by being embalmed with fragrant oils and resins, and it remained as entire as if it were immortal!

NIRUKTA: 'Etymology, glossary.' One of the Vedangas. The Nirukta is devoted to the explanation of difficult Vedic words. The only work of the kind now known to us is that of Yaska, who was a predecessor of Panini; but such works were no doubt numerous, and the names of seventeen writers of Niruktas are mentioned as having preceded Yaska. The Nirukta consists of three parts:—(1.) Naighantuka, a collection of synonymous words; (2.) Naigama, a collection of words peculiar to the Vedas; (3.) Daivata, words relating to deities and sacrifices. These are mere lists of' words, and are of themselves of little value. They may have been compiled by Yaska himself, or he may have found them ready to his hand. The real Nirukta, the valuable portion of the work, is Yaska's commentary which follows. In this he explains the meaning of words, enters into etymological investigations, and quotes passages of the Vedas in illustration. These are valuable from their acknowledged antiquity, and as being the oldest known examples of a Vedic gloss. They also throw a light upon the scientific and religious condition of their times, but the extreme brevity of their style makes them obscure and difficult to understand. The text of the Nirukta has been published by Roth.

NRISINHA: The Narasinha or manlion incarnation.

NYAYA: The logical school of philosophy.

O

OM: A word of solemn invocation, affirmation, benediction, and consent, so sacred that when it is uttered no one must hear it. The word is used at the commencement of prayers and religious ceremonies, and is generally placed at the beginning of books. It is a compound of the three letters a, u, m, which are typical of the three Vedas; and it is declared in the Upanishads, where it first appears, to have a mystic power and to be worthy of the deepest meditation. In later times the monosyllable represents the Hindu triad or union of the three gods, a being Vishnu, u Siva, and m Brahma. This monosyllable is called Udgitha.

P

PADA: The Pada text of the Vedas, or of any other work, is one in which each word (pada) stands separate and distinct, not joined with the next according to the rules of sandhi (coalition).

PADMA-PURANA: This Purana generally stands second in the list of Puranas, and is thus described:—"That which contains an account of the period when the world was a golden lotus (padma), and of all the occurrences of that time, is therefore, called Padma by the wise. It contains 55,000 stanzas." The work is divided into five books or Khandas:-" (1.) Srishti Khanda, or section on creation; (2.) Bhumi Khanda, on the earth; (3.) Swarga Khanda, on heaven; (4.) Patala Khanda, on the regions below the earth; (5.) Uttara Khanda, last or supplementary chapter. There is also current a sixth division, the Kriya-yoga-sara, a treatise on the practice of devotion." These denominations of the various divisions convey but an imperfect and partial notion of their heterogeneous contents, and it seems probable that the different sections are distinct works associated together under one title. There is no reason to consider any of them as older than the twelfth century. The tone of the whole Purana is strongly Vaishnava; that of the last section especially so. In it Siva is represented as explaining to Parvati the nature and attributes of Vishnu, and in the end the two join in adoration of that deity. A few chapters have been printed and translated into Latin by Wollheim.

PAHLAVA: Name of a people. Manu places the Pahlavas among the northern nations, and perhaps the name is connected with the word Pahlavi, i.e., Persian. They let their beards grow by command of King Sagara. According to Manu, they were Kshatriyas who had become outcasts, but the Mahabharata says they were created from the tail of Vasishtha's cow of fortune; and the Ramayana states that they sprang from her breath. They are also called Pahnavas.

PANCHAJANYA: Krishna's conch, formed from the shell of the sea-demon Panchajana.

PANCHALA: Name of a country. From the Mahabharata it would seem to have occupied the Lower Doab; Manu places it near Kanauj. It has sometimes been identified with the Panjab, and with "a little territory in the more immediate neighbourhood of Hastinapur." Wilson says, "A country extending north and west from Delhi, from the foot of the Himalayas to the Chambal." It was divided into Northern and Southern Panchalas, and the Ganges separated them. Cunningham considers North Panchala to be Rohilkhand, and South Panchala the Gangetic Doab. The capital of the former was Ahichhatra, whose ruins are found near Ramnagar, and of the latter Kampilya, identical with the modem Kampila on the old Ganges between Badaun and Farrukhabad.

PANCHATANTRA: A famous collection of tales and fables in five (pancha) books (tantra). It was compiled by a Brahmin named Vishnusarman, about the end of the fifth century A.D., for the edification of the sons of a king, and was the original of the better-known Hitopadesa. This work has reappeared in very many languages both of the East and West, and has been the source of many familiar and widely known stories.

It was translated into Pahlavi or old Persian by order of Naushirvan in the sixth century A.D. In the ninth century it appeared in Arabic as Kalila o Damna, then, or before, it was translated into Hebrew, Syriac, Turkish, and Greek; and from these, versions were made into all the languages of Europe, and it became familiar in England as Pilpay's Fables (Fables of Bidpai). In modern Persia it is the basis of the Anwari Suhaili and Iyar-i Danish. The latter has reappeared in Hindustani as the Khirad-afroz. The stories are popular throughout Hindustan, and have found their way into most of the languages and dialects. There are various editions of the text and several translations.

PANCHAVATI: A place in the great southern forest near the sources of the Godavari, where Rama passed a long period of his banishment. It has been proposed to identify it with the modern Nasik, because Lakshmana cut off Surpanakha's nose at Panchavati.

PANDAVAS: The descendants of Pandu.

PANDU: 'The pale.' Brother of Dhritarashtra, king of Hastinapura and father of the Pandavas or Pandu princes.

PANDYA: Pandya, Chola, and Chera were three kingdoms in the south of the country for some centuries before and after the Christian era. Pandya was well known to the Romans as the kingdom of King Pandian, who is said to have sent ambassadors on two different occasions to Augustus Caresar. Its capital was Madura, the Southern Mathura. Pandya seems to have fallen under the ascendancy of the Chola kings in the seventh or eighth century.

PANINI: The celebrated grammarian, author of the work called Paniniyam. This is the standard authority on Sanskrit grammar, and it is held in such respect and reverence that it is considered to have been written by inspiration. So in old times Panini was placed among the Rishis, and in more modern days he is represented to have received a large portion of his work by direct inspiration from the god Siva. It is also said that he was so dull a child that he was expelled from school, but the favour of Siva placed him foremost in knowledge. He was not the first grammarian, for he refers to the works of several who preceded him.

The grammars which have been written since his time are numberless, but although some of them are of great excellence and much in use, Panini still reigns supreme, and his rules are incontestable. "His work," says Professor Williams, "is perhaps the most original of all productions of the Hindu mind." The work is written in the form of Sutras or aphorisms, of which it contains 3996, arranged in eight (ashta) chapters (adhyaya), from which the work is sometimes called Ashtadhyayi. These aphorisms are exceedingly terse and complicated. Special training and study are required to reach their meaning. Colebrooke remarks that "the endless pursuit of exceptions and limitations so disjoins the general precepts, that the reader cannot keep in view their intended connection and mutual relations. He wanders in an intricate maze, and the key of the labyrinth is continually slipping from his hand."

But it has been well observed that there is a great difference between the European and Hindu ideas of a grammar. In Europe, grammar has hitherto been looked upon as only a means to an end, the medium through which a knowledge of language and literature is acquired. With the Pandit, grammar was a science; it was studied for its own sake, and investigated with the most minute criticism; hence, as Goldstucker says, "Panini's work is indeed a kind of natural history of the Sanskrit lauguage." Panini was a native of Salatura, in the country of Gandhara, west of the Indus, and so is known as Salottariya. He is described as a descendant of Panin and grandson of Devala. His mother's name was Daksha, who probably belonged to the race of Daksha, and he bears the metronymic Daksheya. He is also called Ahika. The time when he lived is uncertain, but it is supposed to have been about four centuries B.C. Goldstucker carries him back to the sixth century, but Weber is inclined 10 place him considerably later. Panini's grammar has been. printed by Bohtlingk, and also in India.

PANIS: 'Niggards.' In the Rigveda, "the senseless, false, evil-speaking, unbelieving, unpraising, unworshipping Panis were Dasyus or envious demons who used to steal cows and hide them in caverns." They are said to have stolen the cows recovered by Sarama.

PARAMATMAN: The supreme soul of the universe.

PARASARA: A Vedic Rishi to whom some hymns of the Rigveda are attributed. He was a disciple of Kapila, and he received the Vishnu Purana from Pulastya and taught it to Maitreya. He was also a writer on Dharmasastra, and texts of his are often cited in books on law. Speculations as to his era differ widely, from 575 B.C. to 1391 B.C., and cannot be trusted. By an amour with Satyavati he was father of Krishna Dwaipayana, the Vyasa or arranger of the Vedas. According to the Nirukta, he was son of Vasishtha, but the Mahabharata and the Vishnu Purana make him the son of Saktri and grandson of Vasishtha.

The legend of his birth, as given in the Mahabharata, is that King Kalmashapada met with Saktri in a narrow path, and desired him to get out of the way. The sage refused, and the Raja struck him with his whip. Thereupon the sage cursed the Raja so that he became a man-eating Rakshasa. In this state he ate up Saktri, whose wife, Adrisyanti, afterwards gave birth to Parasara. When this child grew up and heard the particulars of his father's death, he instituted a sacrifice for the destruction of all the Rakshasas, but was dissuaded from its completion by Vasishtha and other sages. As he desisted, he scattered the remaining sacrificial fire upon the northern face of the Himalaya, where it still blazes forth at the phases of the moon, consuming Rakshasas, forests, and mountains.

PARASURAMA: 'Rama with the axe.' The first Rama and the sixth Avatara of Vishnu. He was a Brahmin, the fifth son of Jamadagni and Renuka. By his father's side he descended from Bhrigu, and was, par excellence, the Bhargava; by his mother's side he belonged to the royal race of the Kusikas. He became manifest in the world at the beginning of the Treta Vuga, for the purpose of repressing the tyranny of the Kshatriya or regal caste. His story is told in the Mahabharata and in the Puranas. He also appears in the Ramayana, but chiefly as an opponent of Ramachandra. Aceording to the Mahabharata, he instructed Arjuna in the use of arms, and had a combat with Bhishma, in which both suffered equally. He is also represented as being present at the great war council of the Kaurava princes. This Parasu-rama, the sixth Avatara of Vishnu, appeared in the world before Rama or Ramachandra, the seventh Avataira, but they were both living at the same time, and the elder incarnation showed some jealousy of the younger.

The Mahabharata represents Parasurama as being struck senseless by Ramachandra, and the Ramayana relates how Parasurama, who was a follower of Siva, felt aggrieved by Rama's breaking the bow of Siva, and challenged him to a trial of strength. This ended in his defeat, and in some way led to his being "excluded from a seat in the celestial world." In early life Parasurama was under the protection of Siva, who instructed him in the use of arms, and gave him the parasu, or axe, from which he is named. The first act recorded of him by the Mahabharata is that, by command of his father, he cut off the head of his mother, Renuka. She had incensed her husband by entertaining impure thoughts, and he called upon each of his sons in succession to kill her. Parasurama alone obeyed, and his readiness so pleased his father that he told him to ask a boon. He begged that his mother might be restored pure to life, and, for himself, that he might be invincible in single combat and enjoy length of days.

Parasurama's hostility to the Kshatryas evidently indicates a severe struggle for the supremacy between them and the Brahmins. He is said to have cleared the earth of the Kshatriyas twenty-one times, and to have given the earth to the Brahmins. The origin of his hostility to the Kshatriyas is thus related:—Kartavirya, a Kshatriya, and king of the Haihayas, had a thousand arms. This king paid a visit to the hermitage of Jamadagni in the absence of that sage, and was hospitably entertained by his wife, but when he departed he carried off a sacrificial calf belonging to their host. This act so enraged Parasurama that he pursued Kartavirya, cut off his thousand arms and killed him. In retaliation the sons of Karta-virya killed Jamadagni, and for that murder Parasurama vowed vengeance against them and the whole Kshatriya race. "Thrice seven times did he clear the earth of the Kshatriya caste, and he filled with their blood the five large lakes of Samanta-panchaka." He then gave the earth to Kasyapa, and retired to the Mahendra mountains, where he was visited by Arjuna.

Tradition ascribes the origin of the country of Malabar to Parasurama. According to one account, he received it as a gift from Varuna, and according to another, he drove back the ocean and cut fissures in the Ghats with blows of his axe. He is said to have brought Brahmins into this country from the north, and to have bestowed the land upon them in expiation of the slaughter of the Kshatriyas. He bears the appellations Khandaparasu, 'who strikes with the axe,' and Nyaksha, 'inferior.'

PARIKSHIT: Son of Abhimanyu by his wife Uttara, grandson of Arjuna, and father of Janamejaya. He was killed by Aswatthama in the womb of his mother and was born dead, but he was brought to life by Krishna, who blessed him and cursed Aswatthama. When Yudhishthira retired from the world, Parikshit succeeded him on the throne of Hastinapura. He died from the bite of a serpent, and the Bhagavata Purana is represented as having been rehearsed to him in the interval between the bite and his death.

PARJANYA: 1. A Vedic deity, the rain-god or rain personified. Three hymns in the Rigveda are addressed to this deity, and one of them is very poetical and picturesque in describing rain and its effects. The name is sometimes combined with the word vata (wind), Parjanya-vata, referring probably to the combined powers and effects of rain and wind. In later times he is regarded as the guardian deity of clouds and rain, and the name is applied to Indra. 2. One of the Adityas.

PARTHA: A son of Pritha or Kunti. A title applicable to the three elder Pandavas, but especially used for Arjuna.

PARVATI: 'The mountaineer.' A name of the wife of Siva.

PATALA: The infernal regions, inhabited by Nagas (serpents), Daityas, Danavas, Yakshas, and others. They are seven in number, and their names, according to the Vishnu Purana, are Atala, Vitala, Nitala, Gabhastimat, Mahatala, Sutala, and Patala, but these names vary in different authorities. The Padma Purana gives the names of the seven regions and their respective rulers as follow:—(1.) Atala, subject to Mahamaya; (2.) Vitalas, ruled by a form of Siva called Hatakeswara; (3.) Sutala, ruled by Bali; (4.) Talatala, ruled by Maya; (5.) Mahatala, where reside the great serpents; (6.) Rasatala, where the Daityas and Danavas dwell; (7.) Patala, the lowermost, in which Vasuki reigns over the chief Nagas or snake-gods. In the Siva Puraua there are eight: Patala, Tala, Atala, Vitala, Tala, Vidhi-patala, Sarkara-bhumi, and Vijaya. The sage Narada paid a visit to these regions, and on his return to the skies gave a glowing account of them, declaring them to be far more delightful than Indra's heaven, and abounding with every kind of luxury and sensual gratification.

PATALIPUTRA: The Palibothra of the Greek writers, and described by them as being situated at the confluence of the Erranaboas (the Sone river) with the Ganges. It was the capital of the Nandas, and of the Maurya dynasty, founded by Chandragupta, which succeeded them as rulers of Magadha. The city has been identified with the modern Patna; for although the Sone does not now fall into the Ganges there, the modern town is smaller in extent than the ancient one, and there is good reason for believing that the rivers have changed their courses.

PATANJALI: The founder of the Yoga philosophy. The author of the Mahabhashya, a celebrated commentary on the

Grammar of Panini, and a defence of that work agaiust tre criticisms of Katyayana. He is supposed to have written about 200 B.C. Ram Krishna Gopal Bhandarkar, a late inquirer, says, "He probably wrote the third chapter of his Bhashya between 144 and 142 B.C." Weber, however, makes his date to be 25 A.D. He is also called Gonardiya and Gonikaputra. A legend accounting for his name represents that he felt as a small snake from heaven into the palm of Panini (*pata*, fallen; *anjali*, palm).

PATHA: 'Reading.' There are three forms, called Pathas, in which the Vedic text is read and written:—(1.) Sanhita-patha, the ordinary form, in which the words coalesce according to the rules of Sandhi; (2.) Pada-patha, in which each word stands separate and independent; (3.) Krama-patha, in which each word is given twice, first joined with the word preceding and then with the word following.

PIPPALADA: A school of the Atharvsveda, founded by a sage of that name.

PISACHAS (mas.), PISACHI (fem.): Fiends, evil spirits, placed by the Vedas as lower than Rakshasas. The vilest and most malignant order of malevolent beings. Accounts differ as to their origin. The Brahmana and the Mahabharata say that they were created by Brahma, together with the Asuras and Rakshasas, from the stray drops of water which fell apart from the drops out of which gods, men, gandharvas, etc., had been produced. According to Manu they sprang from the Prajapatis. In the Puranas they are represented as the offspring of Kasyapa by his wife Krodhavasa, or Pisacha, or Kapisa.

PITHASTHANA: 'Seat,' or lit. 'place of a seat.' "Fifty-one places where, according to the Tantras, the limbs of Sati fell when scattered by her husband Siva, as he bore her dead body about and tore it to pieces after she had put an end to her existence at Daksha's sacrifice. This part of the legend seems to be an addition to the original fable, made by the Tantras, as it is not in the Puranas. It bears some analogy to the Egyptian fable of Isis and Osiris. At the Pithasthanas, however, of Jwalamukhi, Vindhyavasini, Kalighat, and others, temples are erected to the differentforms of Devi or Sati, not to the phallic emblem of Mahadeva, which, if present, is there as an accessory, not as a principal; and the chief object of worship is a figure of the goddess—a circumstance in which there is an essential difference between the temples of Durga and the shrines of Osiris."—Wilson.

PITRIS: Patres; the fathers; the Manes. This name is applied to three different classes of beings:—1. The Manes of departed forefathers, to whom pindas (balls of rice and flour) and water are offered at stated periods. 2. The ten Prajapatis or mythical progenitors of the human race. 3. "According to a legend in the Harivansa and in the Vayu Purana, the first Pitris were the sons of the gods. The gods having offended Brahma by neglecting to worship him, were cursed by him to become fools; but, upon their repentance, he directed them to apply to their sons for instruction. Being taught accordingly the rites of expiation and penance by their sons, they addressed them as fathers; whence the sons of the gods were the Pitris." The account given of the Pitris is much the same in all the Puranas. "They agree in distinguishing them into seven classes, three of which are without form, or composed of intellectual, not elementary substance, and assuming what forms they please; and four are corporeal. When the Puranas come to the enumeration of the particular classes, they somewhat differ, and the accounts in all the works are singularly imperfect."

The incorporeal Pitris, according to one enumeration, are the Vairajas, Agnishwattas, and Barhishads. The first of these seem also to be called Subhaswaras, Somasads, and Saumyas. The corporeal are the Sukalas or Sukalins, Angirasas,

Suswadhas, and Somapas. The Sukalas are also called Manasas; the Somapas are also called Ushmapas; the Angirasas seem also to be called Havishmats, Havirbhajas, and Upahutas; and the Suswadhas are apparently the same as the Ajyapas and Kaavyas or Kavyas. The Vairajas are the Manes of great ascetics and anchorites, the Agnish Wattas are the Pitris of the gods, the Barhishads of demons, the Somapas of Brahmins, the Havishmats of Kshatriyas, the Ajyapas of Vaisyas, and the Sukalins of the Sudras; but one authority, the Harivansa, makes the Somapas belong to the Sudras, and the Sukalins to the Brahmins, and there appears to be good reason for this.

Other names are given by Dr. F. Hall from various authorities: Rasmipas, Phenapas, Sudhavats, Garhapatyas, Ekasringas, Chaturvedas, and Kalas. Besides these there are the Vyamas, 'fumes,' the Pitris of the barbarians. The Rigveda and Manu make two independent classes, the Agni-dagdhas and the An-agni-dagdhas, those who when alive kept up or did not keep up the household flame, and presented or did not present oblations with fire. The Vishnu Purana makes the Barhishads identical with the former, and the Agnishwattas with the latter. Yama, god of the dead, is king of the Pitris, and Swadha, 'oblation,' is sometimes said to be their mother, at others their wife.

PRABODHA-CHANDRODAYA: 'The rise of the moon of knowledge.' A philosophical drama by Krishna Misra, who is supposed to have lived about the twelfth century. It has been translated into English by Dr. Taylor, and into German by Rosenkranz and by Hirzel.

PRACHETAS: 1. One of the Prajapatis. 2. An ancient sage and lawgiver. 3. The ten Prachetasas were sons of Prachinabarhis and great-grandsons of Prithu, and, according to the Vishnu Purana, they passed ten thousand years in the great ocean, deep in meditation upon Vishnu, and obtained from him the boon of becoming the progenitors of mankind. They took to wife Marisha, daughter of Kandu, and Daksha was their son.

PRADYUMNA: A son of Krishna by Rukmini. When a child only six days old, he was stolen by the demon Sambara and thrown into the ocean. There he was swallowed by a fish, which was afterwards caught and carried to the house of Sambara. When the fish was opened, a beautiful child was discovered, and Mayadevi or Mayavati, the mistress of Sambara's household, took him under her care. The sage Narada informed her who the child was, and she reared him carefully. When he grew up she fell in love with him, and informed him who he was and how he had been carried off by Sambara. He defied the demon to battle, and after a long conflict slew him. Then he flew through the air with Mayavati, and alighted in the inner apartments of his father's palace. Krishna presented him to his mother Rukmini "with the virtuous Mayavati his wife," declaring her really to be the goddess Rati. Pradyumna also married Kakudmati, the daughter of Rukmin, and had by her a son named Aniruddha. Pradyumna was killed at Dwaraka in the presence of his father during a drunken brawl.

Though Pradyumna passed as the son of Krishna, he was, according to the legend, a revival or resuscitation of Kama, the god of love, who was reduced to ashes by the fiery glance of Siva, and so the name Pradyumna is used for Kama. The Vishnu Purana puts the following words into the mouth of Narada when he presented Pradyumna to Rukmini:—" When Manmatha (the deity of love) had perished, the goddess of beauty (Rati), desirous to secure his revival, assumed a delusive form, and by her charms fascinated the demon Sambara, and exhibited herself to him in various illusory enjoyments. Thus thy son is the descended Kama; and this is the goddess Rati, his wife. There is no occasion for any uncertainty; this is thy daughter-in-law." In the Harivansa he has a wife named Prabhavati, daughter of King Vajranabha. When he went to see her for the first time, he changed himsclf into a been and lived in a garland of flowers which had been prepared for her. According to the Mahabharata, he was Sanat-kumara, tho son of Brahma.

PRAGJYOTISHA: A city situated in the east, in Kamarupa on the borders of Assam.

PRAHLADA: A Daitya, son of Hiranyakasipu and father of Bali. Hiranyakasipu, in his wars with the gods, had wrested the sovereignty of heaven from Indra and dwelt there in luxury. His son Prahlada, while yet a boy, became an ardent devotee of Vishnu, which so enraged his father that he ordered the boy to be killed; but not the weapons of the Daityas, the fangs of the serpents, the tusks of the celestial elephants, nor the flames of fire took any effect, and his father was constrained to send him back to his preceptor, where he continued so earnest in performing and promoting the worship of Vishnu that he eventually obtained final exemption from existence. According to some accounts, it was to avenge Prahlada, as well as to vindicate his own insulted majesty, that Vishnu became incarnate as the Narasinha, 'man-lion,' and slew Hiranyakasipu.

After the death of his father, Prahlada became king of the Daityas and dwelt in Patala; but, according to the Padma Purana, he was raised to the rank of Indra for life, and finally united with Vishnu. The Padma Purana carries the story farther back to a previous birth. In this previous existence Prahlada was a Brahmin named Somasarman, fifth son of Sivasarman. His four brothers died and obtained union with Vishnu, and he desired to follow them. To accomplish this he engaged in profound meditation, but he allowed himself to be disturbed by an alarm of the Daityas, and so was born again as one of them. He took the part of his race in the war between them and the gods, and was killed by the discus of Vishnu, after that he was again born as son of Hiranyakasipu.

PRAJAPATI: 'Lord of creatures,' a progenitor, creator. In the Veda the term is applied to Indra, Savitri, Soma, Hiranyagarbha, and other deities. In Manu the term is applied to Brahma as the active creator and supporter of the universe; so Brahma is the Prajapati. It is also given to Manu Swayambhuva himself, as the son of Brahma and as the secondary creator of the ten Rishis, or "mind-born sons" of Brahma, from whom mankind has descended. It is to these ten sages, as fathers of the human race, that the name Prajapati most commonly is given. They are Marichi, Atri, Angiras, Pulastya Pulaha, Kratu, Vasishtha, Prachetas or Daksha, Bhrigu, and Narada. According to some authorities, the Prajapatis are only seven in number, being identical with the seven great Rishis. The number and names of the Prajapatis vary in different authorities; the Mahabharata makes twenty-one.

PRAKRITA: The Prakrits are provincial dialects of the Sanskrit, exhibiting more or less deterioration from the original language; and they occupy an intermediate position between that language and the modern vernaculars of India, very similar to that of the Romance languages between the Latin and the Modern languages of Europe. They resemble the European languages also in another respect: they have in them a small proportion of words which have not been affiliated on the original classical language, and are apparently remnants of a different tongue and an older race. The Prakrits are chielly known from the dramas in which kings and Brahmins speak Sanskrit, while characters of inferior position speak in different Prakrits. Sometimes these Prakrit passages are so very debased that it hardly seems possible for them to be specimens of really spoken vernaculars. Such passages may perhaps be comic exaggerations of provincial peculiarities. The Prakrits have received careful study, and the Prakrita-prakasa, a grammar by Vararuchi, translated by Professor Cowell, was probably written about the beginning of the Christian era.

PRANA: 'Breath of life.' In the Atharvaveda it is personified and a hymn is addressed to it.

PRATISAKHYAS: Treatises on the phonetic laws of the language of the Vedas, dealing with the euphonic combination of letters and the peculiarities of their pronunciation as they prevailed in the different Sakhas or Vedic schools. These treatises are very ancient, but they are considerably later than the hymns, for the idiom of the hymns must have become obscure and obsolete before these treatises were necessary. Four such treatises are known:—

Rigveda: One which is considered to belong to the Sakala-sakha of this Veda, and is ascribed to Saunaka. It has been edited and translated into German by Max Muller, and into French by M. Regnier.

Yajurveda: Taittiriya-pratisakhya, belonging to the Black Yajur, printed in the Bibliotheca Indica and also in the Journal of the American Oriental Society, with a translation by Professor Whitney.

Vajasaneyi-pratisakhya: Belonging to the White Yajur. It is attributed to Katyayana, and has been edited and translated by Weber.

Atharvaveda: The Saunakiya Chaturadhyayika, i.e., Saunaka's treatise in four chapters. Edited and translated into English by Whitney.

No Pratisakhya of the Samaveda has been discovered.

PRAYAGA: The modern Allahabad. The place where the Ganges, Jumna, and the fabled subterranean Saraswati unite, called also Triveni, 'the triple braid.' It has always been a celebrated place of pilgrimage.

PRISNI: In the Vedas and Puranas, the earth, the mother of the Maruts. The name is used in the Vedas also for a cow. There were several females of this name, and one of them is said to have been a new birth of Devaki.

PRITHI, PRITHU, PRITHI-VAINYA: Prithi or Prithi-vainya, i.e., Prithi, son of Vena, is mentioned in the Rigveda, and he is the declared Rishi or author of one of the hymns. The Atharvaveda says, "She (Viraj) ascended: she came to men. Men called her to them, saying, 'Come, Iravati.' Manu Vaivaswata was her calf, and the earth her vessel. Prithivainya milked her; he milked from her agriculture and grain. Men subsist on agriculture and grain." The Satapatha Brahmana refers to Prithi as "first of men who was installed as a king." These early allusions receive a consistent form in the Puranas, and we have the following legend:-Prithi was son of Vena, son of Anga. He was called the first king, and from him the earth received her name Prithivi.

The Vishnu Purana says that the Rishis "inaugurated Vena monarch of the earth," but he was wicked by nature and prohibited worship and sacrifice. Incensed at the decay of religion, pious sages beat Vena to death with blades of holy grass. In the absence of a king robbery and anarchy arose, and the Munis, after consultation, proceeded to rub the thigh of the dead king in order to produce a son. There came forth a man like a charred log, with flat face and extremely short." This man became a Nishada, and with him came out the sons of the departed king. The Brahmins then rubbed the right arm of the corpse, "and from it sprang the majestic Prithu, Vena's son, resplendent in body, glowing like the manifested Agni.

At his birth all creatures rejoiced, and through the birth of this virtuous son Vena, delivered from the hell called Put, ascended to heaven."

Prithu then became invested with universal dominion. His subjects, who had suffered from famine, besought him for the edible plants which the earth withheld. In anger he seized his bow to compel her to yield the usual supply. She assumed the form of a cow and fled before him. Unable to escape, she implored him to spare her, and promised to restore all the needed fruits if a calf were given to her, through which she might be able to secrete milk. "He therefore, having made Swayambhuva Manu the calf, milked the earth, and received the milk into his own hand for the benefit of mankind. Thence proceeded all kinds of corn and vegetables upon which people subsist now and perpetually. By granting life to the earth Prithu was as her father, and she thence derived the patronymic appellation Prithivi." This milking the earth has been made the subject of much allegory and symbolism. The Matsya Purana specifies a variety of milkers, gods, men, Nagas, Asuras, etc., in the following style:—"The Rishis milked the earth through Brihaspati; their calf was Soma, the Vedas were the vessel, and the milk was devotion." Other Puranas agree with only slight deviations. "These mystifications," says Wilson, "are all, probably, subsequent modifications of the original simple allegory which typified the earth as a cow, who yielded to every class of beings the milk they desired, or the object of their wishes."

PRITHU: A king of the Solar race, a descendant of Ikshwaku. There are many Prithus.

PULASTYA: One of the Prajapatis or mind-born sons of Brahma, and one of the great Rishis. He was the medium through which some of the Puranas were communicated to man. He received the Vishnu Purana from Brahma and communicated it to Parasara, who made it known to mankind. He was father of Visravas, the father of Kuvera and Ravana, and all the Rakshasas are supposed to have sprung from him.

PURANA: 'Old,' hence an ancient legend or tale of olden times. The Puranas succeed the Itihasas or epic poems, but at a considerable distance of time, and must be distinguished from them. The epics treat of the legendary actions of heroes as mortal men, the Puranas celebrate the powers and works of positive gods, and represent a later and more extravagant development of Hinduism, of which they are in fact the Scriptures. The definition of a Purana by Amara Sinha, an ancient Sanskrit "exicographer, is a work" which has five distinguishing topics:—(1.) The creation of the universe; (2.) Its destruction and renovation; (3.) The genealogy of gods and patriarchs; (4.) The reigns of the Manus, forming the periods called Manwantaras and (5.) The history of the Solar and Lunar races of kings." These are the Panchalakshanas or distinguishing marks, but no one of the Puranas answers exactly to the description; some show a partial conformity with it, others depart from it very widely.

The Vishnu Purana is the one which best accords with the title. Wilson says, "A very great portion of the contents of many is genuine and old. The sectarial interpolation or embellishment is always sufficiently palpable to be set aside without injury to the more authentic and primitive material; and the Puranas, although they belong especially to that stage of the Hindu religion in which faith in some one divinity was the prevailing principle, are also a valuable record of the form of Hindu belief which came next in order to that of the Vedas, which grafted hero-worship upon the simpler ritual of the latter, and which had been adopted, and was extensively, perhaps universally, established in India at the time of the Greek invasion." According to the same authority, Pantheism "is one of their invariable characteristics," and underlies their whole teaching, "although the particular divinity who is all things, from whom all things proceed, and to whom all things return, is diversified according to their individual sectarian bias."

The Puranas are all written in verse, and their invariable form is that of a dialogue between an exponent and an inquirer, interspersed with the dialogues and observations of other individuals. Thus Pulastya received the Vishnu Purana from Brahma; he made it known to Parasara, and Parasara narrated it to his disciple Maitreya. The Puranas are eighteen in number, and in addition to these there are eighteen Upa Puranas or subordinate works. The Puranas are classified in three categories, according to the prevalence in them of the qualities of purity, gloom, and passion. Those in which the quality of Satwa or purity prevail are—(1.) Vishnu, (2.) Naradiya, (3.) Bhagavata, (4.) Garuda, (5.) Padma, (6.) Varaha. These are Vaishnava Puranas, in which the god Vishnu holds the pre-eminence. The Puranas in which Tamas, the quality of gloom or ignorance, predominates are—(1.) Matsya, (2.) Kurma, (3.) Linga, (4.) Siva, (5.) Skanda, (6.) Agni. These are devoted to the god Siva. Those in which Rajas or passion prevails relate chiefly to the god Brahma. They are—(1.) Brahma, (2.) Brahmanda, (3.) Brahma-vaivarta, (4.) Markandeya, (5.) Bhavishya, (6.) Vamana. The works themselves do not fully justify this classification. None of them are devoted exclusively to one god, but Vishnu and his incarnations fill the largest space.

One called the Vayu Purana is in some of the Puranas substituted for the Agni, and in others for the Siva. This Vayu is apparently the oldest of them, and may date as far back as the sixth century, and it is considered that some of the others may be as late as the thirteenth or even the sixteenth century. One fact appears certain, they must all have received a supplementary revision, because each one of them enumerates the whole eighteen. The Markandeya is the least sectarian of the Puranas; and the Bhagavata, which deals at length with the incarnations of Vishnu, and particularly with his form Krishna, is the most popular. The most perfect and the best known is the Vishnu, which has been entirely translated into English by Professor Wilson, and a second edition, with many valuable notes, has been edited by Dr. F. E. Hall. The Puranas vary greatly in length. Some of them specify the number of couplets that each of the eighteen contains. According to the Bhagavata, the sum total of couplets in the whole eighteen is 400,000; the Skanda is the longest, with 81,000, the Brahma and the Vamana the shortest, with 10,000 couplets each.

The Upa Puranas are named—(1.) Sanatkumara, (2.) Narasinha nr Nrisinha, (3.) Naradiya or Vrihan (old) Naradiya, (4.) Siva, (5.) Durvasa,(6.) Kapila, (7.) Manava, (8.) Ausanasa, (9.) Varuna, (10.) Kalika, (11.) Samba, (12.) Nandi, (13.) Saura, (14.) Parasara, (15.) Aditya, (16.) Maheswara, (17.) Bhagavata, (18.) Vasishtha. These works are not common. Other modern works exist to which the term Purana has been applied.

PURU: The sixth king of the Lunar race, youngest son of Yayati and Sarmishtha. He and his brother Yadu were founders of two great branches of the Lunar race. The descendants of Puru were called Pauravas, and of this race came the Kauravas and Pandavas. Among the Yadavas or descendants of Yadu was Krishna.

PURUKUTSA: A son of Mandhatri, into whose person Vishnu entered for the purpose of destroying the subterranean Gandharvas, called Mauneyas. He reigned on the banks of the Narmada, and that river personified as one of the Nagas was his wife. By her he had a son, Trasadasyu. The Vishnu Purana is said to have been narrated to him by "Daksha and other venerable sages."

PURURAVAS: In the Vedas, a mythical personage connected with the sun and the dawn, and existing in the middle region of the universe. According to the Rigveda he was son of *nil*, and a beneficent pious prince; but the, Mahabharata says, "We have heard that Ila was both his mother and his father. The parentage usually assigned to him is that he was son of Budha by Ila, daughter of Manu, and grandson of the moon." Through his mother he received the city of Pratishthana. He is the hero of the story and of the drama of Vikrama and Urvasi, or the "Hero and the Nymph." Puraravas is the Vikrama or hero, and Urvasi is an Apsaras who came down from Swarga through having incurred the imprecation of Mitra and Varuna. On earth Puraravas and she became enamoured of each other, and she agreed to live with him upon certain conditions. "I have two rams," said the nymph, "which I love as children. They must be kept near my bed side, and never suffered to be carried away. You must also take care never to be seen by me undressed; and clarified butter alone must be my food."

The inhabitants of Swarga were anxious for the return of Urvasi, and knowing the comtract made with Puraravas, the Gandharvas came by night and stole her rams. Puraravas was undressed, and so at first he refrained from pursuing the robbers, but the cries of Urvasi impelled him ro seize his sword and rush after them. The Gandharvas then brought a vivid flash of lightning to the chamber which displayed the person of Puraravas. So the charm was broken and Urvasi disappeared. Puraravas wandered about demented in search of her, and at length found her at Kurukshetra bathing with four other nymphs of heaven. She declared herself pregnant, and told him to come there again at the end of a year, when she would deliver to him a son and remain with him for one night. Puraravas, thus comforted, returned to his capital.

At the end of the year he went to the trysting-place and received from Urvasi his eldest son, Ayus. The annual interviews were repeated until she had borne him five more sons. Some authorities increase the number to eight, and there is considerable variety in their names. She then told him that the Gandharvas had determined to grant him any boon he might desire. His desire was to pass his life with Urvasi. The Gandharvas then brought him a vessel with fire and said, "Take this fire, and, according to the precepts of the Vedas, divide it into three fires; then, fixing your mind upon the idea of living with Urvasi, offer oblations, and you shall assuredly obtain your wishes." He did not immediately obey this command, but eventually he fulfilled it in an emblematic way, and obtained a seat in the sphere of the Gandharvas. and was no more separated from his love." As a son of Ila, his metronymic is Aila. There is a hymn in the Rig-veda which contains an obscure conversation between Pururavas and Urvasi. The above story is first told in the Satapatha Brahmana, and afterwards reappears in the Puranas. The Bhagavata Purana says, "From Puraravas came the triple Veda in the beginning of the Treta."

The story is supposed to have a mythic origin. Max Muller considers it "one of the myths of the Vedas which expresses the correlation of the dawn and the sun. The love between the mortal and the immortal, and the identity of the morning dawn and the evening twilight, is the story of Urvasi and Puraravas." The word Urvasi, according to the same writer, "was originally an appellation, and meant dawn." Dr. Goldstucker's explanation differs, but seems more apposite. According to this, Pururavas is the sun and Urvasi is the morning mist; when

Pururavas is visible Urvasi vanishes, as the mist is absorbod when the sun shines forth. Urvasi in the story is an Apsaras, and the Apsa-rases are "personifications of the vapours which are attracted by the sun and form into mists or clouds."

PURUSHA-SUKTA: A hymn of the Rigveda in which the four castes are first mentioned. It is considered to be one of the latest in date.

PURVA-MIMANSA: A school of philosophy.

PUSHAN: A deity frequently mentioned in the Vedas, but he is not of a distinctly defined character. Many hymns are addressed to him. The word comes from the root "push," and the primary idea is that of "nourisher" or Providence. So the Taittiriya Brahmana says, "When Prajapati formed living creatures, Pushan nourished them." The account given in Bohtlingk and Roth's Dictionary, and adopted by Dr. Muir, is as follows:—"Pushan is a protector and multiplier of cattle and of human possessions in general. As a cowherd he carries an ox-goat, and he is drawn by goats. In the character of a Solar deity, he beholds the entire universe, and is a guide on roads and journeys and to the other world. He is called the lover of his sister Surya. He aids in the revolution of day and night, and shares with Soma the guardianship of living creatures. He is invoked along with the most various deities, but most frequently with Indra and Bhaga."

He is a patron of conjurors, especially of those who discover stolen goods, and he is connected with the marriage ceremonial, being besought to take the bride's hand and bless her. In the Nirukta, and in works of later date, Pushan is identified with the sun. He is also called the brother of Indra, and is enumerated among the twelve Adityas. Pushan is toothless, and feeds upon a kind of gruel, and the cooked oblations offered to him are of ground materials, hence he is called Karambhad. The cause of his being toothless is variously explained. According to the Taittiriya Sanhita, the deity Rudra, being excluded from a certain sacrifice, shot an arrow at the offering and pierced it. A portion of this sacrifice was presented to Pushan, and it broke his teeth. In the Mahabharata and in the Puranas the legend takes a more definite shape. "Rudra (Siva), of dreadful power, ran up to the gods present at Daksha's sacrifice, and in his rage knocked out the eyes of Bhaga with a blow, and, incensed, assaulted Pushan with his foot, and knocked out his teeth as he was eating the purodasa offering." In the Purunas it is not Siva himself, but his manifestation the Rudras, who disturbed the sacrifice of the gods and knocked Pushan's teeth down his throat. Pushan is called Aghrini, 'splendid;' Dasia, Dasma, and Dasmavarchas, 'of wonderful appearance or power,' and Kapardin.

PUSHPAKA: A self-moving aerial car of large dimensions, which contained within it a palace or city. Kuvera obtained it by gift from Brahma, but it was carried off by Ravana, his half-brother, and constantly used by him. After Ramachandra had slain Ravana, he made use of this capacious car to convey himself and Sita, with Lakshmana and all his allies, back to Ayodhya; after that he returned it to its owner, Kuvera. It is also called Ratna-varshaka, "that rains jewels."

PUTANA: A female demon, daughter of Bali. She attempted to kill the infant Krishna by suckling him, but was herself sucked to death by the child.

R

RADHA: 1. Wife of Adhiratha and foster-mother of Karna. 2. The favourite mistress and consort of Krishna while he lived as Gopala among the cowherds in Vrindavana. She was wife of Ayanaghosha, a cowherd. Considered by some to be an incarnation of Lakshmi, and worshipped accordingly. Some have discovered a mystical character in Radha, and consider her as the type of the human soul drawn to the ineffable god, Krishna, or as that pure divine love to which the fickle lover returns.

RAGHU: A king of the Solar race. According to the Raghuvansa, he was the son of Dilipa and great-grandfather of Rama, who from Raghu got the patronymic Raghava and the title Raghu-pati, chief of the race of Raghu. The authorities disagree as to the genealogy of Raghu, but all admit him to be an ancestor of Rama.

RAGHUVANSA: 'The race of Raghu.' The name of a celebrated poem in nineteen cantos by Kalidasa on the ancestry and life of Rama. It has been translated into Latin by Stenzler, and into English by Griffith. There are other translations and many editions of the text.

RAHU: Rahu and Ketu are in astronomy the ascending and descending nodes. Rahu is the cause of eclipses, and the term is used to designate the eclipse itself. He is also considered as one of the planets, as king of meteors, and as guardian of the south-west quarter. Mythologially Rahu is a Daitya who it supposed to seize the sun and moon and swallow them, thus obscuring their rays and causing eclipses. He was son of Viprachitti and Sinhika, and is called by his metronymic Sainhikeya. He had four arms, and his lower part ended in a tail. He was a great mischief-maker, and when the gods had produced the Amrita by churning the ocean, he assumed a disguise, and insinuating himself amongst them, drank some of it. The sun and moon detected him and informed Vishnu, who cut off his head and two of his arms, but, as he had secured immortality, his body was placed in the stellar sphere, the upper parts, represented by a dragon's head, being the ascending node, and the lower parts, represented by a dragon's tail, being Ketu the descending mode Rahu wreaks his vengeance on the sun and moon by occasionally swallowing them.

The Vishnu Purana says, "Eight black horses draw the dusky chariot of Rahu, and once harnessed are attached to it for ever. On the Parvans (nodes, or lunar and solar eclipses) Rahu directs his course from the sun to the moon, and back again from the moon to the sun. The eight horses of the chariot of Ketu, swift as the wind, are of the dusky red colour of lac, or of the smoke of burning straw." Rahu is called Abhra-pisacha, 'the demon of the sky;' Bharani-bhu, 'born' from the asterism Bharani;' Graha, 'the seizer;' Kabandha,' the headless.'

RAIBHYA: A sage who was the friend of Bharadwaja. He had two sons, Arvavasu and Paravasu. The latter, under the curse of Bharadwaja, killed his father, mistaking him for an antelope, as he was walking about at night covered with an antelope's skin. Arvavasu retired into the forest to obtain by devotion a remission of his brother's guilt. When he returned, Paravasu charged him with the crime, and he again retired to his devotions. These so pleased the gods that they drove away Paravasu and restored Raibhya to life.

RAJAGRIHA: The capital of Magadha. Its site is still traceable in the hills between Patna and Gaya.

RAJARSHI (**Raja-rishi**): A Rishi or saint of the regal caste; a Kshatriya who, through pure and holy life on earth has been raised as a saint or demigod to Indra's heaven, as Viswamitra, Puraravas, etc.

RAJASUYA: 'A royal sacrifice' A great sacrifice performed at the installation of a king, religious in its nature but political in its operation. because it implied that he who instituted the sacrifice was a supreme lord, a king over kings, and his tributary princes were required to be present at the rite.

RAKSHASAS: Goblins or evil spirits. They are not all equally bad, but have been classified as of three sorts—one as a set of beings like the Yakshas, another as a sort of Titans or enemies of the gods, and lastly, in the common acceptation of the term demons and friends who haunt cemeteries, disturb sacrifices, harass devout men, animate dead bodies, devour human beings, and vex and affict mankind in all sorts of ways. These last are the Rakshasas of whom Ravana was chief, and according to some authorities, they are descended, like Ravana himself, from the sage Pulastya. According to other authorities, they sprang from Brahma's foot. The Vishnu Purana also makes them descendants of Kasyapa and Khasa, a daughter of Daksha, through their son Rakshas; and the Ramayana states that when Brahma created the waters, he formed certain beings to guard them who were called Rakshasas (from the root *raksh*, to guard, but the derivation from this root may have suggested the explanation), and the Vishnu Purana gives a somewhat similar derivation. It is thought that the Rakshasas of the epic poems were the rude barbarian races of India who were subdued by the Aryans.

When Hanuman entered the city of Lanka to reconnoitre in the form of a cat, he saw that "the Rakshasas sleeping in the houses were of every shape and form. Some of them disgusted the eye, while some were beautiful to look upon. Some had long arms and frightful shapes; some were very fat and some were vcry lean: some were mere dwarfs and some were prodigiously tall. Some had only one eye and others only one ear. Some had monstrous bellies, hanging breasts, long projecting teeth, and crooked thighs; while others were exceedingly beautiful to behold and clothed in great splendour. Some had two legs, some three legs, and some four legs. Some had the heads of serpents, some the heads of donkeys, some the heads of horses, and some the heads of elephants."—(Ramayana.)

The Rakshasas have a great many epithets descriptive of their characters and actions. They are called Anusaras, Asaras, and Hanashas, 'killers or hurters;' Ishti-pachas, 'stealers of offerings;' Sandhya-balas, 'strong in twilight;' Kshapiitas, Naktan-charas, Ratri-charas, and Samani-shadas, 'night-walkers;' Nrijagdhas or Nrichakshas, 'cannibals;' Palalas, Paladas, Palan-kashas, Kravyads, 'carnivorous;' Asra-pas, Asrik-pas, Kaunapas, Kilala-pas, and Rakta-pas, 'blood-drinkers;' Dandasukas, 'biters;' Praghasas, 'gluttons;' Malina-mukhas, 'black-faced;' Karburas, etc. But many of these epithets are not reserved exclusively for Rakshasas.

RAKTA-VIJA: An Asura whose combat with the goddess Chamunda is celebrated in the Devi-Mahatmya. Each drop of his blood as it fell on the ground produced a new Asura, but Chamunda put an end to this by drinking his blood and devouring his flesh.

RAMA, RAMACHANDRA: Eldest son of Dasaratha, a king of the Solar race, reigning at Ayodhya. This Rama is the seventh incarnation of the god Vishnu, and made his appearance in the world at the end of the Treta or second age. His story is briefly told in the Vana Parva of the Mahabharata,but it is given in full length as the grand subject of the Ramayana. King Dasarathawas childless, and performed the aswamedha sacrifice with scrupulous care, in the hope of obtaining offspring. His devotion was accepted by the gods, and he received the promise of four sons. At this time the gods were in great terror and alarm at the deeds and menaces of Ravana, the Rakshasa king of Lanka, who had obtained extraordinary power, in virtue of severe penances and austere devotion to Brahma. In their terror the gods appealed to Vishnu for deliverance, and he resolved to become manifest in the world with Dasaratha as his human father. Dasaratha was performing a sacrificewhen Vishnu appeared to him as a glorious being from out of the sacrificial fire, and gave to him a pot of nectar for his wives to drink. Dasaratha gave half of the nectar to Kausalya, who brought forth Rama with a half of the divine essence, a quarter to Kaikeyi, whose son Bharata was endowed with a quarter of the deity, and the fourth part to Sumitra, who brought forth two sons, Lakshmana and Satrughna, each having an eighth part of the divine essence. The brothers were all attached to each other, but Lakshmana was more especially devoted to Rama and Satrughna to Bharata.

[The two sons of Sumitra and the pairing off of the brothers have not passed without notice. The version of the Ramayana given by Mr. Wheeler endeavours to account for these circumstances. It says that Duaratha divided the divine nectar between his senior wives, Kausalya and Kaikeyi, and that when the younger, Sumitra, asked for some, Dasaratha desired there to share their portions with her. Each gave her half, so Sumitra received two quarters and gave birth to two sons: "from the quarter which she received from Kausalya she gave birth to Lakshmana, who became the ever-faithful friend of Rama, and from the quarter she received from Kaikeyi she gave birth to Satrughna, who became the ever-faithful friend of Bharata." This account is silent as to the superior divinity of Rama, and according to it all four brothers must have been equals as manifestations of the deity.]

The four brothers grew up together at Ayodhya, but while they were yet striplings, the sage Viswamitra sought the aid of Rama to protect him from the Rakshasas. Dasaratha, though very unwilling, was constrained to consent to the sage's request. Rama and Lakshmana then went to the hermitage of Viswamitra, and there Rama killed the female demon Taraka, but it required a good deal of persuasion from the sage before he was induced to kill a female. Viwamitra supplied Rama with celestial arms, and exercised a considerable influence over his actions. Viswamitra afterwards took Rama and his brothers to Mithila to the court of Janaka, king of Videha. This king had a lovely daughter named Sita, whom he offered in marriage to anyone whg could bend the wonderful bow which had once belonged to Siva. Rama not only bent the bow but broke it, and thus won the hand of the princess, who became a most virtuous and devoted wife. Rama's three brothers also were married to a sister and two cousins of Sita.

This breaking of the bow of Siva brought about a very curious incident, which is probably an interpolation of a later date, introduced for a sectarian purpose. Parasurama, the sixth incarnation of Vishnu, the Brahmin exterminator of the Kshatriyas, was still living upon earth. He was a follower of Siva, and was offended at the breaking of that deity's bow. Notwithstanding that he and Rama were both incarnations of Vishnu, he challenged Rama to a trial of strength and was discomfited, but Rama spared his life because he was a Brahmin.

Preparations were made at Ayodhya for the inauguration of Rama as successor to the throne. Kaikeyi, the second wife of Dasaratha, and mother of Bharata, was her husband's favourite. She was kind to Rama in childhood and youth, but she had a spiteful humpbacked female slave named Manthara. This woman worked upon the maternal affection of her mistress until she aroused a strong feeling of jealousy against Rama. Kaikeyi had a quarrel and a long struggle with her husband, but he at length consented to install Bharata and to send Rama into exile for fourteen years. Rama departed with his wife Sita and his brother Lakshmana, and travelling southwards, he took up his abode at Chitrakuta, in the Dandaka forest, between the Yamuna and Godavari. Soon after the departure of Rama, his father Dasaratha died, and Bharata was called upon to ascend the throne. He declined, and set out for the forest with an army to bring Rama back. When the brothers met there was a long contention. Rama refused to return until the term of his father's sentence was completed, and Bharata declined to ascend the throne.

At length it was arranged that Bharata should return and act as his brother's vicegerent, As a sign of Rama's supremacy Bharata carried back with him a pair of Rama's shoes, and these were always brought out ceremoniously when business had to be transacted. Rama passed ten years of his banishment moving from one hermitage to another, and went at length to the hermitage of the sage Agastya, near the Vindhya mountains. This holy man recommended Rama to take up his abode at Panchavati, on the river Godavari, and the party accordingly proceeded thither. This district was infested with Rakshasas, and one of them named Surpanakha, a sister of Ravana, saw Rama and fell in love with him. He repelled her advances, and in her jealousy she attacked Sita. This so enraged Lakshmana that he cut off her ears and nose. She brought her brothers Khara and Dushana with an army of Rakshasas to avenge her wrongs, but they were all destroyed. Smarting under her mutilation she repaired to her brother Ravana in Lanka, and inspired him by her description with a fierce passion for it.

Ravana proceeded to Rama's residence in an aerial car, and his accomplice Maricha having lured Hanuman from home, Ravana assumed the form of a religious mendicant and lulled Sita's apprehensions until he found an opportunity to declare himself and carry her off by force to Lanka. Rama's despair and rage at the loss of his faithful wife were terrible. He and Lakshmana went in pursuit and tracked the ravisher. On their way they killed Kabandha, a headless monster, whose disembodied spirit counselled Rama to seck the aid of Sugriva, king of the monkeys. The two brothers accordingly went on their way to Sugriva, and after overcoming some obstacles and assisting Sugriva to recover Kishkindha, his capital, from his usurping brother Bali, they entered into a firm alliance with him. Through this connection Rama got the appellations of Kapiprabhu and Kapiratha. He received not only the support of all the forces of Sugriva find his allies, but the active aid of

Hanuman, son of the wind, minister and general of Sugriva. Hanuman's extraordinary powers of leaping find flying enabled him to all the work of reconnoitring. By superhuman efforts their armies were transported to Lanka by "Rama's bridge," and after many fiercely contested battles the city of Lanka was taken, Ravana was killed and Sita rescued.

The recovery of his wife filled Rama with joy, but he was jealous of her honour, received her coldly, and refused to take her back. She asserted her purity in touching and dignified language, and determined to prove her innocence by the ordeal of fire. She entered the flames in the presence of men and gods, and Agni, god of fire, led her forth and placed her in Rama's arms unhurt. Rama then returned, taking with him his chief allies to Ayodhya. Reunited with his three brothers, he was solemnly crowned and began a glorious reign, Lakshmana being associated with him in the government. The sixth section of the Ramayana here concludes; the remainder of the story is told in the Uttara-kanda, a subsequent addition.

The treatment which Sita received in captivity was better than might have been expected at the hands of a Rakshasa. She had asserted and proved her purity, and Rama believed her; but jealous thoughts would cross his sensitive mind, and when his subjects blamed him for taking back his wife, he resolved, although she was pregnant, to send her to spend the rest of her life at the hermitage of Valmiki. There she was delivered of her twin sons Kusa and Lava, who bore upon their persons the marks of their high paternity. When they were about fifteen years old they wandered accidentally to Ayodhya and were recognised by their father, who acknowledged them, and recalled Sita to attest her innocence. She returned, and in a public assembly declared her purity, and called upon the earth to verify her words. It did so. The ground opened and received "the daughter of the furrow," and Rama lost his beloved and only wife. Unable to endure life without her, he resolved to follow, and the gods favoured his determination. Time appeared to him in the form of an ascetic and told him that he must stay on earth or ascend to heaven and rule over the gods. Lakshmana with devoted fraternal affection endeavoured to save his brother from what he deemed the baleful visit of Time. He incurred a sentence of death for his interference, and was conveyed bodily to Indra's heaven. Rama with great state and ceremony wcnt to the river Sarayu, and walking into the water was hailed by Brahma's voice of welcome from heaven, and entered "into the glory of Vishnu."

The conclusion of the story as told in the version of the Ramayana used by Mr. Wheeler differs materially. It represents that Sita remained in exile until her sons were fifteen or sixteen years of age. Rama had resolved upon performing the Aswamedha sacrifice; the horse was turned loose, and Satrughna followed it with an army. Kusa and Lava took the horse and defeated and wounded Satrughna. Rama then sent Lakshmana to recover the horse, but he was defeated and left for dead. Next Bharata was sent with Hanuman, but they were also defeated. Rama then set out himself to repair his reverses. When the father and sons came into each other's presence, nature spoke out, and Rama acknowledged his sons. Sita also, after receiving an admonition from Valmiki, agreed to forgive her husband. They returned to Ayodhya. Rama performed the Aswamedha, and they passed the remainder of theit lives in peace and joy.

The incidents of the first six kandas of the Ramayana supply the plot of Bhavabhuti's drama Mahavira-charita. The Uttarakanda is the basis of his Uttara-ramacharita. This describes Rama's jealousy, the banishment of Sita, and the birth of her sons; but the subsequent action is more human and affecting than in the poem. Rama repents of his unjust treatment of his wife, and goes forth to seek her. The course of his wanderings is depicted with great poetic beauty, and his meeting with his sons and his reconciliation with Sita are described with exquisite pathos and tenderness. The drama closes when "All conspire to make their happiness complete."

The worship of Rama still holds its ground, particularly in Awadh and Bihar, and he has numerous worshippers. "It is noteworthy," says Professor Williams, "that the Rama legends have always retained their purity, and, unlike those of Brahma. Krishna, Siva, and Durga, have never been mixed up with indecencies and licentiousness. In fact, the worship of Rama has never degenerated to the same extent as that of some of these other deities." This is true; but it may be observed that Rama and his wife were pure; there was nothing in their characters suggestive of license; and if "the husband of one wife" and the devoted and affectionate wife had come to be associated with impure ideas, they must have lost all that gave them a title to veneration. The name of Rama, as 'Ram! Ram!' is a common form of salutation.

RAMAYANA: 'The House of Rama.' The oldest of the Sanskrit epic poems, written by the sage Valmiki. It is supposed to have been composed about five centuries B.C., and to have received its present form a century or two later. The MSS of the Ramayana vary greatly. There are two well-known distinct recensions, the Northern and the Bengal. The Northern is the older and the purer; the additions and alterations in that of Bengal are so numerous that it is not trustworthy, and has even been called "spurious." Later researches have shown that the variations in MSS. found in different parts of India are so diverse that the versions can hardly be classed in a certain number of different recensions. Unfortunately, the inferior edition is the one best known to Europeans. Carey and Marshman translated two books of it, and Signor Gorresio has given an Italian translation of the whole. Schlegel published a Latin translation of the first book of the Northern recension. The full texts of both these recensions have been printed, and Wheeler has given an epitome of the whole work after the Bengal recension. There is also a poetical version by Griffiths.

Besides the ancient Ramayana, there is another popular work of comparative modem times called the Adhyatma Ramayana. The authorship of it is ascribed to Vyasa, but it is generally considered to be a part of the Brahmanda Purana. It is a sort of spiritualised version of the poem, in which Rama is depicted as a saviour and deliverer, as a god rather than a man. It is divided into seven books, whieh bear the same names as those of the original poem, but it is not so long.

The Ramayana celebrates the life and exploits of Rama the loves of Rama and his wife Sita, the war of the latter by Ravana, the demon king of Lanka, the carried on by Rama and his monkey allies against Ravana, ending in the destruction of the demon and the rescue of Sita, the restoration of Rama to the throne of Ayodhya, his jelousy and banishment of Sita, her residence at the hermitage of Valmiki, the birth of her twin sons Kusa and Lava, the father's discovery and recognition of his children, the recall of Sita, the attestation of her innocence, her death, Rama's resolution to follow her, and his departure to heaven.

The Ramayana is divided into seven kandas or sections, and contains about 50,000 lines. The last of the seven sections is probahly of later date than the rest of the work.

1. Bala-kanda. The boyhood of Rama.

2. Ayodhya-kanda. The scenes at Ayodhya, and the banishment of Rama by his father, King Dasaratha.

3. Aranya-kanda. 'Forest section.' Rama's life in the forest, and the Kidnapping of Sita by Ravana.

4- Kishkindha-kanda. Rama's residence at Kishkindha, the capital of his monkey ally, King Sugriva.

5. Sundara-kanda. 'Beautiful section.' The marvellous passage of the straits by Rama and his allies and their arrival in Lanka.

6. Yuddha-kanda. 'War section.' The war with Ravana, his defeat and death, the recovery of Sita, the return to Ayodhya and the coronation of Rama. This is sometimes called the Lanka Kanda.

7. Uttara-kanda. ' Later section.' Rama's life in Ayodhya, his banishment of Sita, the hirth of his two sons, his recognition of them and of the innocence of his wife, their reunion, her death, and his departure to heaven.

The writer or the compilers of the Ramayana had a high estimate of its value, and it is still held in very great veneration. A verse in the introduction says, "He who reads and repeats this holy life-giving Ramayana is liberated from all his sins and exalted with all his posterity to the highest heaven;" and in the second chapter Brahma is made to say, "As long as the mountains and rivers shall continue on the surface of the earth, so long shall the story of the Ramayana be current in the world."

RANTIDEVA: A pious and benevolent king of the Lunar race, sixth in descent from Bharata. He is mentioned in the Mahabharata and Puranas as being enormously rich, very religious, and charitable and profuse in his sacrifices. The former authority says that he had 200,000 cooks, that he had 2000 head of cattle and as many other animals slaughtered daily for use in his kitchen, and that he fed innumerable beggars daily.

RATI: 'Love, desire; The Venus of the Hindus, the goddess of sexual pleasures, wife of Kama, the god of love, and daughter of Daksha. She is also called Reva, Kami, Priti, Kamapatni, 'wife of Kama;' Kama-kala, 'part of Kama;' Kamapriya, 'beloved of Kama; , Raga-lata, 'vine of love;' Mayavati, 'deceiver;' Kelikila, 'wanton;' Subhangi, 'fair-limbed.'

RAVANA: The demon king of Lanka, from which he

expelled his half-brother Kuvera. He was son of Visravas by his wife Nikasha, daughter of the Rakshasa Sumali. He was half-brother of Kuvera, and grandson of the Rishi Pulastya; and as Kuvera is king of the Yakshas, Ravana is king of the demons called Rakshasas. Pulastya is said to be the progenitor, not only of Ravana, but of the whole race of Rakshasas. By penance and devotion to Brahma, Ravana was made invulnerable against gods and demons, but he was doomed to die through a woman. He was also enabled to assume any form he pleased. All Rakshasas are malignant and terrible, but Ravana as their chief attained the utmost degree of wickedness, and was a very incarnation of evil.

He is described in the Ramayana as having "ten heads (hence his names Dasanana, Dasa-kantha, and Panktigriva), twenty arms, and copper-coloured eyes, and bright teeth like the young moon. His form was as a thick cloud or a mountain, or the god of death with open mouth. He had all the marks of royalty, but his body bore the impress of wounds inflicted by all the divine arms in his warfare with the gods. It was scarred by the thunderbolt of Indra, by the tusks of Indra's elephant Airavata, and by the discus of Vishnu. His strength was so great that he could agitate the seas and split the tops of mountains. He was a breaker of all laws and a ravisher of other men's wives. Tall as a mountain peak, he stopped with his arms the sun and moon in their course, and prevented their rising." The terror he inspires is such that where he is "the sun does not give out its heat, the winds do not blow, and the ocean becomes motionless."

His evil deeds cried aloud for vengeance, and the cry reached heaven. Vishnu declared that, as Ravana had been too proud to seek protection against men and beasts, he should fall under their attacks, so Vishnu became incarnate as Ramachandra for the express purpose of destroying Ravana, and vast numbers of monkeys and bears were created to aid in the enterprise. Rama's wars against the Rakshasas inflicted such losses upon them as greatly to incense Ravana. Burning with rage, and excited by a passion for Sita, the wife of Rama, he left his island abode, repaired to Rama's dwelling, assumed the appearance of a religious mendicant, and carried off Sita to Lanka.. Ravana urged Sita to become his wife, and threatened to kill and eat her if she refused. Sita persistently resisted,and was saved from death by the interposition of ono of Ravana's wives.

Rama called to his assistance his allies Sugriva and Hanuman, with their hosts of monkeys and bears. They built Rama's bridge, by which they passed over into Lanka, and after many battles and wholesale slaughter Ravana was brought to bay at the city of Lanka.. Rama and Ravana fought together on equal terms for a long while, victory sometimes inclining to one sometimes to the other. Rama with a sharp arrow cut off one of Ravana's heads, "but no sooner did the head fall on the ground than another sprang up in its place." Rama then took an arrow which had been made by Brahma, and discharged it at bis foe. It entered his breast, came out of his back, went to the ocean, and then returned clean to the quiver of Rama. "Ravana fell to the ground and expired, and the gods sounded celestial music in the heavens, and assembled in the sky and praised Rama as Vishnu, in that he had slain that Ravana who would otherwise have caused their destruction."

Ravana, though he was chief among Rakshasas, was a Brahmin on his father's side; he was well versed in Sanskrit, used the Vedic ritual, and his body was burnt with Brahminical rites. There is a story that Ravana made each of the gods perform some menial office in his household: thus Agni was his cook, Varuna supplied water, Kuvera furnished money, Vayu swept the house, etc. The Vishnu Purana relates that Ravana, "elevated with wine, came on his tour of triumph to the city of Mahishmati, but there he was taken prisoner by King Kartavirya, and confined like a beast in a corner of his capital." The same authority states that, in another birth, Ravana was Sisupala. Ravana's chief wife was

Mandodari, but he had many others, and they were burnt at his obsequies. His sons were Meghanada, also called Indrajit, Ravani, and Aksha; Trisikha or Trisiras, Devantaka, Narantaka and Atikaya.

RENUKA: Daughter of King Prasenajit or Renu, wife of Jamadagni, and mother of Parasurama. A sight of the connufial endearments of King Chitraratha and his wife inspired her with impure thoughts, and her husband, perceiving that she had "fallen from perfection," desired her sons to kill her. Rumanwat, Sushena, and Vasu, the three seniors, declined, and their father cursed them so that they became idiots. Parasurama, the fourth son, cut off her head, which act so gratified his father that Jamadagni promised him whatever blessings he desired. Among other things, Parasurama asked that his mother might be brought back to life in ignorance of her death and in perfect purity. He also desired that his brothers might be restored to their senses. All this Jamadagni bestowed. She was also called Konkana.

RIBHU: 'Clever, skilful.' An epithct uscd for Indra, Agni, and the Adityas. In the Puranic mythology, Ribhu is a "son of the supreme Brahma, who, from his innate disposition, was of a holy character and acquainted with true wisdom." His pupil was Nidagha, a son of Pulastya, and he took special interest in his instruction, returning to him after two intervals of a thousand years "to instruct him further in true wisdom." The Vishnu Purana, "originally composed by the Rishi Narayana, was communicated by Brahma to Ribhu." He was one of the four Kumaras.

RIBHUS: Three sons of Sudhanwa, a descendant of Angiras, severally named Ribhu, Vibhu, and Vaja. Through their assiduous performance of good works they obtained divinity, exercised superhuman powers, and became entitled to receive praise and adoration. They are supposed to dwell in the solar sphere, and there is an indistinct identification of them with the rays of the sun; but, whether typical or not, they prove the admission, at an early date, of the doctrine that men might become divinitics. They are celebrated in the Rigveda as skilful workmen, who fashioned Indra's chariot and horses, and made their parents young again. By command of the gods, and with a promise of exaltation to divine honours, they made a single new sacrificial cup into four. They are also spoken of as supporters of the sky.

RISHI: An inspired poet or sage. The inspired persons to whom the hymns of the Vedas were revealed, and under whose names they stand. "The seven Rishis" Saptarshi, or the Prajapatis, "the mind-born sons" of Brahma, are often referred to. In the Satapatha Brahmana their names are given as Gotama, Bharadwaja, Viswamitra, Jamadagni, Vasishtha, Kasyapa, and Atri. The Mahabharata gives them as Marichi, Atri, Angiras, Pulaha, Kratu, Pulastya, and Vasishtha. The Vayu Purana adds Bhrigu to this list, making eight, although it still calls them "seven." The Vishnu Purana, more consistently, adds Bhrigu and Daksha, and calls them the nine Brahmarshis. The names of Gautama, Kanwa, Valmiki, Vyasa, Manu, and Vibhandaka are also enumerated among the great Rishis by different authorities. Besides these great Rishis there are many other Rishis. The seven Rishis are representped in the sky by the seven stars of the Great Bear, and as such are called Riksha and Chitrasikhandina, 'having bright crests.'

RISHYASRINGA: 'The deer-horned.' A hermit, the son of Vibhandaka, descended from Kasyapa. According to the Ramayana and Mahabharata he was born of a doe and had a small horn on his forehead. He was brought up in the forest by his father, and sawno other human being till he was vergingupon manhood. There was great drought in the country of Anga, and the king, Lomapada, was advised by his Brahmins to send for the youth Rishyasringa, who should marry his daughter Santa, and be the means of obtaining rain. A number of fair damsels were sent to bring him. He accompanied them back to their city, the desired rain fell, and he married Santa. This Santa was the adopted daughter of Lomapada; her real father was Dasa-ratha, and it was Rishyasringa who performed that sacrifice for Dasaratha which brought about the birth of Rama.

RITU-SANHARA: 'The round of the seasons.' A poem, attributed to Kalidasa. This poem was published by Sir W. Jones, and was the first Sanskrit work ever printed. There are other editions. It has been translated into Latin by Bohlen.

ROHINI: 1. Daughter of Kasyapa and Surabhi, and mother of horned cattle, including Kamadhenu, the cow which grants desires. 2. Daughter of Daksha and fourth of the lunar asterisms, the favourite wife of the moon. 3. One of the wives of Vasudeva, the father of Krishna and mother of Balarama. She was burned with her husband's corpse at Dwaraka. 4- Krishna himself also had a wife so called, and the name is common.

RUDRA: 'A howler or roarer; terrible.' In the Vedas Rudra has many attributes and many names. He is the howling terrible god, the god of storms, the father of the Maruts, and is sometimes identified with the god of fire. On the one hand, he is a destructive deity who brings diseases upon men and cattle, and upon the other he, is a beneficent deity supposed to have a healing influence. These are the germs which afterwards developed into the god Siva. It is worthy of note that Rudra is first called Mahadeva in the White Yajurveda. As applied to the god Siva, the name of Rudra generally designates him in his destructive character. In the Brihadaranyaka Upanishad the Rudras are "ten vital breaths (prana) with the he, art (manas) as eleventh."

In the Vishnu Purana the god Rudra is said to have sprung from the forehead of Brahma, and at the command of that god to have separated his nature into male and female, then to have multiplied each of these into eleven persons, some of which were white and gentle, others black and furious. Elsewhere it is said that the eleven Rudrns were sons of Kasyapa and Surabhi, and in another chapter of the same Purana, it is represented that Brahma desired to create a son, and that Rudra came into existence as a youth. He wept and asked for a name. Brahma gave him the name of Rudra, but he wept seven times more, and so he obtained seven other names: Bhava, Sarva, Isana, Pasupati, Bhima, Ugra, and Mahadeva. Other Puranas agree in this nomenclature. These names are sometimes used for Rudra or Siva himself, and at others for the seven manifestations of him, sometimes called his sons. The names of the eleven Rudras vary considerably in different books.

RUKMINI: Daughter of Bhishmaka, king of Vidarbha. According to the Harivansa, she was sought in marriage by Krishna, with whom she fell in love. But her brother Rukmin was a friend of Kansa, whom Krishna had killed. He therefore opposed him and thwarted the match. Rukmini was then betrothed to Sisupala, king of Chedi, but on her wedding day, as she was going to the temple, "Krishna saw her, took her by the hand, and carried her away in his chariot." They were pursued by her intended husband and by her brother Rukmin, but Krishna defeated them both, and took her safe to Dwaraka, where he married her. She was his principal wife and bore him a son, Pradyumna. By him also she had nine other sons and one daughter. "These other sons were Charudeshna, Sudeshna, Charudeha, Sushena, Charugupta, Bhadracharu, Charuvinda, Sucharu, and the very mighty Charu; also one daughter, Charumati." At Krishna's death she and seven other of his wives immolated themselves on his funeral pile.

S

SAGARA: A king of Ayodhya, of the Solar race, and son of King Bahu, who was driven out of his dominions by the Haihayas. Bahu took refuge in the forest with his wives. Sagara's mother was then pregnant, and a rival wife, being jealous, gave her a drug to prevent her delivery. This poison confined the child in the womb for seven years, and in the interim Bahu died. The pregnant wife wished to ascend his pyre, but the sage Aurva forbade her, predicting that she would give birth to a valiant universal monarch. When the child was born, Aurva gave him the name of Sagara (sa, 'with,' and gara, 'poison'). The child grew up, and having heard his father's history, he vowed that he would exterminate the Haihayas and the other barbarians, and recover his ancestral kingdom. He obtained from Aurva the Agneyastra or fire weapon, and, armed with this, he put nearly the whole of the Haihayas to death and regained the throne. He would also "have destroyed the Sakas, Yavanas, Kambojas, Paradas, and Pahlavas," but they applied to Vasishtha, Sagara's family priest, and he induced Sagara to spare them, but "he made the Yavanas shave their heads entirely; the Sakas he compelled to shave (the upper) half of their heads; the Paradas wore their hair long; and the Pahlavas let their beards grow in obedience to his commands."

Sagara married two wives, Sumati, the daughter of Kasyapa, and Kesini, the daughter of Raja Vidarbha, but having no children, he besought the sage Aurva for this boon. Aurva promised that one wife should have one son; the other, sixty thousand. Kesini chose the one, and her son was Asamanjas, through whom the royal line was continued. Sumati had sixty thousand sons. Asamanjas was a wild immoral youth, and his father a bandoned him. The other sixty thousand sons followed the courses of their brother, and their impiety was such that the gods complained of them to the sage Kapila and the god Vishnu. Sagara engaged in the performance of an Aswamedha or sacrifice of a horse, but although the animal was guarded by his sixty thousand sons,it was carried off to Patala. Sagara directed his sons to recover it. They dug their way to the infernal regions, and there they found the horse grazing and the sage Kapila seated close by engaged in meditation. Conceiving him to be the thief, they menaced him with their weapons.

Disturbed from his devotions, "he looked upon them for an instant, and they were reduced to ashes by the sacred flame that darted from his person. Their remains were discovered by Ansumat, the son of Asamanjas, who prayed Kapila that the victims of his wrath might be raised through his favour to heaven. Kapila promised that the grandson of Ansumat should be the means of accomplishing this by bringing down the river of heaven. Ansumat then returned to Sagara, who completed his sacrifice, and he gave the name of Sagara the chasm which his sons had dug, and Sagara means 'ocean.' The son of Ansumat was Dilipa, and his son was Bhagiratha. The devotion of Bhagiratha brought down from heaven the holy Ganges, which flows from the toe of Vishnu, and its waters having flowed over the ashes of the sons of Sagara, cleansed them from all impurity.

Their Manes were thus made fit for the ceremonies and for admission into Swarga.

The Ganges received the name of Sagara in honour of Sagara, and Bhagirathi from the name of the devout king whose prayers brought her down to earth. The Harivansa adds another marvel to the story. Sagara's wife Sumati was delivered of a gourd containing sixty thousand seeds, which became embryos and grew. Sagara at first placed them in vessels of milk, but afterwards each one had a separate nurse, and at ten months they all ran about. The name of Sagara is frequently cited in deeds conveying grants of land in honour of his generosity in respect of such gifts.

SAHITYA-DARPANA: 'The mirror of composition.' A celebrated work on poetry and rhetoric by Viswanatha Kaviraja, written about the fifteenth century. It has been translated into English for the Bibliotheca Indica. There are several editions of the text.

SAKA: An era commencing 78 A.D., and called the era of Salivahana. Cunningham supposes its epoch to be connected with a defeat of the Sakas by Salivahana.

SAKAS: A northern people, usually associated with the Yavanas. Wilson says, "These people, the Sakai and Sacre of classical writers, the Indo-Scythians of Ptolemy, extended, about the commencement of our era, along the west of India, from the Hindu Koh to the mouths of the Indus." They were probably Turk or Tatar tribes, and were among those recorded as conquered by King Sagara, 'Who compelled them to shave the upper half of their heads. They seem to have been encountered and kept back by King Vikramaditya of Ujjayini, who was called Sakari, 'foe of the Sakas.'

SAKRA: A name of Indra.

SAKTA: A worshipper of the Saktis.

SAKTI: The wife or the female energy of a deity, but specially of Siva.

SAKTI, SAKTRI: A priest and eldest son of Vasishtha. King Kalmashapada struck him with a whip, and he curse the king to become possessed by a man-eating Rakshasa. He himself became the first victim of the monster he had evoked.

SAKUNI: Brother of Queen Gandhari, and so uncle of the Kaurava princes. He was a skilful gambler and a cheat, so he was selected to be the opponent of Yudhishthira in the match in which that prince was induced to stake and lose his all. He also was known by the patronymic Saubala, from Subala, his lather.

SAKUNTALA: A nymph who was the daughter of Viswamitra by the nymph Menaka. She was born and left in a forest, where she was nourished by birds until found by the sage Kanwa. She was brought up by this sage in his hermitage as his daughter, and is often called his daughter. The loves, marriage, separation, and reunion of Sakuntala and King Dushyanta are the subject of the celebrated drama Abhijnana Sakuntala. She was mother of Bharata, the head of a long race of kings, who has given his name to India (Bharatavarsha), and the wars of whose descendants are sung in the Mahabharata.

The story of the loves of Dushyanta and Sakuntala is, that while she was living in the hermitage of Kanwa she was seen in the forest by King Dushyanta, who fell in love with her. He induced her to contract with him a Gandharva marriage, that is, a simple declaration of mutual acceptance. On leaving her to return to his city, he gave her a ring as a pledge of his love. When the nymph went back to the hermitage, she was so engrossed with thoughts of her husband that she heeded not the approach of the sage Durvasa, who had come to visit Kanwa, so that choleric saint cursed her to be forgotten by her beloved. He afterwards relented, and promised that the curse should be removed as soon as Dushyanta should see the ring.

Sakuntala, finding herself with child, set off to her husband, but on her way she bathed in a sacred pool, and there lost the ring. On reaching the palace, the king did not recognise her and would not own her, so she was taken by her mother to the forest, where she gave birth to Bharata. Then it happened that a fisherman caught a large fish and in it found a ring which he carried to Dushyanta. The king recognised his own ring, and he soon afterwards accepted Sakuntala and her son Bharata. Kalidasa's drama of Sakuntala was the first translation made from Sanskrit into English. It excited great curiosity and gained much admiration when it appeared. There are several recensions of the text extant. The text has been often printed, and there are many translations into the languages of Europe. Professor Williams has published a beautifully illustrated translation.

SALAGRAMA: A stone held sacred and worshipped by the Vaishnavas, because its spirals are supposed to contain or to be typical of Vishnu. It is an ammonite found in the river

Gandak, and is valued more or less highly according to the number of its spirals and perforations.

SALIVAHANA: A celebrated king of the south of India, who was the enemy of Vikramaditya, and whose era, the Saka, dates from A.D. 78. His capital was Pratishthana on the Godavari. He was killed in battle at Karar.

SALYA: King of the Madras, and brother of Madri, second wife of Pandu. In the great war he left the side of the Pandavas and went over to the Kauravas. He acted as charioteer of Karna in the great battle. At the death of Karna he succeeded him as general, and commanded the army on the last day of the battle, when he was slain by Yudhishthira.

SAMA-VEDA: The third Veda.

SAMBA: A son of Krishna by Jambavati, but the Linga Purana names Rukmini as his mother. At the swayamvara of Draupadi he carried off that princess, but he was pursued by Duryodhana and his friends and made prisoner. Balarama undertook to obtain his release, and when that hero thrust his ploughshare under the ramparts of Hastinapura and threatened it with ruin, the Kauravas gave up their prisoner, and Balarama took him to Dwaraka, There he lived a dissolute life and scoffed at sacred things.

The devotions of the three great sages, Viswamitra, Durvasa, and Narada, excited the ridicule of Samba and his boon companions. They dressed Samba up to represent a woman with child and took him to the sages, inquiring whether he would give birth to a boy or a girl. The sages answered, "This is not a woman, but the son of Krishna, and he shall bring forth an iron club which shall destroy the whole race of Yadu, . . . and you and all your people shall perish by that club." Samba accordingly brought forth an iron club, which Ugrasena caused to be pounded and cast into the sea. These ashes produced rushes, and the rushes when gathered turned into clubs, or into reeds which were used as swords. One piece could not be crushed. This was subsequently found in the belly of a fish, and was used to tip an arrow, which arrow was used by the hunter Jaras, who with it unintentionally killed Krishna. Under the curse of Durvasa, Samba became a leper and retired to the Panjab, where by fasting, penance, and prayer he obtained the favour of Surya, and was cured of his leprosy. He built a temple to the sun on the banks of the Chandrabhaga (Chinab), and introduced the worship of that luminary.

SAMBARA: In the Vedas, a demon, also called a Dasyu, who fought against King Divodasa, but was defeated and had his many castles destroyed by Indra. He appears to be a mythical personification of drought, of a kindred character to Vritra, or identical with him. In the Puranas a Daitya who carried off Pradyumna and threw him into the sea, but was subsequently slain by him. He was also employed by Hiranya-kasipu to destroy Prahlada.

SAMBUKA: A Sudra, mentioned in the Raghuvansa, who performed religious austerities and penances improper for a man of his caste, and was consequently killed by Ramachandra.

SAMVAT, SAMVATSARA: 'Year.' The era of Vikramaditya, dating from 57 B.C.

SANAKA, SANANDANA, SANATANA, SANATKUMARA: The four Kumaras or mind-born sons of Brahma. Some specify seven. Sanatkumara (or Sanasujata) was the most prominent of them. They are also called by the patronymic Vaidhatra.

SANDHYA: 'Twilight.' It is personified as the daughter of Brahma and wife of Siva. In the Siva Purana it is related that Brahma having attempted to do violence to his daughter, she changed herself into a deer. Brahma then assumed the form of a stag and pursued her through the sky. Siva saw this, and shot an arrow which cut off the head of the stag. Brahma then reassumed his own form and paid homage to Siva. The arrow remains in the sky in the sixth lunar mansion, called Ardra, and the stag's head remains in the fifth mansion, Mrigasiras.

SANDILYA: A descendant of Sandila. A particular sage who was connected with the Chhandogya Upanishad; one who wrote a book of Sutras, one who wrote upon law, and one who was the author of the Bhagavata heresy; two or more of these may be one and the same person. The Sutras or aphorisms have been published in the Bibliotheca Indica.

SANDIPANI: A master-at-arms who gave instruction to Balarama and Krishna.

SANGITA-RATNAKARA: A work on singing, dancing, and pantomime, written by Sarnga Deva.

SANI: The planet Saturn. The regent of that planet, represented as a black man in black garments. Sani was a son of the sun and Chhaya, but another statement is that he was the offspring of Balarama and Revati. He is also known as Ara, Kona, and Kroda, and by the patronymic Saura. His influence is evil, hence he is called Kruradristi and Kruralochana, 'the evil-eyed one.' He is also Manda, 'the slow;' Pangu, 'the lame;' Sanaischara, 'slow-moving;' Saptarchi, 'seven-rayed;' and Asita, 'the dark.'

SANJAYA: 1. The charioteer of Dhritarashtra. He was minister also, and went as ambassador to the Pandavas before the great war broke out. He is represented as reciting to Dhritarashtra the Bhagavad-gita. His patronymic is Gavalgani, son of Gavalgana. 2. A king of Ujjayini and father of Vasavadatta.

SANJNA: 'Conscience.' According to the Puranas, she was daughter of Viswakarma and wife of the sun. She had three children by him, the Manu Vaivaswata, Yama, and Yami (goddess of the Yamuna river). "Unable to endure the fervours of her lord, Sanjna gave him Chhaya (shade) as his handmaid, and repaired to the forests to practise devout exercises." The sun beheld her engaged in austerities in the form of a mare, and he approached her as a horse. Hence sprang the two Aswins and Revanta. Surya then took Sanjna back to his own dwelling, but his effulgence was still so overpowering, that her father, Viswakarma, placed the sun upon his lathe, and cut away an eighth part of his brilliancy. She is also call Dyumayi, 'the brilliant,' and Mahavirya, 'the very powerful.'

SANKARA: 'Auspicious.' A name of Siva in his creative character or as chief of the Rudras.

SANKARACHARYA: (Sankara + acharya). The great religious reformer and teacher of the Vedanta philosophy, who lived in the eighth or ninth century. He was a native of Kerala or Malabar, and lived a very erratic life, disputing with heretics and popularising the Vedanta philosophy by his preaching and writings wherever he went. His travels extended as far as Kashmir, and he died at Kedaranath in the Himalayas at the early age of thirty-two. His learning and sanctity were held in such high estimation and reverence, that he was looked upon as an incarnation of Siva, and was believed to have the power of working miracles. The god Siva was the special object of his worship, and he was the founder of the great sect of Smarta Brahmins, who are very numerous and powerful in the south. He established several maths or monasteries for the teaching and preservation of his doctrines. Some of these still remain. The chief one is at Sringa-giri or Sringeri, on the edge of the Western Ghats in the Mysore, and it has the supreme control of the Smarta sect. The writings attributed to him are very numerous; chief among them are his Bhashyas or commentaries on the Sutras or aphorisms of Vyasa, a commentary on the Bhagavad-gita, some commentaries on the Upanishads, and the Ananda-lahari, a hymn in praise of Parvati, the consort of Siva.

SANKARA-VIJAYA: 'The triumph of Sankara.' A biography of Sankaracharya relating his controversies with heretical sects and his refutation of their doctrines and superstitions. There is more than one work bearing this name: one by Ananda Giri, which is published in the Bibliotheca Indica; another by Madhavacharya; the latter is distinguished as the Sankshepa Sankara-Vijaya. The work of Ananda Giri has been critically examined by Kashinath Trimbak Telang in the Indian Antiquary,

SANKHYA-DARSANA: Kapila's aphorisms on the Sankhya philosophy. They have been printed.

SANKHYA-KARIKA: A work on the Sankhya philosophy, written by Iswara Krishna; translated by Colebrooke and Wilson.

SANNYASI: A Brahmin in the fourth and last stage of his religious life. In the present day the term has a wider meaning, and is applied to various kinds of religious mendicants who wander about and subsist upon alms, most of them in a filthy condition and with very scanty clothing. They are generally devotees of Siva.

SANTANU: A king of the Lunar race, son of Pratipa, father of Bhishma, and in a way the grandfather of Dhritarashtra and Pandu. Regarding him it is said, "Every decrepit man whom he touches with his hands becomes young." He was called Satyavach, 'truth-speaker,' and was remarkable for his "devotion and charity, modesty, constancy, and resolution."

SAPTARSHI (Sapta-rishi): The seven great Rishis.

SAPTA-SINDHAVA: 'The seven rivers.' The term frequently occurs in the Vedas, and has been widely known and somewhat differently applied. It was apparently known to the Romans in the days of Augustus, for Virgil says—

"Ceu septem surgens sedatis amnibus altus
Per tacitum Ganges."—Eneid

They appear in Zend as the Hapta-heando, and the early Muhammadan travellers have translated the term. But their Saba' Sin, 'seven rivers,' according to Biruni, applies to the rivers which flow northwards from the mountains of the Hindu Koh, and "uniting near Turmuz, form the river of Balkh (the Oxus)." The hymn in which the names of the rivers have been given has the following description—"Each set of seven streams has followed a threefold course. The Sindhu surpasses the other rivers in impetuosity. . . . Receive favourably this my hymn, O Ganga, Yamuna, Saraswati, Sutudri, Parushni; hear, O Marud-vridha, with the Asikni and Vitasta, and thou, Arjikiya, with the Sushoma. Unite first in thy course with the Trishtama, the Susartu, the Rasa, and the Sweti; thou meetest with the Gomati, and the Krumu with the Kubha and the Mehatnu."

According to this, the "seven rivers" are—(1.) Ganga (Ganges); (2.) Yamuna (Jumna); (3.) Saraswati (Sarsuti); (4.) Sutudri (Sutlej); (5.) Parushni; (6.) Marud-vridha; (7.) Arjikiya (the Vipasa,Hyphasis, Vyas). Wilson says the Parushni is identified with the Iravati" (Hydraotes, Ravi), but in this hymn it is the Marud-vridha which would seem to be the Iravati, because it is said to unite with the Asikni (Akesines, Chandrabhaga, Chinab) and the Vitasta (Hydaspes or Jhelam). This would leave the Parushni unsettled. The other names, with the exception of the Gomati (Gumti), are not identified. Sushoma has been said to be the Sindhu, but in this hymn the Sindhu is clearly distinct. In the Mahabharata the seven rivers are named in one place: Vaswokasara, Nalini, Pavani, Ganga, Sita, Sindhu, and Jambunadi; and in another, Ganga, Yamuna, Plakshaga, Rathastha, Saryu, Gomati, and Gandaki (Gandak). In the Ramayana and the Puranas the seven rivers are the seven streams into which the Ganges divided after falling from the brow of Siva, the Nalini,

Hladini, and Pavani going east, the Chakshu, Sita, and Sindhu to the west, while the Ganges proper, the Bhagirathi, flowed to the south. The term is also used for the seven great oceans of the world, and for the country of the seven rivers.

SARAMA: 1. In the Rigveda the dog of Indra and mother of the two dogs called after their mother, Sarameyas, who each had four eyes, and were the watchdogs of Yama. Sarama is said to have pursued and recovered the cows stolen by the Panis, a myth which has been supposed to mean that Sarama is the same as Ushas, the dawn, and that the cows represent the rays of the sun carried away by night. 2. The wife of Vibhishana, who attended upon Sita, and showed her great kindness when she was in captivity with Ravana. 3. In the Bhagavata Purana, Sarama is one of the daughters of Daksha, and the mother of wild animals.

SARANYU: 'The fleet runner.' A daughter of Twashtri. She has been identified with the Greek Erinnys. The beginning of this myth is in a hymn of the Rigveda, which says—"1. Twashtri makes a wedding for his daughter. Hearing this, the whole world assembles. The mother of Yama, the wedded wife of the great Vivaswat (the sun), disappeared. 2. They concealed the immortal bride from mortals. Making another of like appearance, they gave her to Vivaswat. Saranyu bore the two Aswins, and when she had done so she deserted the two twins."

In the Nirukta the story is expanded as follows:—"Saranyu, the daughter of Twashtri, bore twins to Vivaswat, the son of Aditi. She then substituted for herself another female of similar appearance, and fled in the form of a mare. Vivaswat in like manner assumed the shape of a horse and followed her; from their intercourse sprang two Aswins, while Manu was the offspring of Savarna or the female of like appearance." The Brihad-devata has another version of the same story:—"Twashtri had twin children, a daughter Saranya and a son Trisiras. He gave Saranya in marriage to Vivaswat, to whom she bore Yama and Yami, who also were twins. Creating a female like herself without her husband's knowledge, and making the twins over in charge to her, Saranyu took the form of a mare and departed. Vivaswat, in ignorance, begot on the female who was left, Manu, a royal Rishi, who resembled his father in glory; but discovering that the real Saranyu, Twashtri's daughter, had gone away, Vivaswat followed her quickly, taking the shape of a horse of the same species as she. Recognising him in that form, she approached him with the desire of sexual connection, which he gratified. In their haste his seed fell on the ground, and she, being desirous of offspring, smelled it. From this act sprang the two Kumaras, Nasatya and Dasra, who were lauded as Aswins (sprung from a horse)."—Muir's Texts,

SARASWATI: 'Watery, elegant.' In the Vedas, Saraswati is primarily a river, but is celebrated in the hymns both as a river and a deity. The Saraswati river was one boundary of Brahmavarta, the home of the early Aryans, and was to them, in all likelihood, a sacred river, as the Ganges has long been to their descendants. As a river goddess, Saraswati is lauded for the fertilising and purifying powers of her waters, and as the bestower of fertility, fatness, and wealth. Her position as Vach, the goddess of speech, finds no mention in the Rigveda, but is recognised by the Brahmanas and the Mahabharata. Dr. Muir endeavours to account for her acquisition of this character. He says, "When once the river had acquired a divine character, it was quite natural that she should be regarded as the patroness of the ceremonies which were celebrated on the margin of her holy waters, and that her direction and blessing should be invoked as essential to their proper performance and success. The connection into which she was thus brought with sacred rites may have led to the further step of imagining her to have an influence on the composition of the hymns which formed so important a part of the proceedings, and of identifying her with Vach, the goddess of speech."

In later times Saraswati is the wife of Brahma, the goddess of speech and learning, inventress of the Sanskrit language and Devanagari letters, and patroness of the arts and sciences. "She is represented as of a white colour, without any superfluity of limbs, and not unfrequently of a graceful figure, wearing a slender crescent on her brow and sitting on a lotus."—Wilson. The same authority states that "the Vaishnavas of Bengal have a popular legend that she was the wife of Vishnu, as were also Lakshmi and Ganga. The ladies disagreed; Saraswati, like the other prototype of learned ladies, Minerva, being something of a termagant, and Vishnu, finding that one wife was much as he could manage, transferred Saraswati to Brahma and Ganga to Siva, and contented himself with Lakshmi alone. Other names of Saraswati are Bharati, Brahmi, Putkari, Sarada, Vagiswari. The river is now called Sarsuti. It falls from the Himalayas and is lost in the sands of the desert. In ancient times it flowed on to the sea. A passage in the Rigveda says of it, "She who goes on pure from the mountains as far as the sea."—Max Muller, According to the Mahabharata it was dried up by the curse of the sage Utathya.

SARMISHTHA: Daughter of Vrishaparvan the Danava, second wife of Yayati and mother of Puru.

SARVA-DARSANA SANGRAHA: A work by Madhavacharya which gives an account of the Darsanas or schools of philosophy, whether orthodox or heretical.

SARVARI: A woman of low caste, who was very devout and looked for the coming of Rama until she had grown old. In reward of her piety a sage raised her from her low caste, and when she had seen Rama, she burnt herself on a funeral pile. She ascended from the pile in a chariot to the heaven of Vishnu.

SASTRA: 'A rule book, treatise.' Any book of divine or recognised authority, but more specially the law-books.

SATADRU: 'Flowing in a hundred channels.' The name of the river Sutlej, the Zaradrus of Ptolemy, the Hesudrus of Pliny.

SATAPATHA-BRAHMANA: A celebrated Brahmana attached to the White Yajurveda, and ascribed to the Rishi Yajnawalkya. It is found in two Sakhas, the Madhyandina and the Kanwa. This is the most complete and systematic as well as the most important of all the Brahmanas. It has been edited by Weber.

SATA-RUPA: 'The hundred-formed.' The first woman. According to one account she was the daughter of Brahman, and from their intercourse the first Manu, named Swayambhuva, was born. Another account makes her the wife, not the mother, of Manu. The account given by Manu is that, Brahma divided himself into two parts, male and female, and from them sprang Manu. She is also called Savitri.

SATI: A daughter of Daksha and wife of Rudra, i.e., Siva. The Vishnu Purana states that she "abandoned her body in consequence of the anger of Daksha. She then became the daughter of Himavat and Mena; and the divine Bhava again married Uma, who was identical with Siva's former spouse." The authorities generally agree that she died or killed herself in consequence of the quarrel between her husband and father; and the Kasi Khanda, a modern work, represents that she entered the fire and became a Sati.

SATRUGHNA: 'Foe-destroyer.' Twin-brother of Lakshmana and half-brother of Rama, in whom an eighth part of the divinity of Vishnu was incarnate. His wife was Srutakirti, cousin of Sita. He fought on the side of Rama and killed the Rakshasa chief Lavana.

SATYABHAMA: Daughter of Satrajita and one of the four chief wives of Krishna. She had ten sons, Bhanu, Subhanu,

Swarbhanu, Prabhanu, Bhanumat, Chandrabhanu, Brihadbhanu, Atibhanu, Sribhanu, and Pratibhanu. Krishna took her with him to Indra's heaven, and she induced him to bring away the Parijata tree.

SATYAKI: A kinsman of Krishna's, who fought on the side of the Pandavas, and was Krishna's charioteer. He assassinated Kritavarma in a drinking bout at Dwaraka, and was himself cut down by the friends of his victim. He is also called Daruka and Yuyudhana, and Saineya from his father, Sini.

Satyavati: 1. Daughter of Uparichara, king of Chedi, by an apsaras named Adrika, who was condemned to live on earth in the form of a fish. She was mother of Vyasa by the Rishi Parasara, and she was also wife of King Santanu, mother of Vichitravirya and Chitrangada, and grandmother of the Kauravas and Pandavas, the rivals in the great war. The sage Parasara met her as she was crossing the river Yamuna when she was quite a girl, and the offspringof their intercourse was brought forth on an island (dwipa)in that river, and was hence called Dwaipayana. She was also called Gandhakali, Gandhavati, and Kalangani; and as her mother lived in the form of a fish, she is called Dasanandini, Daaeyi, Jhajhodari, and Matsyodari, 'fish-born' 2. A daughter of King Gadhi, wife of the Brahmin Richika, mother of Jamadagni and grandmother of Parasurama. She was of the Kusika race, and is said to have been transformed into the Kausiki river.

SATYAVRATA: 1. Name of the seventh Manu.

2. A king of the Solar race, descended from Ikshwaku. He was father of Harischandra, and is also named Vedhas and Trisanku. According to the Ramayana, he was a pious king, and was desirous of performing a sacrifice in virtue of which he might ascend bodily to heaven. Vasishtha, his priest, declined to perform it, declaring it impossible. He then applied to Vasishtha's sons, and they condemned him to become a Chandala for his presumption. In his distress and degradation he applied

to Viswamitra, who promised to raise him in that form to heaven. Viswamitra's intended sacrifice was strongly resisted by the sons of Vasishtha, but he reduced them to ashes, and condemned them to be born again as outcasts for seven hundred births.

The wrathful sage bore down all other opposition, and Trisanku ascended to heaven. Here his entry was opposed by Indra and the gods, but Viswamitra in a fury declared that he would create "another Indra, or the world should have no Indra at all." The gods were obliged to yield, and it was agreed that Trisanku, an immortal, should hang with his head downwards, and shine among some stars newly called into being by Viswamitra.

The Vishnu Purana gives a more simple version. While Satyavrata was a Chandala, and the famine was raging, he supported Viswamitra's family by hanging deer's flesh on a tree on the bank of the Ganges, so that they might obtain food without the degradation of receiving it from a Chandala; for this charity Viswamitra raised him to heaven.

The story is differently told in the Harivansa. Satyavrata or Trisanku,when a prince, attempted to carry off the wife of a citizen in consequence of which his father drove him from home, nor did Vasishtha, the family priest, endeavour to soften the father's decision. The period of his exile was a time of famine, and he greatly succoured the wife and family of Viswamitra, who were in deep distress while the sage was absent far away. He completed his twelve years' exile and penance, and being hungry one day, and having no flesh to eat, he killed Vasishtha's wondrous cow, the Kamadhenu, and ate thereof himself, and gave some to the sons of Viswamitra. In his rage Vasishtha gave him the name Trisanku, as being guilty of three great sins. Visvamitra was gratified by the assistance which Satyavrata bad rendered to his family, "he installed him in his father's kingdom, . . . and, in spite of the resistance of the gods and of Vasishtha, exalted the king alive to heaven."

SAUBHARI: A devout sage, who, when he was old and emaciated, was inspired with a desire of offspring. He went to King Mandhatri, and demanded one of his fifty daughters. Afraid to refuse, and yet unwilling to bestow a daughter upon such a suitor, the king temporised, and endeavoured to evade the request. It was at length settled that, if anyone of the daughters should accept him as a bridegroom, the king would consent to the marriage. Saubhari was conducted to the presence of the girls; but on his way he assumed a fair and handsome form, so that all the girls were captivated, and contended with each other as to who should become his wife. It ended by his marrying them all and taking them home. He caused Viswakarma to build for each a separate palace, furnished in the most luxurious manner, and surrounded with exquisite gardens, where they lived a most happy life, each one of them having her husband always present with her, and believing that he was devoted to her and her only. By his wives he had a hundred and fifty sons; but as he found his hopes and desires for them to daily increase and expand, he resolved to devote himself wholly and solely to penance and the worship of Vishnu. Accordingly, he abandoned his children and retired with his wives to the forest.

SAUNAKA: A sage, the son of Sunaka and grandson of Gritsamada. He was the author of the Brihad-devata, and Anukramani, and other works, and he was a teacher of the Atharvaveda. His pupil was Aswalayana. There was a family of the name, and the works attributed to Saunaka are probably the productions of more than one person.

SAVITRI: 1. The holy verse of the Veda, commonly called Gayatri. 2. A name of Satarupa, the daughter and wife of Brahma, who is sometimes regarded as a personification of the holy verse. 3. Daughter of King Aswapati, and lover of Satyavan, whom she insisted on marrying, although she was warned by a seer that he had only one year to live. When the fatal day arrived, Satyavan went out to cut wood, and she followed him. There he fell, dying, to the earth, and she, as she supported him, saw a figure, who told her that he was Yama, king of the dead, and that he had come for her husband's spirit. Yama carried off the spirit towards the shades, but Savitri followed him. Her devotion pleased Yama, and he offered her any boon except the life of her husband. She extorted three such boons from Yama, but still she followed him, and he was finally constrained to restore her husband to life.

SAVYA-SACHIN: 'Who pulls a bow with either hand.' A title of Arjuna.

SAYANA: Sayanacharya, the celebrated commentator on the Rigveda. "He was brother of Madhavacharya, the prime minister of Vira Bukka Raya, Raja of Vijayanagar, in the fourteenth century, a munificent patron of Hindu literature. Both the brothers are celebrated as scholars, and many important works are attributed to them; not only scholia on the Sanhitas and Brahmanas of the Vedas, but original works on grammar and law; the fact, no doubt, being that they availed themselves of those means which their situation and influence secured them, and employed the most learned Brahmins they could attract to Vijayanagar upon the works which bear their name, and to which they also contributed their own labour and learning; their works were, therefore, compiled under peculiar advantages, and are deservedly held in the highest estimation."—Wilson.

SESHA, SESHANAGA: King of the serpent race or Nagas, and of the infernal regions called Patala. A serpent with a thousand heads which is the couch and canopy of Vishnu whilst sleeping during the intervals of creation. Sometimes Sesha is represented as supporting the world, and sometimes as upholding the seven Patalas or hells. Whenever he yawns he causes earthquakes. At the end of each kalpa he vomits venomous fire which destroys all creation. When the gods churned the ocean they made use of Sesha as a great rope, which they twisted round the mountain Mandara, and so used it as a churn. He is represented clothed in purple and wearing a white necklace, holding in one hand a plough and in the other a pestle. He is also called Ananta, 'the endless,' as the symbol of eternity. His wife was named Anantasirsha. He is sometimes distinct from Vasuki but generally identified with him. In the Puranas he is said to be the son of Kasyapa and Kadru, and according to some authorities, he was incarnate in Balarama. His hood is called Manidwipa, 'the island of jewels,' and his palace Manibhitti, 'jewel-walled,' or Manimandapa,' jewel palace.'

SIDDHAS: A class of semi-divine beings of great purity and holiness, who dwell in the regions of the sky between the earth and the sun. They are said to be 88,000 in number.

SIKHANDI, SIKHANDINI: Sikhandini is said to have been the daughter of Raja Drupada, but according to another statement she was one of the two wives whom Bhishma obtained for his brother Vichitravirya. "She (the widow) perished in the jungle, but before her death she had been assured by Parasurama that she should become a man in a future birth, and cause the death of Bhishma, who had been the author of her misfortunes." Accordingly, she was born again as Sikhandi, son of Drupada. Bhishma fell in battle pierced all over by the arrows of Arjuna, but according to this story, the fatal shaft came from the hands of Sikhandi.

SIKSHA: Phonetics; one of the Vedangas. The science which teaches the proper pronunciation and manner of reciting the Vedas. There are many treatises on this subject.

SINDHU: 1. The river Indus; also the country along that river and the people dwelling in it. From Sindhu came the Hind of the Arabs, the Hindoi or Indoi of the Greeks, and India. 2. A river in Malwa. There are others of the name.

SINHASANA DWATRINSAT: The thirty-two stories told by the images which supported the throne of King Vikramaditya. It is the Singhasan Battisi in Hindustani, and is current in most of the languages of India.

SISUPALA: Son of Damaghosha, king of Chedi, by Srutadeva, sister of Vasudeva; he was therefore cousin of Krishna, but he was Krishna's implacable foe, because Krishna had carried off Rukmini, his intended wife. He was slain by Krishna at the great sacrifice of Yudhishthira in punishment of opprobrious abuse. The Mahabharata states that Sisupala was born with three eyes and four arms. His parents were inclined to cast him out, but were warned by a voice not to do so, as his time was not come. It also foretold that his superfluous members should disappear when a certain person took the child into his lap, and that he would eventually die by the hands of that same person. Krishna placed the child on his knees and the extra eye and arms disappeared; Krishna also killed him.

The Vishnu Purana contributes an additional legend about him. "Sisupala was in a former existence the unrighteous but valiant monarch of the Daityas, Hiranyakasipu, who was killed by the divine guardian of creation in the man-lion Avatara. He was next the ten-headed sovereign Ravana, whose unequalled prowess, strength, and power were overcome by the lord of the three worlds Rama. Having been killed by the deity in the form of Raghava, he had long enjoyed the reward of his virtues in exemption from an embodied state, but had now received birth once more as Sisupala,the son of Damaghosha, king of Chedi. In this character he renewed with greater inveteracy than ever his hostile hatred towards Pundarikaksha (Vishnu), . . . and was in consequence slain by him. But from the circumstance of his thoughts being constantly engrossed by the supreme being, Sisupala was united with him after death, . . . for the lord bestows a heavenly and exalted station even upon those whom he slays in his displeasure." He was called Sumitha, 'virtuous.'

SISUPALA-VADHA: 'The Death of Sisupala;' an epic poem by Magha, in twenty cantos. It has been often printed, and has been translated into French by Fauche.

SITA: 'A furrow.' In the Veda, Sita is the furrow, or husbandry personified, and worshipped as a deity presiding over agriculture and fruits. In the Ramayana and later works she is daughter of Janaka, king of Videha, and wife of Rama. The old Vedic idea still adhered to her, for she sprang from a furrow. In the Ramayana her father Janaka says, "As I was ploughing my field, there sprang from the plough a girl, obtained by me while cleansing my field, and known by name as Sita (the furrow). This girl sprung from the earth grew up as my daughter." Hence she is styled Ayonija, 'not born from the womb.'

She is said to have lived before in the Krita age as Vedavati, and to be in reality the goddess Lakahmi in human form, born in the world for bringing about the destruction of Ravana, the Rakshasa king of Lanka, who was invulnerable to ordinary means, but doomed to die on account of a woman. Sita became the wife of Rama, who won her by bending the great bow of Siva. She was his only wife, and was the embodiment of purity, tenderness, and conjugal affection. She accompanied her husband in his exile, but was carried off from him by Ravana and kept in his palace at Lanka.. There he made many efforts to win her to his will, but she continued firm against all persuasions, threats and terrors, and maintained a dignified serenity throughout.

When Rama had slain the ravisher and recovered his wife, he received her coldly, and refused to take her back, for it was hard to believe it possible that she had retained her honour. She asserted her purity in touching language, and resolved to establish it by the ordeal of fire. The pile was raised and she entered the flames in the presence of gods and men, but she remained unhurt, and the god of fire brought her forth and placed her in her husband's arms. Not with standing this proof of her innocence, jealous thoughts passed through the mind of Rama, and after he had ascended his ancestral throne at Ayodhya, his people blamed him for taking back a wife who had been in the power of a licentious ravisher. So, although she was pregnant, he banished her and sent her to the hermitage of Valmiki, where she gave birth to twin sons, Kusa and Lava.

There she lived till the boys were about fifteen years old. One day they strayed to their father's capital He recognised and acknowledged them and then recalled Sita. She returned and publicly declared her innocence. But her heart was deeply wounded. She called upon her mother earth to attest her purity, and it did so. The ground opened, and she was taken back into the source from which she had sprung. Rama was now disconsolate and resolved to quit this mortallife. Sita had the appellations of Bhumija, Dharanisuta, and Parthivi, all meaning 'daughter of the earth.'

SIVA: The name Siva is unknown to the Vedas, but Rudra, another name of this deity, and almost equally common, occurs in the Veda both in the singular and plural, and from these the great deity Siva and his manifestations, the Rudras, have been developed. In the Rigveda the word Rudra is used for Agni, and the Maruts are called his sons. In other passages he is distinct from Agni. He is lauded as "the lord of songs, the lord of sacrifices,who heals, is brilliant as the sun, the best and most bountiful of gods, who grants prosperity and welfare to horses and sheep, men, women, and cows; the lord of nourishment, who drives away diseases, dispenses remedies, and removes sin; but, on the other hand, he is the wielder of the thunderbolt, the bearer of bow and arrows, and mounted on his chariot is terrible as a wild beast, destructive and fierce."

In the Yajurveda there is a long prayer called Satarudriya which is addressed to him and appeals to him under a great variety of epithets. He is "auspicious, not terrible;" "the deliverer, the first divine physician;" he is "blue-necked and red-coloured, who has a thousand eyes and bears a thousand quivers;" and in another hymn he is called "Tryambaka, the sweet-scented increaser of prosperity;" "a medicine for kine and horses, a medicine for men, and a source of ease to rams and ewes." In the Atharvaveda he is still the protector of cattle, but his character is fiercer. He is "dark, black, destroying, terrible." He is the "fierce god," who is besought to betake himself elsewhere," and not to assail mankind with consumption, poison, or celestial fire."

The Brahmanas tell that when Rudra was born he wept, and his father, Prajapati, asked the reason, and on being told that he wept because he had not received a name, his father gave him the name of Rudra (from the root *rud*, 'weep'). They also relate that at the request of the gods he pierced Prajapati because of his incestuous intercourse with his daughter. In another place he is said to have applied to his father eight successive times for a name, and that he received in succession the names Bhava, Sarva, Pasupati, Ugradeva, Mahadeva, Rudra, Isana, and Asani. In the Upanishads his character is further developed. He declares to the inquiring gods, "I alone was before all things, and I exist and I shall be. No other transcends me. I am eternal and not eternal, discernible and undiscernible, I am Brahma and I am not Brahma." Again it is said, "He is the only Rudra, he is Isana, he is divine, he is Maheswara, he is Mahadeva." " There is only one Rudra, there is no place for a second. He rules this fourth world, controlling and productive; living beings abide with him, united with him. At the time of the end he annihilates all worlds,." "He is without beginning, middle, or end; the one, the pervading, the spiritual and blessed, the wonderful, the consort of Uma, the supreme lord, the three-eyed, the blue-throated, the tranquil. He is Brahma, he is Siva, he is Indra; he is undecaying, supreme, self-resplendent; he is Vishnu, he is breath, he is the spirit, the supreme lord; he is all that hath been or that shall be, eternal Knowing him, a man overpasses death. There is no other way to liberation."

In the Ramayana Siva is a great god, but the references to him have more of the idea of a personal god than of a supreme divinity. He is represented as fighting with Vishnu, and as receiving worship with Brahma, Vishnu, and Indra, but he acknowledges the divinity of Rama, and holds a less exalted position than Vishnu. The Mahabharata also gives Vishnu or Krishna the highest honour upon the whole. But it has many passages in which Siva occupies the supreme place, and receives the homage and worship of Vishnu and Krishna. "Mahadeva," it says, "is an all-pervading god, yet is nowhere seen; he is the creator and the lord of Brahma, Vishnu, and Indra, whom the gods, from Brahma to the Pisachas, worship." The rival claims of Siva and Vishnu to supremacy are clearly displayed in this poem; and many of those powers and attributes are ascribed to them which were afterwards so widely developed in the Puranas. Attempts also are made to reconcile their conflicting claims by representing Siva and Vishnu, Siva and Krishna, to be one, or, as it is expressed at a later time in the Harivansa, there is "no difference between Siva who exists in the form of Vishnu, and Vishnu who exists in the form of Siva."

The Puranas distinctly assert the supremacy of their particular divinity, whether it be Siva or whether it be Vishnu, and they have developed and amplified the myths and allusions of the older writings into numberless legends and stories for the glorification and honour of their favourite god.

The Rudra of the Vedas has developed in the course of ages into the great and powerful god Siva, the third deity of the Hindu triad, and the supreme god of his votaries. He is shortly described as the destroying principle, but his powers and attributes are more numerous and much wider. Under the name of Rudra or Mahakala, he is the great destroying and dissolving power. But destruction in Hindu belief implies reproduction; so as Siva or Sankara, 'the auspicious,' he is the reproductive power which is perpetually restoring that which has been dissolved, and hence he is regarded as Iswara, the supreme lord, and Mahadeva, the great god. Under this character of restorer he is represented by his symbol, the Linga or phallus, typical of reproduction; and it is under this form alone, or combined with the Yoni, the female organ, the representative of his Sakti, or female energy, that he is everywhere worshipped.

Thirdly, he is the Mahayogi, the great ascetic, in whom is centred the highest perfection of austere penance and abstract meditation, by which the most unlimited powers are attained, marvels and miracles are worked, the highest spiritual knowledge is acquired, and union with the great spirit of the universe is eventually gained. In this character he is the naked ascetic Digambara, 'clothed with the elements,' or Dhurjati, 'loaded with matted hair,' and his body smeared with ashes. His first or destructive character is sometimes intensified, and he becomes Bhairava, 'the terrible destroyer,' who takes pleasure in destruction. He is also Bhuteswara, the lord of ghosts and goblins. In these characters he haunts cemeteries and places of cremation, wearing serpents round his head and skulls for a necklace, attended by troops of imps and trampling on rebellious demons.

He sometimes indulges in revelry, and, heated with drink, dances furiously with his wife Devi the dance called Tandava, while troops of drunken imps caper around them. Possessed of so many powers and attributes, he has a great number of names, and is represented under a variety of forms. One authority enumerates a thousand and eight names, but most of these are descriptive epithets, as Trilochnna, 'the three-eyed,' Nilakantha, 'the blue-throated,' and Panchanana, 'the five-faced.'

Siva is a fair man with five faces and four arms. He is commonly represented seated in profound thought, with a third eye in the middle of his forehead, contained in or surmounted by the moon's crescent; his matted locks are gathered up into a coil like a horn, which bears upon it a symbol of the river Ganges, which he caught as it fell from heaven; a necklace of skulls (mundamala) hangs round his neck, and serpents twine about his neck as a collar (nagakundala); his neck is blue from drinking the deadly poison which would have destroyed the world, and in his hand he holds a trisula or trident called Pinaka. His garment is the skin of a tiger, a deer, or an elephant, hence he is called Kritti-vasa; sometimes he is clothed in a skin and seated upon a tiger-skin, and he holds a deer in his hand. He is generally accompanied by his bull Nandi.

He also carries the bow Ajagava, a drum (damaru) in the shape of an hour-glass, the Khatwanga or club with a skull at the end, or a cord (pasa) for binding refractory offenders. His Pramathas or attendants are numerous, and are imps and demons of various kinds. His third eye has been very destructive. With it he reduced to ashes Kama, the god of love, for daring to inspire amorous thoughts of his consort Parvati while he was engaged in penance; and the gods and all created beings were destroyed by its glance at one of the periodical destructions of the universe. He is represented to have cut off one of the heads of Brahma for speaking disrespectfully, so that Brahma has only four heads instead of five. Siva is the great object of worship at Benares under the name of Visweswara. His heaven is on Mount Kailasa.

There are various legends respecting Siva's garments and weapons. It is said that "he once visited a forest in the form of a religious mendicant and the wives of the Rishis residing there fell in love with his great beauty, which the Rishis, perceiving, resented; in order, therefore, to overpower him, they first dug a pit, and by magical arts caused a tiger to rush out of it, which he slew, and taking his skin worc it as a garment; they next caused a deer to spring out upon him, which he took up in his left hand and ever after retained there. They then produced a red-hot iron, but this too he took up and kept in his hand as a weapon. The elephant's skin belonged to an Asura named Gaya, who acquired such power that he would have conquered the gods, and would have destroyed the Munis had they not fled to Benares and taken refuge in a temple of Siva, who then destroyed the Asura, and, ripping up his body, stripped off the elephant hide, which he cast over his shoulders for a cloak."—Williams.

Other names or epithets of Siva are Aghora, 'horrible; Babhru, Bhagavat, 'divine;' Chandrasekhara, 'moon-crested;' Gangadhara,'bearer of the Ganges;' Girisa, 'mountain lord ;' Hara, 'seizer;' lsana, 'ruler;' Jatadhara, 'wearing matted hair;' Jalamurti, 'whose form is water;' Kala, 'time;' Kalanjam; Kapala-malin, 'wearing a garland of skulls;' Mahakala, 'great time;' Mahesa, 'great lord;' Mrityunjaya, 'vanquisher of death;' Pasu-pati, 'lord of animals;' Sankara, Sarva, Sadasiva or Sambhu, 'the auspicious;' Sthanu, 'the firm;' Tryambaka, 'three-eyed;' Ugra, 'fierce;' Virupaksha, 'of misformed eyes;' Viswanatha, 'lord of all'.

SIVI: Son of Usinara, and king of the country also called Usinara, near Gandhara. The great charity and devotion of Sivi are extolled in the Mahabharata by the sage Markandeya. Agni having assumed the form of a pigeon,was pursued by Indra in the shape of a falcon. The pigeon took refuge in the bosom of Sivi, and the falcon would accept nothing from Sivi instead of the pigeon but an equal weight of the king's own flesh. Sivi cut a piece of flesh from his right thigh and placed it in the balance, but the bird was heavier. He cut again and again, and still the pigeon drew the scale, until the king placed his whole body in the balance. This outweighed the pigeon and the falcon flew away. On another occasion, Vishnu went to Sivi in the form of a Brahmin and demanded food, but would accept no food but Sivi's own son Vrihad-garbha, whom he required Sivi to kill and cook. The king did so, and placed the food before the Brahmin, who then told him to eat it himsalf. Sivi took up the head and prepared to eat. The Brahman then stayed his hand, commended his devotion, and restoring the son to life, vanished from sight.

SKANDA: God of war.

SKANDA PURANA: "The Skanda Purana is that in which the six-faced deity Skanda has related the events of the Tatpurusha Kalpa, enlarged with many tales, and subservient to the duties taught by Maheswara. It is said to contain 81,800 stanzas, so it is asserted amongst mankind." "It is uniformly agreed," says Wilson, "that the Skanda Purana, in a collective form, has no existence; and the fragments, in the shape of Sanhitas, Khandas, and Mahatmyas, which are affirmed in various parts of India to be portions of the Purana, present a much more formidable mass of stanzas than even the immense number of which it is said to consist. The most celebrated of these portions in Hindusthan is the Kasi Khanda, a very minute description of the temples of Siva in or adjacent to Benares, mixed with directions for worshipping Maheswara, and a great variety of legends explanatory of its merits and of the holiness of Kasi. Many of them are puerile and uninteresting, but some of them are of a higher character. There is every reason to believe the greater part of the contents of the Kasi Khanda anterior to the first attack upon Benares by Mahmud of Ghazni. The Kasi Khanda alone contains 15,000 stanzas. Another considerable work is the Utkala Khanda, giving an account of the holiness of Orissa." A part of this Purana has been printed at Bombay.

SMRITI: 'What was remembered.' Inspiration, as distinguished from Sruti, or direct revelation. What has been remembered and handed down by tradition. In its widest application, the term includes the Vedangas, the Sutras, the Ramayana, the Mahabharata, the Puranas, the Dharma-sastras, especially the works of Manu, Yajnawalkya, and other inspired lawgivers, and the Niti-sastras or ethics, but its ordinary application is to the Dharma-sastras; as Manu says, " By Sruti is meant the Veda, and by Smriti the institutes of law."

SOMA: The juice of a milky climbing plant (Asclepias acida), extracted and fermented, forming a beverage offered in libations to the deities, and drunk by the Brahmins. Its exhilarating qualities were grateful to the priests, and the gods were represented as being equally fond of it. This soma juice occupies a large space in the Rigveda; one Mandala is almost wholly devoted to its praise and uses. It was raised to the position of a deity, and represented to be primeval, all-powerful, healing all diseases, bestower of riches, lord of other gods, and even identified with the Supreme Being. As a personification, Soma was the god who represented and animated the soma juice, an Indian Dionysus or Bacchus.

"The simple-minded Aryan people, whose whole religion was a worship of the wonderful powers and phenomena of nature, had no sooner perceived that this liquid had power to elevate the spirits and produce a temporary frenzy, under the influence of which the individual was prompted to, and capable of, deeds beyond his natural powers, than they found in it something divine; it was to their apprehension a god, endowing those into whom it entered with godlike powers; the plant which afforded it became to them the king of plants; the process of preparing it was a holy sacrifice; the instruments used therefor were sacred. The high antiquity of this cultus is attested by the references to it found occurring in the Persian Avesta; it seems, however, to have received a new impulse on Indian territory." —Whitney.

In later times, the name was appropriated to the moon, and some of the qualities of the soma juice have been transferred to the luminary, who is Oshadhi-pati, or lord of herbs. So Soma is considered the guardian of sacrifices and penance, asterisms and healing herbs.

In the Puranic mythology, Soma, as the moon, is commonly said to be the son of the Rishi Atri by his wife Anasuya, but the authorities are not agreed. One makes him of Dharma; another gives his paternity to Prabhakara, of the race of Atri; and he is also said to have been produced from the churning of the ocean in another Manwantara. In the Vishnu Purana he is called "the monarch of Brahmins;" but the Brihad Aranyaka, an older work, makes him a Kshatriya. He married twenty-seven daughters of the Rishi Daksha, who are really personifications of the twenty-seven lunar asterisms; but keeping up the personality, he paid such attention to Rohini, the fourth of them, that the rest became jealous, and appealed to their father. Daksha's interference was fruitless, and he cursed his son-in-law, so that he remained childless, and became affected with consumption.

This moved the pity of his wives, and they interceded with their father for him. He could not recall his curse, but he modified it so that the decay should be periodical, not permanent. Hence the wane and increase of the moon. He performed the Rajasuya sacrifice, and became in consequence so arrogant and licentious that he carried off Tara, the wife of Brihaspati, and refused to give her up either on the entreaties of her husband or at the command of Brahma. This gave rise to a widespread quarrel. The sage Usanas, out of enmity to Brihaspati, sided with Soma, and he was supported by the Danavas, the Daityas, and other foes of the gods. Indra and the gods in general sided with Brisaspati. There ensued a fierce contest, and "the earth was shaken to her centre." Soma had his body cut in two by Siva's trident, and hence he is called Bhagnatma. At length Brahma interposed and stopped the fight, compelling Soma to restore Tara to her husband. The result of this intrigue was the birth of a child, whom Tara, after great persuasion, declared to be the son of Soma, and to whom the name of Budha was given; from him the Lunar race sprung.

According to the Puranas, the chariot of Soma has three wheels, and is drawn by ten horses of the whiteness of the jasmine, five on the right half of the yoke, and five on the left.

The moon has many names and descriptive epithets, as Chandra, Indu, Sasi, 'marked like a hare;' Nisakara, 'maker of night;' Nakshatra-natha, 'lord of the constellations;' Sitamarichi, 'having cool rays;' Sitansu, 'having white rays;' Mriganka, 'marked like a deer;' Sivasekhara, 'the crest of Siva;' Kumuda-pati, 'lord of the lotus;' Swetavaji:, 'drawn by white horses.'

SRI: 'Fortune, prosperity.' 1. The wife of Vishnu. 2. An honorific prefix to the names of gods, kings, heroes, and men and books of high estimation.

SRI HARSHA: A great sceptical philosopher, and author of the poem called Naishadha or Naishadhiya. There were several kings of the name.

SRISAILA: The mountain of Sri, the goddess of fortune. It is a holy place in the Dakhin, near the Krishna, and was formerly a place of great splendour. It retains its sanctity but has lost its grandeur. Also called Sriparvata.

SRUTI: 'What was heard.' The revealed word. The Mantras and Brahmanas of the Vedas are always included in the term, and the Upanishads are generally classed with them.

SUBRAHMANYA: A name of Kartikeya, god of war, used especially in the South.

SUDARSANA: A name of Krishna's chakra or discus weapon.

SUDAS: A king who frequently appears in the Rigveda, and at whose court the rival Rishis Vasishtha and Viswamitra are represented as living. He was famous for his sacrifices.

SUDRA: The fourth or servile caste.

SUDRAKA: A king who wrote the play called Mrichchhakatika, 'the toy-cart,' in ten acts.

SUGRIVA: 'Handsome neck.' A monkey king who was dethroned by his brother Bali, but after the latter had been killed, Sugriva was reinstalled by Rama as king at Kishkindha. He, with his adviser Hanuman and their army of monkeys, were the allies of Rama in his war against Ravana, in which he was wounded. He is said to have been the son of the sun, and from his paternity he is called Ravinandana and by other similar names. He is described as being grateful, active in aiding his friends, and able to change his form at will. His wife's name was Ruma.

SUKA-SAPTATI: 'The seventy tales of a parrot.' This is the original of the Tutinamah of the Persian, from which the Hindustani Tota-kahani was translated.

SUKRA: The planet Venus and its regent. Sukra was son of Bhrigu and priest of Bali and the Daityas (Daitya-guru). He is also called the son of Kavi. His wife's name was Susuma or Sata-parwa. His daughter Devayani married Yayati of the Lunar race, and her husband's infidelity induced Sukra to curse him. Sukra is identified with Usanas, and is author of a code of law. The Harivansa relates that he went to Siva and asked for means of protecting the Asuras against the gods, and for obtaining his object he performed "a painful rite, imbibing the smoke of chaff with his head downwards for a thousand years." In his absence the gods attacked the Asuras and Vishnu killed his mother, for which deed Sukra cursed him "to be born seven times in the world of men." Sukra restored his mother to life, and the gods being alarmed lest Sukra's penance should be accomplished, Indra sent his daughter Jayanti to lure him from it. She waited upon him and soothed him, but he accomplished his penance and afterwards married her. Sukra is known by his patromymic Bhargava, and also as Bhrigu. He is also Kavi or Kavya, ' the poet.' The planet is called Asphujit, Magha-bhava, son of Magha; Shodasansu, 'having sixteen rays', and Sweta, 'the white.'

SUMBHA and NISHUMBHA: Two Asuras, brothers, who were killed by Durga. These brothers, as related in the Markandeya Purana, were votaries of Siva, and performed severe penance for 5000 years in order to obtain immortality. Siva refused the boon, and they continued their devotions with such increased intensity for 800 years more, that the gods trembled for their power. By advice of Indra, the god of love, Kama, went to them with two celestial nymphs, Rambha and Tilottama, and they succeeded in seducing the two Asuras and holding them in the toils of sensuality for 5000 years. On recovering from their voluptuous aberration they drove the nymphs back to paradise and recommenced their penance. At the end of 1000 years Siva blessed them "that in riches and strength they should excel the gods." In their exaltation they warred against the gods, who in despair appealed in succession to Brahma, Vishnu, and Siva, but in vain. The latter advised them to apply to Durga and they did so. She contrived to engage the Asuras in war, deafeated their forces, slew their commanders, Chanda and Munda and finally killed them.

SUNAHSEPHA: The legend of Sunahsepha, as told in the Aitareya Brahmana, is as follows:—King Harischandra, of the race of Ikshwaku, being childless, made a vow that if he obtained a son he would sacrifice him to Varuna. A son was born who received the name of Rohita, but the father postponed, under various pretexts, the fulfilment of his vow. When at length he resolved to perform the sacrifice, Rohita refused to be the victim, and went out into the forest, where he lived for six years. He then met a poor Brahmin Rishi called Ajigarta, who had three sons, and Rohita purchased from Ajigarta for a hundred cows, the second son, named Sunasehpha, to be the substitute for himself in the sacrifice. Varuna approved of the substitute, and the sacrifice was about to be performed, the father receiving another hundred cows for binding his son to the sacrificial post, and a third hundred for agreeing to slaughter him. Sunahsepha saved himself by reciting verses in honour of different deities, and was received into the family of Viswamitra, who was one of the officiating priests.

The Ramayana gives a different version of the legend. Ambarisha, king of Ayodhya, was performing a sacrifice when Indra carried off the victim. The officiating priest represented that this loss could be atoned for only by the sacrifice of a human victim. The king, after a long search, found a Brahmin Rishi named Richika, who had two sons, and the younger, Sunahsepha, was then sold by his own consent for a hundred thousand cows, ten millions of gold pieces, and heaps of jewels. Sunahsepha met with his maternal uncle, Viswamitra, who taught him two divine verses which he was to repeat when about to be sacrificed. As he was bound at the stake to be immolated, he celebrated the two gods Indra and Vishnu with the excellent verses, and Indra, being pleased, bestowed upon him long life. He was afterwards called Devarata, and is said to have become son of Viswamitra. The Mahabharata and the Puranas show some variations. A series of seven hymns in the Rigveda is attributed to Sunahsepha.

SURPANAKHA: 'Having nails like winnowing-fans.' Sister of Ravana. This Rakshasi admired the beauty of Rama and fell in love with him. When she made advances to Rama he referred her to Lakshmana, and Lakshmana in like manner sent her back to Rama. Enraged at this double rejection, she fell upon Sita, and Rama was obliged to interfere forcibly for the protection of his wife. He called out to Lakshmana to disfigure the violent Rakshasi, and Lakshmana cut off her nose and ears. She flew to her brothers for revenge, and this brought on the war between Rama and Ravana. She described to Ravana the beauty of Sita, and instigated his carrying her off, and finally she cursed him just before the engagement in which he was killed.

SURYA: The sun or its deity. He is one of the chief deities in the Vedas, as the great source of light and warmth, but the references to him are more poetical than precise. Sometimes he is identical with Savitri and Aditya, sometimes he is distinct.

Sometimes he is called son of Dyaus, sometimes of Aditi. In one passage, Ushas, the dawn, is his wife, in another he is called the child of the dawns; he moves through the sky in a chariot drawn by seven ruddy horses or mares." Surya has several wives, but, according to later legends, his twin sons the Aswins, who are ever young and handsome and ride in a golden car as precursors of Ushas, the dawn, were born of a nymph called Aswini, from her having concealed herself in the form of a mare. In the Ramayana and Puranas, Surya is said to be the son of Kasyapa and Aditi, but in the Ramayana he is otherwise referred to as a son of Brahma.

His wife was Sanjna, daughter of Viswa-karma, and by her he had three children, the Manu Vaivaswata, Yama, and the goddess Yami, or the Yamuna river. His effulgence was so overpowering that his wife gave him Chhaya (shade) for a handmaid, and retired into the forest to devote herself to religion. While thus engaged, and in the form of a mare, the sun saw her and approached her in the form of a horse. Hence sprang the two Aswins and Revanta. Surya brought back his wife Sanjna to his home, and her father, the sage Viswakarma, placed the luminary on his lathe and cut away an eighth of his effulgence, trimming him in every part except the feet. The fragments that were cut off fell blazing to the earth, and from them Viswa-karma formed the discus of Vishnu, the trident of Siva, the weapon of Kuvera, the lance of Kartikeya, and the weapons of the other gods. According to the Mahabharata, Karna was his illegitimate son by Kunti. He is also fabled to be the father of Sani and the monkey chief Sugriva.

The Manu Vaivaswata was father of Ikshwaku, and from him, the grandson of the sun, the Suryavansa, or Solar race of kings, draws its origin. In the form of a horse Surya communicated the White Yajurveda to Yajnawalkya, and it was he who bestowed on Satrajit the Syamantaka gem. A set of terrific Rakshasas called Mandehas made an attack upon him and sought to devour him, but were dispersed by his light. According to the Vishnu Puran, he was seen by Satrajita in "his proper form," "of dwarfish stature, with a body like burnished copper, and with slightly reddish eyes." Surya is represented in a chariot drawn by seven horses, or a horse with seven heads, surrounded with rays. His charioteer is Aruna or Vivaswat, and his city Vivaswati or Bhaswati.

There are temples of the sun, and he receives worship. The names and epithets of the sun are numberless. He is Savitri, 'the nourisher; Vivaswat, 'the brilliant;' Bhaskara, 'light-maker;' Dinakara, 'daymaker;' Arhapati, 'lord of day;' Lokachakshuh, 'eye of the world;' Karmasakshi, 'witness of the deeds (of men);' Graharaja, 'king of the constellations;' Gabhastiman, 'possessed of rays;' Sahasrakirana, 'having a thousand rays;' Vikartana, 'shorn of hie beams' (by Viswa-karma); Martanda, 'descended from Mritanda,' etc. Surya's wives are called Savarna, Swati, and Mahavirya.

SURYA-SIDDHANTA: A celebrated work on astronomy, said to have been revealed by the sun (Surya). It has been edited in the Bibliotheca Indica by Hall, and there are other editions. It has been translated by Whitney and Burgess.

SURYAVANSA: The Solar race. A race or lineage of Kshatriyas which sprang from Ikshwaku, grandson of the sun. Rama was of this race, and so were many other great kings and heroes. Many Rajputs claim deseent from this and the other great lineage, the Lunar race. The Rana of Udaipur claims to be of the Suryavansa, and the Jharejas of Cutch and Sindh assert a descent from the Chandra-vansa. There were two dynasties of the Solar race. The elder branch, which reigned at Ayodhya, descended from Ikshwaku through his eldest son, Vikukshi. The other dynasty, reigning at Mithila, descended from another of Ikshwaku's sons, named Nimi. The lists of these two dynasties on the opposite page are taken from the Vishnu Purana. The lists given by other authorities show some discrepancies, but they agree in general as to the chief names.

SUSRUTA: A medical writer whose date is uncertain, but his work was translated into Arabic before the end of the eighth century. The book has been printed at Calcutta. There is a Latin translation by Hepler and one in German by Vullers.

SUTRA: 'A thread or string.' A rule or aphorism. A verse expressed in brief and technical language, a very favourite form among the Hindus of embodying and transmitting rules. There are Sutras upon almost every subject, but "the Sutras" generally signify those which are connectedwith the Vedas.o

SWADHA: 'Oblation.' Daughter of Daksha and Prasuti according to one statement, and of Agni according to another. She is connected with the Pitris or Manes, and is represented as wife of Kavi or of one class of Pitris, and as mother of others.

SWAHA: 'Offering.' Daughter of Daksha and Prasuti. She was wife of Vahni or Fire, or of Abhimani, one of the Agnis.

SWARGA: The heaven of Indra, the abode of the inferior gods and of beatified mortals, supposed to be situated on Mount Meru. It is called also Sairibha, Misraka-vana,Tavisha, Tridivam, Tri-pishtapam, and Urdhwaloka. Names of heaven or paradise in general are also used for it.

SWASTIKA: A mystical religious mark placed upon persons or things. It is in the form of a Greek cross with the ends bent round.

SWAYAM-BHUVA: A name of the first Manu.

The Surya-Vansa or Solar Race

Ikshwaku

Dynasty of Ayodhya

Vikulkshi
Kakutstha
Anenas
Prithu
Viswagaswa
Ardra
Yuvanaswa
Sravasta
Brihadaswa
Kuvalayaswa (called Dhundhumara)
Dridhaswa
Haryaswa
Nikumbha
Sanhataswa
Krisaswa
Prasenajit
Yuvanaswa
Mandhatri
Purukutsa
Trasadasyu
Sambhuta
Anaranya
Prishadaswa
Haryaswa
Sumanas
Tridhanwan
Satyavrata (Trisanku)
Harischandra
Rohitaswa
Harita
Chunchu
Vijaya
Ruruka
Vrika
Bahuka
Sagara
Asamanjas
Ansumat
Dilipa
Bhagiratha
Sruta
Nabhaga
Ambarisha
Sindhudwipa
Ayutayus
Rituparna
Sarvakama
Sudasa
Saudasa (Kalmashapada)
Asmaka
Mulaka (Narikavacha)
Dasaratha
Ilavila
Viswasaha
Khatwanga
Dirghabahu
Raghu
Aja
Dasaratha
Rama
Kusa
Atithi
Nishadha
Nala
Nabhas
Pundarika
Kshema-dhanwan
Devanika
Ahinagu
Paripatra
Dala
Chhala
Uktha
Vajranabha
Sankhanabha
Dhyushitaswa
Viswasaha
Hiranyanabha
Pushya
Dhruvasandhi
Sudarsana
Agnivarna
Sighra
Maru
Prasusruta
Susandhi
Amarsha
Mahaswat
Visrutavat
Brihadbala

Dynasty of Mithila

Nimi
Janaka
Udavasu
Nandivardhana
Suketu
Devarata
Brihaduktha (or Brihadratha)
Mahavirya
Satyadhriti
Dhrishtaketu
Haryaswa
Maru
Pratibandhaka
Kritaratha
Krita
Vibudha
Mahadhriti
Krtirata
Maharoman
Suvarnaroma
Hraswaroma
Siradhwaja (father of Sita)
Bhanumat
Satadyumna
Suchi
Urjavaha
Satyadhwaja
Kuni
Anjana
Ritujit
Arishtanemi
Srutayus
Suparswa
Sanjaya
Kshemari
Anenas
Minaratha
Satyaratha
Satyarathi
Upagu
Sruta
Saswata
Sudhanwan
Subhasa
Susruta
Jaya
Vijaya
Rita
Sunaya
Vitahavya
Dhriti
Bahulaswa
Kriti

SWETAKETU: A sage who, according to the Mahabharata, put a stop to the practice of married women consorting with other men, especially with Brahmins. His indignation was aroused at seeing a Brahmin take his mother by the hand and invite her to go away with him. The husband saw this, and told his son that there was no ground of offence, for the practice had prevailed from time immemorial. Swetaketu would not tolerate it, and introduced the rule by which a wife is forbidden to have intercourse with another man unless specially appointed by her husband to raise up seed to him.

SWETASWATARA: An Upanishad attached to the Yajurveda. It is one of the most modern. Translated by Dr. Roer for the Bibliotheca Indica.

SYAMANTAKA: A celebrated gem given by the sun to Satrajita. "It yielded daily eight loads of gold, and dispelled all fear of portents, wild beasts, fire, robbers, and famine." But though it was an inexhaustible source of good to the virtuous wearer, it was deadly to a wicked one. Satrajita being afraid that Krishna would take it from him, gave it to his own brother, Prasena, but he, being a bad man, was killed by a lion. Jamvat, king of the bears, killed the lion and carried off the gem, but Krishna, after a long conflict, took it from him, and restored it to Satrajita.

Afterwards Satrajita was killed in his sleep by Satadhanwan, who carried off the gem. Being pursued by Krishna and Balarama, he gave the gem to Akrura and continued his flight, but he was overtaken and killed by Krishna alone. As Krishna did not bring back the jewel, Balarama suspected that he had secreted it, and consequently he upbraided him and parted from him, declaring that he would not be imposed upon by perjuries. Akrura subsequently produced the gem, and it was claimed by Krishna, Balarama, and Satya-bhama. After some contention it was decided that

Akrura should keep it, and so "he moved about like the sun wearing a garland of light."

T

TAITTIRIYA: This term is applied to the Sanhita of the Black Yajurveda. It is also applied to a Brahmana, to an Aranyaka, to an Upanishad, and a Pratisakhya of the same Veda. All these are printed, or are in course of printing, in the Bibliotheca Indica, and of the last there is a translation in that serial.

TAKSHAKA: 'One who cuts off; a carpenter.' A name of Viswakarma. A serpent, son of Kadru, and chief of snakes.

TAKSHASILA: A city of the Gandharas, situated in the Panjab. It was the residence of Taksha, son of Bharata and nephew of Ramachandra, and perhaps took its name from him. It is the Taxila of Ptolemy and other classical writers. Arrian describes it as "a large and wealthy city, and the most populous between the Indus and Hydaspes." It was three days' journey east of the Indus, and General Cunningham has found its remains at Sahhdhari, one mile north-east of Kala-kisarai.

TANTRA: 'Rule, ritual'. The title of a numerous class of religious and magical works, generally of later date than the Puranas, and representing a later development of religion, although the worship of the female energy had its origin at an earlier period. The chief peculiarity of the Tantras is the prominence they give to the female energy of the deity, his active nature being personified in the person of his Sakti, or wife. There are a few Tantras which make Vishnu's wife or Radha the object of devotion, but the great majority of them are devoted to one of the manifold forms of Devi, the Sakti of Siva, and they are commonly written in the form of a dialogue between these two deities.

Devi, as the Sakti of Siva, is the especial energy concerned with sexual intercourse and magic powers, and these are the leading topics of the Tantras. There are five requisites for Tantra worship, the five Makaras or five m's—(1.) Madira, Madya, wine (2.) Mansa, flesh; (3.) Matsya, fish; (4.) Mudra, parched grain and mystic gesticulations; (5.) Maithuna, sexual intercourse. Each Sakti has a twofold nature, white and black, gentle and ferocious. Thus Uma and Gauri are gentle forms of the Sakti of Siva, while Durga and Kali are fierce forms. The Saktas or worshippers of the Saktis are divided into two classes, Dakshinacharis and Vamacharis, the right-handed and the left-handed. The worship of the right-hand Saktas is comparatively decent, but that of the left hand is addressed to the fierce forms of the Saktis, and is most licentious. The female principle is worshipped, not only symbolically, but in the actual woman, and promiscuous intercourse forms part of the orgies. Tantra worship prevails chiefly in Bengal and the Eastern provinces.

TARA, TARAKA: Wife of Brihaspati. According to the Puranas, Soma, the moon, carried her off, which led to a great war between the gods and the Asuras. Brahma put an end to the war and restored Tara, but she was delivered of a child which she declared to be the son of Soma, and it was named Budha.

TARAKA: A female Daitya, daughter of the Yaksha Suketu or of the demon Sunda, and mother of Maricha. She was changed into a Rakshasi by Agastya, and lived in a forest called by her name on the Ganges, opposite the confluence of the Saryu, and she ravaged all the country round. Viswamitra desired Rama-chandra to kill her, but he was reluctant to kill a woman. He resolved to deprive her of the power of doing harm, and cut off her two arms. Lakshmana cut off her nose and ears. She, by the power of sorcery, assailed Rama and Lakshmana with a fearful shower of stones, and at the earnest command of Viswamitra, the former killed her with an arrow.

TILOTTAMA: Name of an Apsaras. She was originally a Brahmin female, but for the offence of bathing at an improper season, she was condemned to be born as an Apsaras, for the purpose of bringing about the mutual destruction of the two demons Sunda and Upasunda.

TRASADASYU: A royal sage and author of hymns. According to Sayana, he was son of Purukutsa. When Purukutsa was a prisoner, "his queen propitiated the seven Rishis to obtain a son who might take his father's place. They advised her to worship Indra and Varuna, in consequence of which Trasadasyu was born." He was renowned for his generosity. According to the Bhagavata Purana, he was father of Purukutsa.

TRETA YUGA: The sccond age of the world, a period of 1,296,000 years.

TRIBHUVANA, TRILOKA: The three worlds, Swarga, Bhumi, Patalaheaven, earth, and hell—

TRILOCHANA: 'Three-eyed,' i.e., Siva. The Mahabharats relates that the third eye burst from Siva's forehead with a great flame when his wife playfully placed her hands over his eyes after he had been engaged in austerities in the Himalaya. This eye has been very destructive. It reduced Kama, the god of love, to ashes.

TRIMURTI: 'Triple form.' The Hindu triad. This was foreshadowed in the Vedic association of the three gods Agni, Vayu, and Surya. The triad consists of the gods Brahma, Siva, and Vishnu, the representatives of the creative, destructive, and preservative principles. Brahma is the embodiment "of the Rajo-guna, the quality of passion or desire, by which the world was called into being; Siva is the embodied Tamoguna, the attribute of darkness or wrath, and the destructive fire by which the earth is annihilated; and Vishnu is the embodied Satwaguna, or property of mercy and goodness by which the world is preserved. The three exist in one and one in three, as the Veda is divided into three and is yet but one; and they are all Asrita, or comprehended within that one being who is parama or 'supreme,' Guhya or 'secret,' and Sarvatma, 'the soul of all things.'

The Padma Purana, which is a Vaishnava work and gives the supremacy to Vishnu, says, "In the beginning of creation, the great Vishnu, desirous of creating the whole world, became three-fold: creator, preserver, and destroyer. In order to create this world, the supreme spirit produced from the right side of his body himself as Brahma; then in order to preserve the world he produced from the left side of his body Vishnu; and in order to destroy the world he produced from the middle of his body the eternal Siva. Some worship Brahma, others Vishnu, others Siva; but Vishnu, one yet threefold, creates, preserves, and destroys, therefore let the pious make no difference between the three." The representation of the Trimarti is one body with three heads: in the middle Brahma, on the right Vishnu, and on the left Siva. The worship of Brahma is almost extinct, but Vishnu and Siva receive unbounded adoration from their respective followers, and each is elevated to the dignity of the supreme being.

TRIPURA: 'Triple city.' 1. According to the Harivansa it was aerial, and was burnt in a war with the gods. 2. A name of the demon Bana, because he received in gift three cities from Siva, Brahma, and Vishnu. He was killed by Siva. His name at full length is Tripurasura. The name is also applied to Siva.

TRITA, TRITA-APTYA: A minor deity mentioned occasionally in the Rigveda, and generally in some relation to Indra. Thus "Indra broke through the defences of Vala, as did

Trita through the coverings of the well." In explanation of this and similar allusions, a legend is told by the commentator to the effect, that Ekata, Dwita, and Trita (first, second, and third), were three men produced in water by Agni, for the purpose of rubbing off the remains of an oblation of clarified butter. Agni threw the cinders of the offerings into water, and from them sprang the three brothers, who, from their origin in water (*ap*), were called Aptyas. Trita went one day to draw water from a well and fell into it. The Asuras then heaped coverings over the mouth of it to prevent his getting out, but he broke through them with ease.

The Niti-manjari tells the story differently. Ekata, Dwita, and Trita were travelling in a desert and suffered from thirst. They came to a well from which Trita drew water and gave it to his brothers. In order to appropriate his property the two brothers threw him into the well, placed a cart-wheel over it, and left him there. Trita prayed earnestly to the gods, and with their help he escaped.

TURVASA, TURVASU: Son of Yayati by Devayani. He refused to bear the curse of premature decrepitude passed upon his father, and so his father cursed him that his posterity should "not possess dominion." His father gave him a part of his kingdom, but after some generations, his linemerge into that of his brother Puru, who bore for a time the curse passed upon his father.

TWASHTRI: In the Rigveda this deity is the ideal artist, the divine artisan, the most skilful of workmen, who is versed in all wonderful and admirable contrivances, and corresponds in many respects with Hephaistos and Vulcan. He sharpens and carries the great iron axe, and he forges the thunderbolts of Indra. He is the beautiful, skilful worker, the omniform, the archetype of all forms, the vivifier and the bestower of long life. He imparts generative power and bestows offspring.

He forms husband and wife for each other, even from the womb. He develops the seminal germ in the womb, and is the shaper of all forms, human and animal. He has generated a strong man, a lover of the gods, a swift horse, and has created the whole world. "As the Satapatha Brahmana expresses it," He has produced and nourishes a great variety of creatures; all worlds or beings are his, and are known to him; he has given to heaven and earth and to all things their forms." He created Brahmanaspati above all creatures, and generated Agni along with heaven and earth, the waters and the Bhrigus.

He is master of the universe, the first-born protector and leader, and knows the region of the gods. He is supplicated to nourish the worshipper and protect his sacrifice. He is the bestower of blessings, and is possessed of abundant wealth, and grants prosperity. He is asked, like other gods, to take pleasure in the hymns of his worshippers and to grant them riches. He is associated with the Ribhus, and is represented as sometimes envying and sometimes admiring their skill He is represented as being occasionally in a state of hostility with Indra, and he had a son named Viswarupa (omniform) or Trisiras, who had three heads, six eyes, and three mouths, who was especially obnoxious to Indra, and was slain by him. He had a daughter, Saranyu, whom he married to Vivaswat, and she was the mother of the Aswins. In the Puranas Twashtri is identified with Viswakarman, the artisan of the gods, and sometimes also with Prajapati. One of the Adityas and one of the Rudras bear this name, as also did a prinee descended from Bharata.

U

UCHCHAIHSRAVA: The model horse. The white horse of Indra, produced at the churning of the ocean. It is fed on ambrosia, and is held to be the king of horses.

UDAYANA: 1. A prince of the Lunar race, and son of Sahasranika, who is the hero of a popular story. He was king of Vatsa, and is commonly called Vatsaraja. His capital was Kausambi Vasavadatta, princess of Ujjayani, saw him in a dream and fell in love with him. He was decoyed to that city, and there kept in captivity by the king, Chandasena; but when he was set at liberty by the minister, he carried off Vasavadatta from her father and a rival suitor. 2. A name of Agastya.

UDDHAVA: The friend and counsellor of Krishna. According to some, he was Krishna's cousin, being son of Devabhaga, the brother of Vasudeva. He was also called Pavanavyadhi.

UGRASENA: A king of Mathura, husband of Karni, and father of Kansa and Devaka. He was deposed by Kansa, but Krishna, after killing the latter, restored Ugrasena to the throne.

UJJAYANI: The modern Oujein or Ujjein. It was the capital of Vikramaditya and one of the seven sacred cities. Hindu geographers calculate their longitude from it, making it their first meridian.

ULUPI: A daughter of Kauravya, Raja of the Nagas, with whom Arjuna contracted a kind of marriage. She was nurse to her stepson, Babhruvahana, and had great influence over him. According to the Vishnu Purina, she had a son named Iravat.

UMA: 'Light.' A name of the consort of Siva. The earliest known mention of the name is in the Kena Upanishad, where she appears as a mediatrix between Brahma and the other gods, and seems to be identified with Vach.

UPANISHADS: 'Esoteric doctrine.' The third division of the Vedas attached to the Brahmana portion, and forming part of the Sruti or revealed word. The Upanishads are generally written in prose with interspersed verses, but some are wholly in verse. There are about 150 of these works, probably even more. They are of later date than the Brahmanas, but it is thought that the oldest may date as far back as the sixth century B.C. The object of these trestises is to ascertain the mystic sense of the text of the Veda, and so they enter into such abstruse questions as the orgin of the universe, the nature of the deity, the nature of soul, and the connection of mind and matter. Thus they contain the beginnings of that metaphysical inquiry which ended in the full development of Hindu philosophy.

The Upanishads have "one remarkable peculiarity, the total absence of any Brahminical exclusiveness in their doctrine. They are evidently later than the older Sanhitas and Brahmanas, but they breathe an entirely different spirit, a freedom of thought unknown in any earlier work except the Rigveda hymns themselves. The grcat teachers of the higher knowledge and Brahmins are continually represented as going to Kshatriya kings to become their pupils."—Professor Cowell. The Rig-veda has the Upanishad called Aitareya attached to the Aitareya Brahmana. The Taittiriya Sanhita of the Yajur has an Upanishad of the same name. The Vajasaneyi Sanhita has the Isa, and attached to the Satapatha Brahmana it has the Brihad Aranyaka, which is the most important of them. The Samaveda has the Kena and Chhandogya. All these have been translated into English. The Atharvaveda has the Katha, Prasna, Mundaka, Mandukya, and others, altogether fifty-two in number. These are the most important of the Upanishads. Many of the Upanishads have been printed, and several of them translated in the Bibliotheca Indica, and by Poley. There is a catalogue by Millier in the Zeitschrift des D.M.G.

UPAVEDAS: Subordinate Vedas. These are sciences which have no connection whatever with the Sruti or revealed Veda. They are four in number—(1.) Ayurveda, medicine;

(2.) Gandharva-veda, music and dancing; (3.) Dhanurveda, archery, military science; (4.) Sthapatyaveda, architecture.

URVASI: A celestial nymph, mentioned first in the Rigveda. The sight of her beauty is said to have caused the generation, in a peculiar way, of the sages Agastya and Vasishtha by Mitra and Varuna. A verse says, "And thou, O Vasishtha, art a son of Mitra and Varuna." She roused the anger of these two deities and incurred their curse, through which she came to live upon the earth, and became the wife or mistress of Pururavas. The story of her amour with Pururavas is first told in the Satapatha Brahmana. The loves of Pururavas, the Vikrama or hero, and of Urvasi, the nymph, are the subject of Kalidasa's drama called Vikramorvasiya.

USHA: A Daitya princess, daughter of Bana and granddaughter of Bali. She is called also Pritijusha. She fell in love with a prince whom she saw in a dream, and was anxious to know if there were such a person. Her favourite companion, Chitralekha, drew the portraits of many gods and men, but Usha's choice fell upon Aniruddha, son of Pradyumna and grandson of Krishna. Chitralekha, by her magic power, brought Aniruddha to Usha. Her father, on hearing of the youth's being in the palace, endeavoured to kill him, but he defended himself successfully. Bana, however, kept Aniruddha, "binding him in serpent bonds." Krishna, Pradyumna, and Balarama went to the rescue; and although Bana was supported by Siva and by Skanda, god of war, his party was defeated, and Aniruddha was carried back to Dwaraka with his wife Usha.

UTATHYA: A Brahman of the race of Angiras, who married Bhadra, daughter of Soma, a woman of great beauty. The god Varuna, who had formerly been enamoured of her, carried her off from Utathya's hermitage, and would not give her up to Narada, who was sent to bring her back. Utathya, greatly enraged, drank up all the sea, still Varuna would not let her go. At the desire of Utathya, the lake of Varuna was then dried up and the ocean swept away. The saint then addressed himself to the countries and to the river:- "Saraswati, disappear into the deserts, and let this land, deserted by thee, become impure." After the country had become dried up, Varuna submitted himself to Utathya and brought back Bhadra. The sage was pleased to get back his wife, and released both the world and Varuna from their sufferings.

UTTARA MIMANSA: A school of philosophy.

UTTARA-RAMACHARITA: 'The later chronicle of Rama. A drama by Bhavabhuti on the latter part of Rama's life. The second part of King Rama, as the Mahavira-charita is the first. The drama is based on the Uttara Kanda of the Ramayana, and quotes two or three verses from that poem. It was probably written about the beginning of the eighth century. It has been translated in blank verse by Wilson, and more literally by Professor C. H. Tawney. There are several editions of the text.

VACH: 'Speech.' In the Rigveda, Vach appears to be the personification of speech by whom knowledge was communicated to man. Thus she is said to have "entered into the Rishis," and to make whom she loves terrible and intelligent, a priest and a Rishi. She was "generated by the gods," and is called "the divine Vach," "queen of the gods," and she is described as "the melodious cow who milked forth sustenance and water," "who yields us nourishment and sustenance." The Brahmanas associate her with Prajapati in the work of creation. In the Taittiriya Brahmana she is called "the mother of the Vedas," and "the wife of Indra, who contains within herself all worlds." In the Satapatha Brahmana she is represented as entering into a sexual connection with Prajapati, who, "being desirous of creating, connected himself with various spouses," and among them, "through his mind, with Vach," from whom "he created the waters;" or, as this last sentence is differently translated, "He created the waters from the world in the form of speech (Vach)." In the Kathaka Upanishad this idea is more distinctly formulated :—"Prajapati was this universe. Vach was a second to him. He associated sexually with her; she became pregnant; she departed from him; she produced these creatures; she again entered into Prajapati."

The Aitareya Brahmana and the Satapatha Brahmana have a story of the Gandharvas having stolen the soma juice, or, as one calls it, "King Soma," and that as the Gandharvas were fond of women, Vach was, at her own suggestion, "turned into a female" by the gods and Rishis, and went to recover it from them.

In the Atharvaveda she is identified with Viraj, and is the daughter of Kama (desire). "That daughter of thine, O Kama, is called the cow, she whom sages denominate Vach-Viraj."

The Mahabharata also calls her "the mother of the Vedas," and says, "A voice derived from Brahma entered into the ears of them all; the celestial Saraswati was then produced from the heavens. Here and in "the later mythology, Saraswati was identified with Vach, and became under different names the spouse of Brahma and the goddess of wisdom and eloquence, and is invoked as a muse," generally under the name of Saraswati, but sometimes as Vach.

The Bhagavata Purana recognises her as "the slender and enchanting daughter" of Brahma, for whom he had a passion, and from whom mankind was produced, that is the female Viraj. Saraswati, as wife of Brahma and goddess of wisdom, represents perhaps the union of power and intelligence which was supposed to operate in the work of creation. According to the Padma Purana, Vach was daughter of Daksha, wife of Kasyapa, and mother of the Gandharvas and Apsarases.

VAIKUNTHA: The paradise of Vishnu, sometimes described as on Mount Meru, and at others as in the Northern Ocean. It is also called Vaibhra. Vishnu himself is sometimes designated by this term.

VAISAMPAYANA: A celebrated sage who was the original teacher of the Black Yajurveda. He was a pupil of the great Vyasa, from whom he learned the Mahabharata, which he afterwards recited to King Janamejaya, at a festival. The Harivansa is also represented as having been communicated by him.

VAISESHIKA: The Atomic school of philosophy.

VAISYA: The third or trading and agricultural caste.

VAITARANI: The river 'to be crossed,' that is, the river of hell, which must be crossed before the infernal regions can be entered. This river is described as being filled with blood, ordure, and all sorts of filth, and to run with great impetuosity. A sccond river stated by the Mahabharata to be in the country of the Kalingas; it must be the river of the same name ("Byeturnee") somewhat higher up in Cuttack.

VAJRA: 1. The thunderbolt of Indra, said to have been made of the bones of the Rishi Dadhichi. It is a circular weapon, with a hole in the centre, according to some, but others represent it as consisting of two transverse bars. It has many names:—Asani, Abhrottha, 'sky-born;' Bahudara, 'much cleaving ;' Bhidira or Chhidaka, 'the splitter;' Dambholi and Jasuri, 'destructive;' Hradin, 'roaring;' Kulisa, 'axe;' Pavi, 'pointed;' Phenavahin, 'foam-bearing; Shat-kona, 'hexagon;' Sambha and Swaru. 2. Son of Aniruddha. His mother is sometimes said to be Aniruddha's wife Subhadra, and at others the Daitya princess Usha. Krishna just before his death made him king over the Yadavas at Indra-prastha.

VALAKHILYAS: I. Eleven hymns of an apocryphal or peculiar character interpolated in the Rigveda. 2. "Pigmy sages no bigger than a joint of the thumb, chaste, pious, resplendent as the rays of the sun." So described by the Vishnu Purana, which says that they were brought forth by Samnati (humility), wife of Kratu, and were 60,000 in number. They are able to fly swifter than birds. The Rigveda says that they sprang from the hairs of Prajapati (Brahma). They are the guards of the chariot of the sun. They are also called Kharwas. Wilson says: "They are not improbably connected with the character of Daumling, Thaumlin, Tamlane, Tom-a-lyn, or Tom Thumb."

VALMIKI: The author of the Ramayana, which he in Vedic phrase is said to have "seen." He himself is represented as taking part in some of the scenes he describes. He received the banished Sita into his hermitage at Chitrakuta, and educated her twin sons Kusa and Lava. Tradition has marked a hill in the district of Banda in Bundlekand as his abode. The invention of the sloka is attributed to him, but it cannot be his, because the metre is found in the Vedas.

VAMADEVA: 1. A Vedic Rishi, author of many hymns. In one of his hymns he represents himself as speaking before his birth, saying, "Let me not come forth by this path, for it it difficult of issue let me come forth obliquely from the side." Sayana, the commentator, says in explanation, "The Rishi Vama-deva, while yet in the womb, was reluctant to be born in the usual manner, and resolved to come into the world through his mother's side. Aware of his purpose, the mother prayed to Aditi, who thereupon came with her son Indra to expostulate with the Rishi." [This story accords with that told by the Buddhists of the birth of Buddha.] In the same hymn Vama-deva says, "In extreme destitution I have cooked the entrails of a dog," and Manu cites this to show that a man is not rendered impure even by eating the flesh of dogs for the preservation of his life. In another hymn he says, "As a hawk I came forth with speed;" and a commentator explains, "Having assumed the form of a hawk, he came forth from the womb by the power of Yoga, for he is considered to have been endowed with divine knowlege from the period of his conception." 2. A Vedic sage mentioned in the Mahibharata as possessor of two horses of marvellous speed called Vamyas. 3. A name of Siva; also of one of the Rudras.

VARAHA MIHIRA: An astronomer who was one of "the nine gems" of the court of Vikramaditya. He was author of Brihat-sanhita and Brihaj-jataka. His death is placed in Saka 509 (A.D. 587).

VARANAVATA: The city in which the Pandavas dwelt in exile.

VARNA: 'Class or caste.' The Chaturvarna, or four castes, as found established in the code of Manu, are-

1. **Brahmin:** The sacerdotal and learned class, the members of which may be, but are not necessarily priests.
2. **Kshatriya:** The regal and warrior caste.
3. **Vaisya:** Trading and agricultural caste.
4. **Sudra:** Servile caste, whose duty is to serve the other three.

The first three castes were called dwija, "twice born or regenerate," from their being entitled to investiture with the sacred thread which effects a second birth. The Brahmins maintain that their caste alone remains, that the other three have been lost or degraded, and it is generally believed that there are no pure Kshatriyas or Vaisyas now existing. The numerous castes which have sprung up from the intercourse of people of different castes or from other causes are called Varnasankara, 'mixed castes.'

VARUNA: Similar to Ouranos. 'The universal encompasser, the all-embracer.' One of the oldest of the Vedic deities, a personifica-tion of the all-investing sky, the maker and upholder of heaven and earth. As such he is king of the universe, king of gods and men, possessor of illimitable knowledge, the supreme deity to whom special honour is due. He is often associated with Mitra, he being the ruler of the night and Mitra of the day; but his name frequently occurs alone, that of Mitra only seldom. In later times he was chief among the lower celestial deities called Adityas, and later still he bccame a sort of Neptune, a god of the seas and rivers, who rides upon the Makara.

This character he still retainas His sign is a fish. He is regent of the west quarter and of one of the Nakshatras or lunar mansions. According to the Mahabharata, he was son of Kardama and father of Pushkara. The Mahabharata relates that he carried off Bhadra, the wife of Utathya, a Brahmin, but Utathya obliged him to submit and restore her. He was in a way the father of the sage Vasishtha. In the Vedas, Varuna is not specially connected with water, but there are passages in which he is associated with the element of water both in the atmosphere and on the earth, in such a way as may account for the character and functions ascribed to him in the later mythology.

Dr. Muir thus sums up in the words of the hymns the functions and attributes of Varuna :—"The grandest cosmical functions are ascribed to Varuna. Possessed of illimitable resources 'or knowledge', this divine being has meted out 'or fashioned' and upholds heaven and earth, he dwells in all worlds as sovereign ruler; indeed the three worlds are embraced within him. He made the golden and revolving sun to shine in the firmament. The wind which resounds through the atmosphere is his breath. He has opened out boundless paths for the sun, and has hollowed out channels for the rivers, which flow by his command. By his wonderful contrivance the rivers pour out their waters into the one ocean but never fill it. His ordinances are fixed and unassailable. They rest on him unshaken as on a mountain. Through the operation of his laws the moon walks in brightness, and the stars which appear in the nightly sky mysteriously vanish in daylight. Neither the birds flying in the air, nor the rivers in their ceaseless flow can attain a knowledge of his power or his wrath. His messengers behold both worlds. He knows the flight of birds in the sky, the paths of ships on the ocean, the course of the far-travelling wind, and beholds all the things that have been or shall be done. No creature can even wink without him. He witnesses men's truth and falsehood. He instructs the Rishi Vasishtha in mysteries; but his secrets and those of Mitra are not to be revealed to the foolish.

He has unlimited control over the destinies of mankind. He has a hundred thousand remedies, and is supplicated to show his wide and deep benevolence and drive away evil and sin, to untie sin like a rope and remove it. He is entreated not to steal away, but to prolong life, and to spare the suppliant who daily transgresses his laws. In many places mention is made of the bonds or nooses with which he seizes and punishes transgressors. Mitra and Varuna conjointly are spoken of in one passage as being barriers against falsehood, furnished with many nooses, which the hostile mortal cannot surmount; and, in another place, Indra and Varuna are described as binding with bonds not formed of rope. On the other hand, Varuna is said to be gracious even to him who has committed sin. He is the wise guardian of immortality, and a hope is held out that he and Yama, reigning in blessedness, shall be beheld in the next world by the righteous.

"The attributes and functions ascribed to Varuna impart to his character a moral elevation and sanctity far surpassing that attributed to any other Vedic deity."

The correspondence of Varuna with Ouranos is notable, but "the parallel will not hold in all points. There is not in the Vedic mythology any special relation between Varuna and Prithivi 'the earth' as husband and wife, as there is between Ouranos and Gaia in the theogony of Hesiod; nor is Varuna represented in the Veda, as Ouranos is by the Greek poet, as the progenitor of Dyaus (Zeus), except in the general way in which he is said to have formed and to preserve heaven and earth" (Muir's Texts,). Manu also refers to Varuna as "binding the guilty in fatal cords."

In the Puranas, Varuna is sovereign of the waters, and one of his accompaniments is a noose, which the Vedic deity also carried for binding offenders: this is called Nagapasa, Pulakanga, or Viswajit. His favourite resort is Pushpa-giri, 'flower mountain,' and his city Vasudha-nagara or Sukha. He also possesses an umbrella impermesble to water, formed of the hood of a cobra, and called Abhoga. The Vishnu Purana mentions an incident which shows a curious coincidence between Varuna and Neptune. At the marriage of the sage Richika, Varuna supplied him with the thousand fleet of white horses which the bride's father had demanded of him. Varuna is also called Prachetas, Amburija, Jalapati, Kesa, 'lord of the waters;' Uddama, 'the surrounder;' Pasabhrit, 'the noose-carrier;' Viloma, Variloma, 'watery hair;' Yadahpati, 'king of aquatic animals. His son is named Agasti.

VASAVADATTA: A princess of Ujjayini, who is the heroine of a popular story by Subandhu. The work has been printed by Dr. F. Hall in the Bibliotheca Indica. He considers it to have been written early in the seventh century.

VASISHTHA: 'Most wealthy.' A celebrated Vedic Sage to whom many hymns are ascribed. According to Manu, he was one of the seven great Rishis and of the ten Prajapatis. There was a special rivalry between him and the sage Viswamitra, who raised himself from the Kshatriya to the Brahmin caste. Vasishtha was the possessor of a "cow of plenty," called Nandini, who had the power of granting him all things (vasu) he desired, hence his name. A law-book is attributed to him, or to another of the same name.

Though Vasishtha is classed among the Prajapatis who sprang from Brahma, a hymn in the Rigveda and the commentaries thereon assign him a different origin, or rather a second birth, and represent him and the sage Agastya to have sprung from Mitra and Varuna. The hymn says, "Thou, O Vasishtha, art a son of Mitra and Varuna, born a Brahmin from the soul of Urvasi. All the gods placed in the vessel thee the drop which had fallen through divine contemplation." The comment on this hymn says, "When these two Adityas 'Mitra and Varuna' beheld the Apsara Urvasi at a sacrifice their seed fell from them. . . . It fell on many places, into a jar, into water, and on the ground. The Muni Vasishtha was produced on the ground, while Agastya was born in the jar."

There is a peculiar hymn attributed to Vasishtha in the Rigveda, beginning "Protector of the dwelling," which the commentators explain as having been addressed by him to a house-dog which barked as he entered the house of Varuna by night to obtain food alter a three days' fast. By it tho dog was appeased and put to sleep, "wherefore these verses are to be recited on similar occasions by thieves and burglars."

In the same Veda and in the Aitareya Brahmana, Vasishtha appears as the family priest of King Sudas, a position to which his rival Viswamitra aspired. This is amplified in the Mahabharata, where he is not the priest of Sudas but of his son Kalmasha-pada, who bore the patronymic Saudasa. It is said that his rival Viswamitra was jealous, and wished to have this office for himself, but the king preferred Vasishtha. Vasishtha had a hundred sons, the eldest of whom was named Saktri. He, meeting the king in the road, was ordered to get out of the way; but he civilly replied that the path was his, for by the law a king must cede the way to a Brahmin. The king struck him with a whip, and he retorted by cursing the king to become a man-eater. Viswamitra was present, but invisible, and he maliciously commanded a man-devouring Rakshasa to enter the king. So the king became a man-eater, and his first victim was Saktri.

The same fate befell all the hundred sons, and Vasishtha's grief was boundless. He endeavoured to destroy himself in various ways. He cast himself from the top of Mount Meru, but the rocks he fell upon were like cotton. He passed through a burning forest without harm. He threw himself into the sea with a heavy stone tied to his neck, but the waves cast him on dry land. He plunged into a river swollen by rain, but although he had bound his arms with cords, the stream loosened his bonds and landed him unbound (*vipasa*) on its banks. From this the river received the name of Vipasa (Vyas). He threw himself into another river full of alligators, but the river rushed away in a hundred directions, and was consequently called Satadru (Sutlej).

Finding that he could not kill himself, he returned to his hermitage, and was met in the wood by King Kalmasha-pada, who was about to devour him, but Vasishtha exorcised him and delivered him from the curse he had borne for twelve years. The sage then directed the king to return to his kingdom and pay due respect to Brahmins. Kalmashapada begged Vasishtha to give him offspring. He promised to do so, and "being solicited by the king to beget an heir to the throne, the queen became pregnant by him and brought forth a son at the end of twelve years."

Another legend in the Mahabharata represents Viswamitra as commanding the river Saraswati to bring Vasishtha, so that he might kill him. By direction of Vasishtha the river obeyed the command, but on approaching Viswamitra, who stood ready and armed, it promptly carried away Vasishtha in another direction.

The enmity of Vasishtha anti Viswamitra comes out very strongly in the Ramayana. Viswamitra ruled the earth for many thousand years as king, but he coveted the wondrous cow of plenty which he had seen at Vasishtha's hermitage, and attempted to take her away by force. A great battle followed between the hosts of King Viswamitra and the warriors produced by the cow to support her master. A hundred of Viswamitra's sons were reduced to ashes by the blast of Vasishtha's mouth, and Viswamitra being utterly defeated, he abdicated and retired to the Himalaya. The two met again after an interval and fought in single combat. Viswamitra was again worsted by the Brahminical power, and "resolved to work out his own elevation to the Brahminical order," so as to be upon an equality with his rival. He accomplished his object and became a priest, and Vasishtha suffered from his power. The hundred sons of Vasishtha denounced Viswamitra for presuming, though a Kshatriya, to act as a priest. This so incensed Viswamitra that he "by a curse doomed the sons of Vasishtha to be reduced to ashes and reborn as degraded outcasts for seven hundred births." Eventually, Vasishtha, being propitiated by the gods, became reconciled to Viswamitra, and recognised his claim to all the prerogatives of a Brahmin Rishi, and Viswamitra paid all honour to Vasishtha.

A legend in the Vishnu Purana represents Vasishtha as being requested by Nimi, a son of Ikshwaku, to officiate at a sacrifice which was to last for a thousand years. The sage pleaded a prior engagement to Indra for five hundred years, but offered to come at the end of that period. The king made no remark, and Vasishtha, taking silence as assent, returned as he had proposed. He then found that Nimi had engaged the Rishi Gautama to perform the sacrifice, and this so angered him that he cursed the king to lose his corporeal form. Nimi retorted the curse, and in consequence "the vigour of Vasishtha entered into the vigour of Mitra and Varuna. Vasishtha, however, received from them another body when their seed had fallen from them at the sight of Urvasi."

In the Markandeya Purana he appears as the family priest of Harischandra. He was so incensed at the treatment shown to that monarch by Viswamitra, that he cursed that sage to be transformed into a crane. His adversary retorted by dooming him to become another bird, and in the forms of two monstrous birds they fought so furiously that the course of the universe was disturbed, and many creatures perished. Brahma at length put an end to the conflict by restoring them to their natural forms and compelling them to be reconciled.

Aceording to the Vishnu Purana, Vasishtha had for wife Urja, one of the daughters of Daksha, and by her he had seven sons. The Bhagavata Purana gives him Arundhati for wife. The Vishnu Purana also makes him the family priest "of the house of Ikshwaku;" and he was not only contemporary with lkshwaku himself, but with his descendants down to the sixty first generation. "Vasishtha, according to all aceounts (says Dr. Muir), must have been possessed of a vitality altogether superhuman," for it appears that the name Vasishtha is "used not to denote merely a person belonging to a family so called, but to represent the founder of the family himself as taking part in the transactions of many successive ages."

"It is clear that Vasishtha, although he is frequently designated in post-Vedic writings as a Brahmin, was, according to some authorities, not really such in any proper sense of the word, as in the accounts which are given of his birth he is declared to have been either a mind-born son of Brahma, or the son of Mitra and Varana and the Apsara Urvasi, or to have had some other supernatural origin." (Muir,) Vasishtha's descendants are called Vasishthas and Vashkalas.

VASU: The Vasus are a class of deities, eight in number, chiefly known as attendants upon Indra. They seem to have been in Vedic times personifications of natural phenomena. They are Apa (water), Dhruva (pole-star), Soma (moon), Dhara (earth), Anila (wind), Anala (fire), Prabhasa (dawn), and Pratyusha (light). According to the Ramayana, they were children of Aditi.

VASUDEVA: Son of Sura, of the Yadava branch of the Lunar race. He was father of Krishna, and Kunti, the mother of the Pandava princes, was his sister. He married seven daughters of Ahuka, and the youngest of them, Devaki, was the mother of Krishna. After the death of Krishna and Balarama he also died, and four of his wives burnt themselves with his corpse. So says the Maha-bharata, but according to the Vishnu Purana, he and Devaki and Rohini burnt themselves at Dwaraka. He received the additional name of Anaka-dundubhi, because the gods, conscious that he was to be the putative father of the divine Krishna, sounded the drums of heaven at his birth. He was also called Bhukasyapa and Dundu, 'drum.'

VATAPI: Vatapi and Ilwala, two Rakshasas, sons either of Hrada or Viprachitti. They are mentioned in the Ramayana as dwelling in the Dandaka forest. Vatapi assumed the form of a ram which was offered in sacrifice and afterwards eaten by Brahmins. Ilwala then ealled upon him to come forth, and accordingly, he tore his way out of the stomachs of the Brahmins. He tried the same trick upon Agastya, but that austere sage ate and digested him. Ilwala, as before, called his brother to come forth, and assaulted the sage, who told him that his brother would never return. Then Ilwala was burnt up by fire from the eyes of Agastya. The Mahabharata's story varies slightly.

VATSYAYANA: A sage who wrote upon erotic subjects, and was author of the Kama-sutras and Nyaya-bhashya. He is also called Mallanaga.

VAYU: 'Air, wind.' The god of the wind, Eolus. In the Vedas he is often associated with Indra, and rides in the same car with him, Indra being the chariotcer. The chariot has a framework of gold which touches the sky, and is drawn by a thousand horses. There are not many hymns addressed to him. According to the Nirukta, there are three gods specially connected with each other. "Agni, whose place is on earth: Vayu or Indra, whose place is in the air; and Surya, whose place is in the heaven." In the hymn Purusha-sukta Vayu is said to have sprung from the breath of Purusha, and in another hymn he is called the son-in-law of Twashtri. He is regent of the north-west quarter, where he dwells.

According to the Vishnu Purana, he is king of the Gandharvas. The Bhagavata Purana relates that the sage Narada incited the wind to break down the summit of Mount Meru. He raised a terrible storm which lasted for a year, but Vishnu's bird, Garuda, shielded the mountain with his wings, and all the blasts of the wind-god were in vain. Narada then told him to attack the mountain in Garuda's absence. He did so, and breaking off the summit of the mountain, he hurled it into the lea, where it became the island of Lanka.

Vayu is the reputed father of Bhima and of Hanumat, and be is said to have made the hundred daughters of King Kusanabha, crooked because they would not comply with his licentious desires, and this gave the name Kanya-kubja, 'hump-backed damsel,' to their city.

Other names of vayu (wind) are Anila, Marut, Pavana vata, Gandhavaha, 'bearer of perfumes;' Jalakantara, 'whose garden is water;' Sadagata, Satataga, 'ever moving,' etc.

VAYU PURANA: "The Purana in which Vayu has declared the laws of duty, in connection with the Sweta kalpa, and which comprises the Mahatmya of Rudra, is the Vayu Purana; it contains twenty-four thousand verses." No MS. containing this number of verses has yet been discovered, but there are indications of the work being imperfect. The Purana is divided into four sections, the first beginning with the creation, and the last treating of the ages to come. It is devoted to the praise of Siva, and is connected with the Siva Purana, for when one of them is given in a list of Puranas the other is omitted.

VEDA. Root, *vid*, 'know.' 'Divine knowledge.' The Vedas are the holy books which are the foundation of the Hindu religion. They consist of hymns written in an old form of Sanskrit; and according to the most generally received opinion, they were composed between 1500 and 1000 B.C. But there is no direct evidence as to their age, and opinions about it vary considerably. Some scholars have thought that the oldest of the hymns may be carried back a thousand years farther. It seems likely that some of the hymns were composed before the arrival of the Aryan immigrants in India, and there is no doubt that the hymns vary greatly in age and spread over a very considerable period.

There are various statements as to the origin of the Vedas. One is that the hymns emanated like breath from Brahma, the soul of the universe. It is agreed that they were revealed orally to the Rishis or sages whose names they bear; and hence the whole body of the Veda is known as Sruti, 'what was heard.'

The Vedas are four in number:—(1.) Rig, (2.) Yajur, (3.) Sama, (4.) Atharva; but the Atharva is of comparatively modern origin. The other three are spoken of by Manu as the "three Vedas," and are said by him to have been "milked out as it were," from fire, air, and the sun. In reality the Rigveda is the Veda, the original work; for the Yajur and the Sarm are merely different arrangements of its hymns for special purposes.

Each Veda is divided into two parts, Mantra and Brahmana. The Mantra, or 'instrument of conveying thought,' consists of prayer and praise embodied in the metrical hymns. The Brahmana, a collective term for the treatises called Brahmanas, is of later date than the Mantra. It is written in prose, and contains liturgical and ritualistic glosses, explanations, and applications oi the hymns illustrated by numerous legends. To the Brahmanas are added the Aranyakas and Upanishads, mystical treatises in prose and verse, which speculate upon the nature of spirit and of God, and exhibit a freedom of thought and speculation which was the beginning of Hindu philosophy. All the Vedic writings are classified in two great divisions, exoteric and esoteric: the Karma-kanda, 'department of works,' the ceremonial; and the Jnana-kanda, 'department of knowledge.' The hymns and prayers of the Mantra come under the first, the philosophical speculations of the Brahmanas, and especially of the Upanishads, under the second division. All are alike Sruti or revelation.

The Mantra or metrical portion is the most ancient, and the book or books in which the hymns are collected are called San-hitas. The Rig-veda and the Sama-veda have each one Sanhitau and the Yajurveda has two Sanhitas.

As before stated, the Rigveda is the original Veda from which the Yajur and Sama are almost exclusively derived. It consists of 1017 Suktas or hymns, or with eleven additional hymns called Valakhilyas of an apocryphal character, 1028. These are arranged in eight Ashtakas, 'octaves,' or Khandas, 'sections,' which are again subdivided into as many Adhyayas, 'chapters,' 2006 Vargas or 'classes,' 10,417 Riks or 'verses,' and 153,826 Padas or 'words.' There is another division, which runs on concurrently with this division, in ten Mandalas, 'circles' or 'classes,' and 85 Anuvakas or 'sections.' The total number of hymns is the same in both arrangements. It is a generally received opinion that the hymns of the tenth Mandala are later in date than the others.

A few hymns of the Rigveda, more especially some of the later hymns in the tenth Mandala, appear to contain some vague, hazy conception of one Supreme Being; but as a whole they are addressed directly to certain personifications of the powers of nature, which personifications were worshipped 83 deities having those physical powers under their control.

From these powers the Vedic poets invoked prosperity on themselves and their flocks; they extolled the prowess of these elemental powers in the struggles between light and darkness, warmth and cold, and they offered up joyous praise and thanksgiving for the fruits of the earth and personal protection. Chief among the deities so praised and worshipped were Agni, Indra, and Surya. More hymns are addressed to Agni, 'fire,' than to any other deity, and chiefly in its sacrificial character, though it receives honour also for its domestic uses. Indra was honoured as the god of the atmosphere, who controlled the rains and the dew, so all-important to an agricultural people. Surya, 'the-sun,' was 'the source of heat,' but he shared this honour with Agni, the sun being considered a celestial fire.

Among the most ancient of the myths was that of Dyaus-pitar, 'heavenly father,' the regent of the sky. Others were Aditi, 'the infinite expanse;' Varuna, 'the investing sky,' afterwards god of the waters; Ushas, 'the dawn,' daughter of the sky; the two Aswins, 'twin sons of the sun,' ever young and handsome, and riding in a golden car as precursors of the dawn. Prithivi, 'the broad one,' as the earth was called, received honour as the mother of all beings. There were also the Maruts or storm-gods, personifications of the wind, the special foes of Vritra, the spirit of drought and ungenial weather, who was in constant conflict with Indra; Rudra, the howling, furious god, who ruled the tempest and the storm; Yama, the god of the dead and judge of departed spirits, also received his meed of reverence; last, though apparently not least in the estimation of the Aryan worshippers, was Soma, the personification of the fermented juice of the plant so named. This exhilarating liquid was alike acceptable to the gods and their worshippers, and many hymns are addressed to it as a deity.

To each hymn of the Rigveda there is prefixed the name of the Rishi to whom it was revealed, as Vasishtha, Viswamitra, Bharadwaja, and many others; and these sages are frequently Spoken of as authors of the hymns bearing their names. It is quite unknown when the hymns were first committed to writing. They were transmitted orally from generation to generation, and continued to be so handed down even after they had been collected and arranged by Krishna Dwaipayana, 'the arranger.' The oral teaching of the Vedas produced what are called the Sakhas or 'schools' of the Vedas. Different learned men, or bodies of men, became famous for their particular versions of the text, and taught these versions to their respective pupils. These different versions constitute the Sakhas; they present, as might be expected, many verbal variations, but no very material discrepancies.

The Yajur or second Veda is composed almost exclusively of hymns taken from the Rig, but it contains some prose passages which are new. Many of the hymns show considerable deviations from the original text of the Rig. These differences may perhaps be attributable either to an original difference of the traditional text or to modifications required by the ritualistic uses of the Yajur. The Yajurveda is the priests' office-book, arranged in a liturgical form for the performance of sacrifices. As the manual of the priesthood, it became the great subject of study, and it has a great number of different Sakhas or schools. It has two Sanhitas, one called the Taittiriya Sanhita, the other Vajasaneyi Sanhita, commonly known as the Black and White Yajur. Of these, the former is the more ancient, and seems to have been known in the third century B.C. These Sanhitas contain upon the whole the same matter, but the arrangement is different. The White Yajur is the more orderly and systematic, and it contains some texts which are not in the Black.

The Sanhita of the Taittiriya or Black Yajur is arranged in 7 Kandas or books, 44 Prasnas or chapters, 651 Anuvakas or sections, and 2198 Kandikas or pieces, "fifty words as a rule forming a Kandika." The Sanhita of the Vajasaneyi or White Yajur is in 40 Adhyayas or chapters, 303 Anuvakas, and 1975 Kandikas.

How the separation into two Sanhitas arose has not been ascertained. It probably originated in a schism led by the sage Yajnawalkya; but if it did not, it produced one, and the adherents of the two divisions were hostile to each other and quarrelled like men of different creeds. In later days a legend was invented to account for the division, which is thus given by the Vishnu and Vayu Puranas: The Yajurveda, in twenty-seven branches (Sakhas), was taught by Vaisampayana to his disciple Yajnawalkya. Vaisampayana had the misfortune to kill his sister's child by an accidental kick, and he then called upon his disciples to perform the appropriate expiatory penance. Yajnawalkya refused to join the "miserable inefficient

Brahmins," and a quarrel ensued. The teacher called upon the disciple to give up all that he had learnt from him; and the disciple, with the same quick temper, vomited forth the Yajur texts which he had acquired, and they fell upon the ground stained with blood. The other pupils were turned into partridges (Tittiri), and they picked up the disgorged texts; hence the part of the Veda which was thus acquired was called Taittiriya and Black Yajnawalkya sorrowfully departed, and by the performance oi severe penances induced the Sun to impart to him those Yajur texts which his master had not possessed.

The Sun then assumed the form of a horse (Vajin), and communicated to him the desired texts. The priests of this portion of the Veda were called Vajins, while the Sanhita itself was called Vajasaneyi, and also White, or bright, because it was revealed by the sun. The statement that Yajnawalkya received this Veda from the sun is, however, earlier than the Puranas, for it is mentioned by the grammarian Katyayana. A more reasonable and intclligible explanation is, that Vajasaneyi is a patronymic of Yajnawalkya, the offspring of Vajasani, and that Taittiriya is derived from Tittiri, the name of a pupil of Yaska's.

Weber, the man best acquainted with this Veda, says, "However absurd this legend of the Puranas may be, a certain amount of sense lurks beneath its surface. The Black Yajur is, in fact, a motley undigested jumble of different pieces; and I am myself more inclined to derive the name Taittiriya from the variegated partridge (Tittiri) than from the Rishi Tittiri." GoldStucker's view is, that the "motley character of the Black Yajurveda arises from the circumstance that the distinction between the Mantra and Brahmana portions is not so clearly established in it as in the other Vedas, hymns and matter properly belonging to the Brahmanas being there intermixed. This defect is remedied in the White Yajurveda, and it points, therefore, to a period when the material of the old Yajur was brought into a system consonant with prevalent theories, literary and ritualistic."

The Samaveda Sanhita is wholly metrical. It contains 1549 verses, only seventy-eight of which have not been traced to the Rigveda. The readings of the text in this Veda frequently differ, like those of the Yajur, from the text as found in the Rig, and Weber considers that the verses "occurring in the Sama Sanhitia generally stamp themselves as older and more original by the greater antiquity of their grammatical forms." But this opinion is disputed. The verses of the Sama have been selected and arranged for the purpose of being chanted at the sacrifices or offerings of the Soma. Many of the invocations are addressed to Soma, some to Agni, and some to Indra. The Mantra or metrical part of the Sama is poor in literary and historical interest, but its Brahmanas and the other literature belonging to it are full and important.

There were different sets of priests for each of the three Vedas. Those whose duty it was to recite the Rigveda were called Hotris or Bahvrichas, and they were required to know the whole Veda. The priests of the Yajur, who muttered its formulas in a peculiar manner at sacrifices, were called Adhwaryus, and the chanters of the verses of the Sama were called Udgatris.

The Atharvaveda, the fourth Veda, is of later origin than the others. This is acknowledged by the Brahmins, and is proved by the internal evidence of the book itself. It is supposed to date from about the same period as the tenth Mandala of the Rigveda, and as Manu speaks of only "the three Vedas," the Atharva could hardly have been acknowledged in his time. Professor Whitney thinks its contents may be later than even the tenth Mandala of the Rig, although these two "stand nearly connected in import and origin." There are reasons for supposing it to have had its origin among the Saindhavas on the banks of the Indus. One-sixth of the whole work is not metrical, "and about one-sixth of the hymns is also found among the hymns of the Rigveda, and mostly in the tenth book of the latter; the rest is peculiar to the Atharva."

The number of the hymns is about 760, and of the verses about 6000. Professor Whitney, the editor of the Atharva, speaks of it thus: "As to the internal character of the Atharva hymns, it may be said of them, as of the tenth book of the Rig, that they are productions of another and a later period, and the expressions of a different spirit from that of the earlier hymns in the other Vedas. In the latter, the gods are approached with reverential awe indeed, but with love and confidence also; a worship is paid them that exalts the offerer of it; the demons embraced under the general name Rakshasa are objects of horror whom the gods ward off and destroy; the divinities of the Atharva are regarded rather with a kind of cringing fear, as powers whose wrath is to be deprecated and whose favour curried, for it knows a whole host of imps and hobgoblins, in ranks and classes, and addresses itself to them directly, offering them homage to induce them to abstain from doing harm.

"The Mantra prayer, which in the older Veda is the instrument of devotion, is here rather the tool of superstition; it wrings from the unwilling hands of the gods the favours which of old their goodwill to men induced them to grant, or by simple magical power obtains the fulfilment of the utterer's wishes. The most prominent characteristic feature of the Atharva is the multitude of incantations which it contains; these are pronounced either by the person who is himself to be benefited, or more often by the sorcerer for him, and are directed to the procuring of the greatest veriety of desirable ends; most frequently perhape long life or recovery from grievous sickness is the object sought; then a talisman, such as a necklace, is sometimes given, or in very numerous cases some plant endowed with marvellous virtues is to be the immediate external means of the cure; further, the attainment of wealth or power is aimed at, the downfall of enemies, success in love or in play, the removal of petty pests, and so on, even down to the growth of hair on a bald pate.

"There are hymns, too, in which a single rite or ceremony is taken up and exalted, somewhat in the same strain as the Soma in the Pavamana hymns of the Rig. Others of a speculative mystical character are not wanting; yet their number is not so great as might naturally be expected, considering the development which the Hindu religion received in the periods following after that of the primitive Veda. It seems in the main that the Atharva is of popular rather than of priestly origin; that in making the transition from the Vedic to modern times, it forms an intermediate step rather to the gross idolatries and superstitions of the ignorant mass than to the sublimated Pantheism of the Brahmins." Such is the general character of the fourth Veda, but Max Muller has translated a hymn in his Ancient Sanskrit Literature, of which Professor Wilson said in the Edinburgh Review, "We know of no passage in Vedic literature which approaches its simple sublimity." This hymn is addressed to Varuna, "the great one who rules over these worlds, and beholds all as if he were close by; who sees all that is within and beyond heaven and earth."

This Veda is also called the Brahmin Veda, "because it claims to be the Veda for the chief sacrificial priest, the Brahmin." It has a Brahmana called Gopatha and many Upanishads. An entirely new recension of this Veda has lately been found in Kashmir. It is in the hands of Professor Roth, and is believed to show many important variations.

The whole of the Rigveda, with the commentary of Sayana, has been magnificently printed in six large quarto vols under the editorship of Max Muller, at the expense of the Government of India. Editions of the text separately in the Sanhita and in the Pada forms have been published by him; also another edition with the Sanhita and Pada texts on opposite pages. There is also a complete edition of the text in Roman characters by Aufrecht, and a portion of the text was published by Roer in the Bibliotheca Indica. Dr. Rosen published the first Ashtaka of the text, with a Latin translation, in 1838. Four volumes of Wilson's incomplete translation have appeared. There is a French translation by Langlois, and Max Muller has printed a critical translation of twelve hymns to the Maruts. There are other translations of portions. Translations by Ludwig and by Grassmann have also lately appeared. The text, with an English and Marathi translation, is appearing in monthly parts at Bombay.

The Sanhita of the Black Yajurveda has been published by Roer and Cowell in the Bibliotheca Indica. The White has been printed by Weber, and another edition has been published in Calcutta.

Of the Sama Sanhita, the text and a translation have been published by Dr. Stevenson. Benfey has also published the text with a German translation and a glossary; and an edition with the commentary of Sayana is now coming out in the Bibliotheca Indica.

The text of the Atharva-veda Sanhita has been printed by Roth and Whitney, and a part of it also by Aufrecht.

VEDANGAS: (Veda+angas.) 'Members of the Veda.' The Shadangas or six subjects necessary to be studied for the reading, understanding, and proper sacrificial employment of the Vedas:—

1. **Siksha:** Phonetics or pronunciation, embracing accents, quantity, and euphony in general.

2. **Chhandas:** Metre.

3. **Vyakarana–Grammar:** Said to be represented by Panini, but rather by older grammars culminating in his great work.

4. **Nirukta:** Etymology or glossary, represented by the glossary of Yaska.

5. **Jyotisha–Astronomy:** Such knowledge of the heavenly bodies as was necessary for compiling a calendar fixing the days and hours suitable for the performance of Vedic sacrifices and ceremonies.

6. **Kalpa–Ceremonial:** Rules for applying the Vedas to the performance of sacrifices. These rules are generally written in the form of Sutras or short aphorisms, and so they are known as the Kalpa-sutras or Srauta-sutras.

VEDANTA: The orthodox school of philosophy.

VENA: Son of Anga, and a descendant of Manu Swayambhuva. When he became king he issued this proclamation:—"Men must not sacrifice or give gifts or present oblations. Who else but myself is the enjoyer of sacrifices? I am for ever the lord of offerings." The sages remonstrated respectfully with him, but in vain; they admonished him in stronger terms; but when nothing availed, they slew him with blades of consecrated grass. After his death the sages beheld clouds of dust, and on inquiry found that they arose from bands of men who had taken to plundering because the country was left without a king. As Vena was childless, the sages, after consultation, rubbed the thigh (or, according to the Harivansa, the right arm) of the king to produce a son. From it there came forth "a man like a charred log, with flat face, and extremely short." The sages told him to sit down (Nishida). He did so, and thus became a Nishada, from whom "sprang the Nishadas dwelling in the Vindhya mountains, distinguished by their wicked deeds." The Brahmins then rubbed the right hand of Vena, and from it "sprang the majestic Prithu, Vena's son, resplendent in body, glowing like the manifested Agni".

The above is the story as told, with little variation, in the Mahabharata, the Vishnu and Bhagavata Puranas, and the Hari-vansa. The Padma Purana says that Vena began his reign well, but fell into the Jaina heresy. For this the sages pummelled him until the first of the Nishadas came forth from his thigh and Prithu from his right arm. Being freed from sin by the birth of the Nishada, he retired to a hermitage on the Narmada, where he engaged in penance. Vishnu was thus conciliated, and granted him the boon of becoming one with himself.

VENI-SANHARA: 'The binding of the braid.' A drama by Bhatta Narayana. The plot is taken from the Mahabharata. Draupadi, the wife of the Pandu princes, was dragged by the hair of her head into the hall of the Kauravas by Duhsasana, and she vowed that it should remain dishevelled until the insult was avenged. Alter the death of the Kauravas she again braided her hair. Wilson has given an analysis of the drama. There are several editions of the text.

VETALA-PANCHAVINSATI: The twenty-five stories of the Vetala. It is the Baital Pachisi of Hindustani, and has been translated into all the languages of India. The work is ascribed to an author named Jambhala-datta.

VIDEHA: An ancient country, of which the capital was Mithila. It corresponds with the modern Tirhut or North Bihar.

VIDURA: A son of Vyasa by a Sudra slave girl, who took the place of his consort. Vidura was called Kshatri, a term ordinarily applied to the child of a Sudra father and Brahmin mother. He enjoyed the character of the "wisest of the wise," and gave good advice to both Kauravas and Pandavas, but in the war he sided with the latter.

VIDYARANYA, VIDYARANYA-SWAMI: 'Forest of learning.' A title of Madhavacharya, as patron of the city of Vidyanagara, afterwards altered to Vijayanagara, the capital of the last great Hindu dynasty of the Dakhin.

VIKRAMADITYA: A celebrated Hindu king who reigned at Ujjayini. He is said to have been the son of a king named Gardabhilla. His name has been given to the Samvat era, commencing 57 B.C. He was a great patron of learning, and his court was made illustrious by the Nava-ratna, or nine gems of literature, who flourished there. He is a great hero of romance, and many improbable stories are told of him. His real position is uncertain. He appears to have driven out the Sakas, and to have established his authority over Northern India. He is said to have fallen in battle with his rival Salivahana, king of the Dakhin, who also has an era called Saka dating from 78 A.D.

VIKRAMORVASIYA: 'The hero and the nymph.' A celebrated drama by Kalidasa, translated in Wilson's Hindu Theatre. There are many editions and translations.

VINDHYA: The mountains which stretch across India, and divide what Manu calls the Madhya-desa or 'middle land,' the land of the Hindus, from the south, that is, they divide Hindustan from the Dakhin. The mountain is personified, and according to a legend, he was jealous of the Himalaya, and called upon the sun to revolve round him as he did round Meru. When the sun refused the mountain began to raise its head to obstruct that luminary, and to tower above Himalaya and Meru. The gods invoked the aid of Agastya, the spiritual guide of Vindhya. That sage called upon the mountain to bow down before him, and afford him an easy passage to and from the south. It obeyed, and Agastya passed over. But he never returned, and so the mountain remaind in its humbled condition, far inferior to the Himalaya.

VISAKHA-DATTA: Author of the drama Mudra-rakshasa. He is said to be of royal descent, but his family has not been identified.

VISHNU: Root, *vish*, 'to pervade.' The second god of the Hindu triad. In the Rigveda Vishnu is not in the first rank of gods. He is a manifestation of the solar energy, and is described as striding through the seven regions of the universe in three steps, and enveloping all things with the dust of his beams. These three steps are explained by commentators as denoting the three manifestations of light—fire, lightning, and the sun; or the three places of the sun—its rising, culmination, and setting. In the Veda he is occasionally associated with Indra. He has very little in common with the Vishnu of later times, but he is called "the unconquerable preserver," and this distinctly indicates the great preserving power which he afterwards became.

In the Brahmanas Vishnu acquires new attributes, and is invested with legends unknown to the Vedas, but still very far distant from those of the Puranas. In Manu, the name is mentioned, but not as that of a grest deity. In the Mahabharata and in the Puranas he is the second member of the triad, the embodiment of the Satwa-guna, the quality of mercy and goodness, which displays itself as the preserving power, the self-existent, all-pervading spirit. As such, his votaries associate him with the watery element which spread everywhere before the creation of the world. In this character he is called Narayana, 'moving in the waters,' and is represented pictorially in human form slumbering on the serpent Sesha and floating on the waters. This, too, is the position he assumes during the periods of temporary annihilation of the universe.

The worshippers of Vishnu recognise in him the supreme being from whom all things emanate. In the Mahabharata and in the Puranas he is the Prajapati (creator) and supreme god.

As such, he has three Avasthas or conditions:—1. That of Brahma, the active creator, who is represented as springing from a lotus which grew from Vishnu's navel while he was sleeping afloat upon the waters. 2. Vishnu himself, the preserver, in an Avatara or incarnate form, as in Krishna. 3. Siva or Rudra, the destructive power, who, according to a statement of the Mahabharata, sprang from his forehead. But though the Mahabharata generally allows Vishnu the supremacy, it does not do so invariably and exclusively. There are passages which uphold Siva as the greatest of the gods, and represent Vishnu as paying him homage.

The Siva Puranas of course make Siva supreme. Vishnu's preserving and restoring power has been manifested to the world in a variety of forms called Avataras, literally 'descents,' but more intelligibly 'incarnations,' in which a portion of his divine essence was embodied in a human or supernatural form possessed of superhuman powers. All these Avataras became manifest for correcting some great evil or effecting some great good in the world. The Avataras are ten in number, but the Bhagavata Purana increases them to twenty-two, and adds that in reality they are innumerable. All the ten Avataras are honoured, but the seventh and eighth, Rama and Krishna, are honoured as great mortal heroes and receive worship as great gods. Krishna is more especially looked upon as a full manifestation of Vishnu, and as one with Vishnu himself, and he is the object of a widely extended and very popular worship.

The holy river Ganges is said to spring from the feet of Vishnu. As preserver and restorer, Vishnu is a very popular deity, and the worship paid to him is of a joyous character. He has a thousand names Sahasranama, the repetition of which is a meritorious act of devotion. His wife is Lakshmi or Sri, the goddess of fortune, his heaven is Vaikuntha, and his vehicle is the bird Garuda. He is represented as a comely youth of a dark-blue colour, and dressed like an ancient king. He has four hands. One holds the Panchajanya, a Sankha or conch-shell; another the Sudarsana or Vajranabha, a chakra or quoit weapon; the third, a Gada or club called Kaumodaki; and the fourth, a Padma or lotus. He has a bow called Sarnga, and a sword called Nandaka. On his breast are the peculiar marks or curls called Srivatsa and the jewel Kaustubha, and on his wrist is the jewel Syamantaka. He is sometimes represented seated on a lotus with Lakshmi beside him, or reclining on a leaf of that plant. Sometimes he is portrayed reclining on the serpent Sesha, and at others as riding on his gigantic bird Garuda.

Of the thousand names of Vishnu the following are some of the most common:—Achyuta, 'unfallen, imperishable;' Ananta, 'the endless;' Ananta-sayana, 'who sleeps on the serpent Ananta;' Chaturbhuja, 'four-armed;' Damodara, 'bound round the belly with a rope,' as Krishna; Govinda or Gopala, 'the cowkeeper' (Krishna); Hari; Hrishikesa, 'lord of the organs of sense;' Jala-sayin, 'who sleeps on the waters;' Janardana, 'whom men worship;' Kesava, 'the hairy, the radiant;' Kiritin, 'wearing a tiara;' Lakshmipati, 'lord of Lakshmi ;' Madhusudana, 'destroyer of Madhu;' Madhava, 'descendant of Madhu;' Mukunda, 'deliverer;' Murari, 'the foe of Mura;' Nara, 'the man;' Narayana, 'who moves in the waters;' Panchayudha, 'armed with five weapons;' Padmanabha, 'lotus-navel;' Pitambara, 'clothed in yellow garments;' Purusha, 'the man, the spirit;' Purushottama, 'the highest of men, the supreme spirit;' Sarngin or Sarngi-pani, 'carrying the bow Sarnga;' Vasudeva Krishna, Son of Vasudeva; Varshneya, 'descendant of Vrishni' Vaikuntha-natha, 'lord of Vaikuntha (paradise);' Yajnesa, Yajneswara, 'lord of sacrifice.'

VISHNU PURANA: This Purana generally stands third in the lists, and is described as "that in which Parasara, beginning with the events of the Varaha Kalpa, expounds all duties, is called the Vaishnava, and the learned know its extent to be 23,000 stanzas." The actual number of stanzas does not amount to 7000, and there is no appearance of any part being wanting. The text is in print.

Wilson, the translator of this Purana, says, "Of the whole series of Puranas the Vishnu most closely corresponds to the definition of a Pancha-lakshana Purana, or one which treats of five specified topics (Primary Creation, Secondary Creation, Genealogies of Gods and Patriarchs, Reigns of the Manus, History). It comprehends them all; and although it has infused a portion of extraneous and sectarial matter, it has done so with sobriety and judgment, and has not suffered the fervour of its religious zeal to transport it to very wide deviations from the prescribed path. The legendary tales which it has inserted are few, and are conveniently arranged, so that they do not distract the attention of the compiler from objects of more permanent interest and importance." The whole work has been translated with numerous elucidatory notes by Wilson, and a second edition has been published with additional valuable notes by Dr. F. Hall.

VISRAVAS: Son of the Prajapati Pulastya, or, according to a statement of the Mahabharata, a reproduction of half Pulastya himself. By a Brahmin wife, daughter of the sage Bharadwaja, named Idavida, or Davida, he had a son, Kuvera, the god of wealth. By a Rakshasi named Nikasha or Kaikasi, daughter of Sumali, he had three sons, Ravana, Kumbhakarna, and Vibhishana and a daughter named Surpanakha. The Vishnu Purana substitutes Kesini for Nikasha. The account given by the Mahabharata is that Pulastya, being offended with Kuvera for his adulation of Brahma, reproduced half of himself as Visravas, and Kuvera to recover his favour gave him three Rakshasi handmaids: Pushpotkata, the mother of Ravana and

Kumbhakarna; Malini, the mother of Vibhishana; and Raka, the mother of Khara and Surpanakha.

VISWADEVAS, VISWE-DEVAS: 'All the gods.' In the Vedas they form a class nine in number. All the deities of junior order. They are addressed in the Veda as preservers of men, bestowers of rewards. In later times, a class of deities particularly interested in exequial offerings. The accounts of them are rather vague. They are generally said to be ten in number, but the lists vary, both as to the number and the names. The following is one list:—(1.) Vasu, (2.) Satya, (3.) Kraṭu, (4.) Daksha, (5.) Kala, (6.) Kama, (7.) Dhriti, (8.) Kuru, (9.) Puru-ravas, (10.) Madravas. Two others are sometimes added, Rochaka or Lochana and Dhuri or Dhwani.

VISWAKARMA: 'Omnificent.' This name seems to have been originally an epithet of any powerful god, as of Indra and Surya, but in course of time it came to designate a personification of the creative power. In this character Viswakarma was the great architect of the universe, and is described in two hymns of the Rigveda as the one "all-seeing god, who has on every side eyes, faces, arms, and feet, who, when producing heaven and earth, blows them forth or shapes them with his arms and wings; the father, generator, disposer, who knows all worlds, gives the gods their names, and is beyond the comprehension of mortals." In these hymns also he is said to sacrifice himself or to himself, and the Nirukta explains this by a legend which represents that "Viswa-karma, son of Bhuvana, first of all offered up all worlds in a Sarvamedha (general sacrifice), and ended by sacrificing himself,"

In the Epic and Puranic periods Viswakarma is invested with the powers and offices of the Vedic Twashtri, and is sometimes so called. He is not only the great architect, but the general artificer of the gods and maker of their weapons. It was he who made the Agneyastra or "fiery weapon," and it was he who revealed the Sthapatya-veda, or science of architecture and mechanics. The Mahabharata describes him as "the lord of the arts, executor of a thousand handicrafts, the carpenter of the gods, the fashioner of all ornaments, the most eminent of artisans, who formed the celestial chariots of the deities, on whose craft men subsist, and whom, a great and immortal god, they continually worship."

In the Ramayana, Viswakarma is represented as having built the city of Lanka for the Rakshasas, and as having generated the ape Nala, who constructed Rama's bridge from the continent to Lanka.

The Puranas make Viswakarma the son of Prabhasa, the eighth Vasu, by his wife "the lovely and virtuous Yoga-siddha." His daughter Sanjna was married to Surya, the sun, but as she was unable to endure his effulgence, Viswakarma placed the sun upon his lathe and cut away an eighth part of his brightness. The fragments fell to the earth, and from these Viswakarma formed "the discus of Vishnu, the trident of Siva, the weapon of Kuvera the god of wealth, the lance of Kartikeya, god of war, and the weapons of the other gods." Viswakarma is also represented as having made the great image of Jagannatha.

In his creative capacity he is sometimes designated Prajapati. He also has the appellations Kara, 'workman;' Takshaka, 'woodcutter;' Devavardhika, 'the builder of the gods;' Sudhanwa, 'having a good bow.'

VISWAMITRA: A celebrated sage, who was born a Kshatriya, but by intense austerities raised himself to the Brahmin caste, and became one of the seven great Rishis. According to the Rig-veda he was son of a king named Kusika, a descendant of Kusa, but later authorities make him the son of Gathin or Gadhi, king of Kanyakubja, and a descendant of Puru; so Viswamitra is declared in the Harivansa to be "at once a Paurava and a Kausika by lineage. According to some, Gadhi was of the Kusika race, descended from Kusika.

Viswamitra is called Gadhija and Gadhinandana, 'son of Gadhi.' The story of Viswamitra's birth, as told in the Vishnu Purana, is that Gadhi had a daughter named Satyavati, whom he gave in marriage to an old Brahmin of the race of Bhrigu named Richika. The wife being a Kshatriya, her husband was desirous that she might bear a son having the qualities of a Brahmin, and he gave her a dish of food which he had prepared to effect this object. He also gave her mother a dish intended to make her conceive a son with the character of a warrior. At the instigation of the mother the dishes were exchanged, so the mother gave birth to Viswamitra, the son of a Kshatriya with the qualities of a Brahmin; and Satyavati bore Jamadagni, the father of Parasurama, the warrior Brahmin and destroyer of the Kshatriyas.

The most noteworthy and important feature in the legends of Viswamitra is the active and enduring struggle between him and the Brahmin Rishi Vasishtha, a fact which is frequently alluded to in the Rigveda, and is supposed to typify the contentions between the Brahmins and the Kshatriyas for the superiority. Both these Rishis occupy a prominent position in the Rigveda, Viswamitra being the Rishi of the hymns in the third Mandala, which contains the celebrated verse Gayatri, and Vasishtha of those of the seventh. Each of them was at different times the Purohita or family priest of King Sudas, a position of considerable importance and power, the possession of which stimulated if it did not cause their rivalry. The two sages cursed each other, and carried their enmity into deeds of violence.

Viswamitra's hundred sons are represented as having been eaten or burnt up by the breath of Vasishtba. On the other hand, the hundred sons of Vasishtha were, according to one legend, eaten up by King Kalmashapada, into whom a man-eating Rakshasa had entered under the influence of

Viswamitra, or, according to another legend, they were reduced to ashes by Viswamitra's curse "and reborn as degraded outcasts for seven hundred births." The Aitareya Brahmana states that Viswamitra had a hundred sons, but that when he adopted his nephew Sunahsepha he proposed to make him the eldest of his sons. Fifty of them assented, and them Viswamitra blessed that they should "abound in cattle and sons;" the other and elder fifty dissented, and them he cursed "that their progeny should possess the furthest ends of the country," and from them have descended many of the border tribes and most of the Dasyus. The Mahabharata has a legend of Viswamitra having commanded the river Saraswati to bring his rival Vasishtha that he might kill him, and of having turned it into blood when it flowed in another direction and carried Vasishtha out of his reach.

Viswamitra's relationship to Jamadagni naturally places him in a prominent position in the Ramayana. Here the old animosity between him and Vasishtha again appears. He as a king paid a visit to Vasishtha's hermitage, and was most hospitably entertained; but he wished to obtain Vasishtha's wondrous cow, the Kamadhenu, which had furnished all the dainties of the feast. His offers were immense, but were all declined. The cow resisted and broke away when he attempted to take her by force, and when he battled for her, his armies were defeated by the hosts summoned up by the cow, and his "hundred sons were reduced to ashes in a moment by the blast of Vasishtha's mouth." A long and fierce combat followed between Vasishtha and Viswamitra, in which the latter was defeated; the Kshatriya had to submit to the humiliation of acknowledging his inferiority to the Brahmin, and he therefore resolved to work out his own elevation to the Brahminical order.

While he was engaged in austerities for accomplishing his object of becoming a Brahmin he became connected with King

Trisanku. This monarch was a descendant of King Ikshwaku, and desired to perform a sacrifice in virtue of which he might ascend bodily to heaven. His priest, Vasishtha, declared it to be impossible, and that priest's hundred sons, on being applied to, refused to undertake what their father had declined. 'When the king told them that he would seek some other means of accomplishing his object, they condemned him to become a Chandala. In this condition he had resort to Viswamitra, and he, taking pity on him, raised him to heaven in his bodily form, notwithstandingthe opposition of the sons of Vasishtha. The Harivansa version of this story is different. Trisanku, also called Satyavrata, had attempted the abduction of the young wife of a citizen. For this his father banished him, and condemned him to "the performance of a silent penance for twelve years." During his exile there was a famine, and Trisanku succoured and supported the wife and family of Viswamitra, who were reduced to the direst extremity in that sage's absence. Vasishtha, the family priest, had done nothing to assuage the wrath of the aggrieved father, and this offended Trisanku. At the end of his penance, being in want of meat, he killed Vasishtha's wonder-working cow and partook of her flesh; for this act Vasishtha gave him the name of Trisanku, 'guilty of three sins.' Viswamitra was grateful for the assistance rendered by Trisanku, and gave him the choice of a boon. He begged that he might ascend bodily to heaven. Viswamitra then installed Trisanku in his father's kingdom, "and in spite of the resistance of the gods and of Vasishtha he exalted the king alive to heaven."

The Mahabharata and the Ramayana tell the story of Viswamitra's amour with Menaka. His austerities had so alarmed the gods that Indra sent this Apsara to seduce Viswamitra "by the display of her charms and the exercise of all her allurements." She succeeded, and the result was the birth of Sakuntala. Viswamitra at length became ashamed of his passion, and "dismissing the nymph with gentle accents, he retired to the northern mountains, where he practised severe austerities for a thousand years. He is said also to have had an amour with the nymph Rambha.

The result of the struggle between Vasishtha and Viswamitra is thus told in the Ramayana:—"Vasishtha, being propitiated by the gods, became reconciled to Viswamitra, and reeognised his claim to all the prerogatives of a Brahmin Rishi. . . . Viswamitra, too, having attained the Brahminical rank, paid all honour to Vasishtha."

The Ramayana gives many particulars of Viswamitra's connection with Rama. It was Viswamitra who prevailed upon King Dasaratha to send his son Rama for the protection of the Brahmins against the attacks of Ravana and his Rakshasas. He acted as his guru, and returned with Rama to Ayodhya, where the prince obtained the hand of Sita.

In the Markandeya and other Puranas the story is told of Viswamitra's implacable persecution of King Harischandra, one result of which was that Vasishtha and Viswamitra cursed each other so that they were turned into birds, and fought together most furiously till Brahma put an end to the conflict, restored them to their natural forms, and compelled them to be reconciled.

VITAHAVYA: A king of the Haihayas. His son attacked and slew all the family of Divodasa, king of Kasi. A son, named Pratardana, was subsequently born to Divodasa, and he attacked the Haihayas and compelled Vitahavya to fly to the sage Bhrigu for protection. Pratardana pursued him, and demanded that he should be given up. Then "Vitahavya, by the mere word of Bhrigu, became a Brahmin Rishi and an utterer of the Veda." (Mahabharata) His son, Gritsamada, was a highly honoured Rishi, and author of several hymns in the Rigveda. He was the founder of the tribe of Haihayas called Vita-havyas.

VOPADEVA: A grammarian of great repute, who lived about the thirteenth century A.D. at Devagiri, and wrote the Mugdha-bodha.

VRATYA: "Persons whom the twice-born beget on women of their own classes, but who omit the prescribed rites and have abandoned the Gayatri, are to be designated as Vratyas."—Manu.

VRIHATKATHA: 'Great story.' A large collection of tales from which the Kathasarit-sagara was drawn. There is a critical examination of this work by Dr. Buhler in the Indian Antiquary.

VRIHAT-SANHITA: The astronomical work of Varaha Mihira.

VRINDAVANA: A wood in the district of Mathura where Krishna passed his youth, under the name of Gopala, among the cowherds.

VRISHNI: A descendant of Yadu, and the ancestor from whom Krishna got the name Varshneya.

VRITRA: In the Vedas he is the demon of drought and ungenial weather, with whom Indra, the god of the firmament, is constantly at war, and whom he is constantly overpowering, and releasing the rain. Sometimes called Vritraisura.

VYAHRITIS: Three mystical words said by Manu to have been milked from the Vedas by Prajapati—the word *bhur*, from the Rigveda; the word *bhuvah*, from the Yajurveda; and the word *swar*, from the Samaveda. The Satapatha Brahmana defines them as "three luminous essences" which Prajapati produced from the Vedas by hearting them. "He uttered the word *bhur*, which became this carth; *bhuvah*, which became this firmament; and *swah*, which became that sky." A fourth word, *mahar*, is sometimes added, and is propably intended to represent the Atharvaveda.

VYAKARANA: 'Grammar.' One of the Vedangas. The science of grammar has been carefully studied among the Hindus from very ancient times, and studied for its own sake as a science rather than as a means of acquiring or regulating language. The grammar of Panini is the oldest of those known to survive, but Panini refers to several grammarians who preceded himself. One of them was named Sakatayana, a portion of whose work is said to have been discovered lately.

VYASA: ' An arranger.' This title is common to many old authors and compilers, but it is specially applied to Vedavyasa the arranger of the Vedas, who, from the imperishable nature of his work, is also called Saswatas, 'the immortal'. The name is given also to the compiler of the Mahabharata, the founder of the Vedanta philosophy, and the arranger of the Puranas; all these persons being held to be identical with Vedavyasa. But this is impossible, and the attribution of all these works to one person has arisen either from a desire to heighten their antiquity and authority, or from the assumed identity of several different "arrangers." Vedavyasa was the illegitimate son of the Rishi Parasara and Satyavati, and the child, who was of a dark colour, was brought forth on an island (dwipa) in the Yamuna. Being illegitimate he was called Kanina, the 'bastard;' from his complexion he received the name Krishna, and from his birthplace he was called Dwaipayana. His mother afterwards married King Santanu, by whom she had two sons. The elder was killed in battle, and the younger, named Vichitravirya, died childless. Krishna Dwaipayana preferred a life of religious retirement, but in accordance with law and at his mother's request, he took the two childless widows of her son, Vichitravirya. By them he had two sons, Dhritarashtra and Pandu, between whose descendants the great war of the Mahabharata was fought.

The Puranas mention no less than twenty-eight Vyasas, incarnations of Vishnu ur Brahma, who descended to the earth in different ages to arrange and promulgate the Vedas.

Y

YADAVA: A descendant of Yadu. The Yadavas were the celebrated race in which Krishna was born. At the time of his birth they led a pastoral life, but under him they established a kingdom at Dwaraka in Gujarat. All the Yadavas who were present in that city after the death of Krishna perished in it when it was submerged by the ocean. Some few were absent, and perpetuated the race, from which many princes and chiefs still a claim their descent. The great Rajas of Vijayanagara asserted themselves as its representatives. The Vishnu Purana says of this race, "Who shall enumerate the whole of the mighty men of the Yadava race, who were tens of ten thousands and hundreds of hundred thousands in numbert?"

YADU: Son of King Yayati of the Lunar race, and founder of the line of the Yadavas in which Krishna was born. He refused to bear the curse of decrepitude passed upon his father by the sage Sukra, and in consequence he incurred the paternal curse, "Your posterity shall not possess dominion." Still he received from his father the southern districts of his kingdom, and his posterity prospered.

YAJNA: 'Sacrifice.' Sacrifice personified in the Puranas as son of Ruchi and husband of Dakshina. He had the head of a deer, and was killed by Virabhadra at Daksha's sacrifice. According to the Harivansa, he was raised to the planetary sphere by Brahma, and made into the constellation Mrigasiras (deer-head).

YAJNAWALKYA: A celebrated sage, to whom is attributed the White Yajurveda, the Satapatha Brahmana, the Brihad Aranyaka, and the code of law called Yajnawalkya-smriti. He lived before the grammarian Katyayana, and was probably later than Manu; at any rate, the code bearing his name is posterior to that of Manu. He was a disciple of Bashkali, and more particularly of Vaisampayana. The Mahabharata makes him present at the Rajasuya sacrifice performed by Yudhishthira; and according to the Satapatha Brahmana, he flourished at the court of Janaka, king of Videha and father of Sits. Janaka had long contentions with the Brahmins, in which he was supported, and probably prompted, by Yajnawalkya.

This sage was a dissenter from the religious teaching and practices of his time, and is represented as contending with and silencing Brahmins at the court of his patron. A Brahmin named Vidagdha Sakalya was his special adversary, but he vanquished him and cursed him, so that "his head dropped off, and his bones were stolen by robbers." Yajnawalkya also is represented as inculcating the duty and necessity of religious retirement and meditation, so he is considered as having been the originator of the Yoga doctrine, and to have helped in preparing the world for the preaching of Buddha. He had two wives, Maitreyi and Katyayani, and he instructed the former in his philosophical doctrine. Max Muller quotes a dialogue between them from the Satapatha Brahmana (Ancient Sanskrit Literature), in which the sage sets forth his views.

The White Yajurveda originated in a schism, of which Yajnawalkya was a leader, if not the author. He was the originator and compiler of this Veda, and according to some it was called Vajasaneyi Sanhita, from his surname Vajasaneya.

What share Yajnawalkya had in the production of the Satapatha Brahmana and Brihad Aranyaka is very doubtful. Some part of these may, perhaps, have sprung directly from him, and they were probably compiled under his superintendence; but it may be, as some think, that they are so called because they treat of him and embody his teaching. One portion of the Brihad Aranyaka, called the Yajnawalkiya Kanda, cannot have been his composition, for it is devoted to his glorification and honour, and was probably written after his death.

The Smriti, or code of law which bears the name of Yajnawalkya, is posterior to that of Manu, and is more precise and stringent in its provisions. Its authority is inferior only to that of Manu, and as explained and developed by the celebrated commentary Mitakshara, it is in force all over India except in Bengal proper, but even there the original text-book is received. The second century A.D. has been named as the earliest date of this work. Like Manu, it has two recensions, the Brihad and Vriddha, perhaps more. The text has been printed in Calcutta, and has been translated into German by Stenzler and into English by Roer and Montriou.

YAKSHAS: A class of supernatural beings attendant on Kuvera, the god of wealth. Authorities differ as to their origin. They have no very special attributes, but they are generally considered as inoffensive, and so are called Punyajanas, 'good people,' but they occasionally appear as imps of evil. It is a Yaksha in whose mouth Kalidasa placed his poem Meghaduta (cloud messenger).

YAMA: 'Restrainer.' Pluto, Minos. In the Vedas Yams is god of the dead, with whom the spirits of the departed dwell. He was the son of Vivaswat (the Sun), and had a twin-sister named Yami or Yamuna. These are by some looked upon as the first human pair, the originators of the race; and there is a remarkable hymn, in the form of a dialogue, in which the female urges their cohabitation for the purpose of perpetuating the species. Another hymn says that Yama "was the first of men that died, and the first that departed to the celestial world." He it was who found out the way to the home which cannot be taken away: "Those who are now born follow by their own paths to the place whither our ancient fathers have departed." "But," says Dr. Muir, "Yama is nowhere represented in the Rig-veda as having anything to do with the punishment of the wicked." So far as is yet known, "the hymns of that Veda contain no prominent mention of any such penal retribution. . . . Yama is still to some extent an object of terror. He is represented as having two insatiable dogs, with four eyes and wide nostrils, which guard the road to his abode, and which the departed are advised to hurry past with all possible speed. These dogs are said to wander about among men as his messengers, no doubt for the purpose of summoning them to their master, who is in another place identified with death, and is described as sending a bird as the herald of doom."

In the epic poems Yama is the son of the Sun by Sanjna (conscience), and brother of Vaivaswata Manu. Mythologically he was the father of Yudhishthira. He is the god of departed spirits and judge of the dead. A soul when it quits its mortal form repairs to his abode in the lower regions; there the recorder, Chitragupta, reads out his account from the great register called Agra-sandhani, and a just sentence follows, when the soul either ascends to the abodes of the Pitris (Manes), or is sent to one of the twenty-one hells according to its guilt, or it is born again on earth in another form. Yama is regent of the south quarter, and as such is called Dakshinasapati. He is represented as of a green colour and clothed with red. He rides upon a buffalo, and is armed with a ponderous mace and a noose to secure his victims.

In the Puranas a legend is told of Yama having lifted his foot to kick Chhaya, the handmaid of his father. She cursed him to have his leg affected with sores and worms, but his father gave him a cock which picked off the worms and cured the discharge. Through this incident he is called Sirnapada, 'shrivelled foot.'

Yama had several wives, as Hemamala, Susila, and Vijaya. He dwells in the lower world, in his city Yamapura. There, in his palace called Kalichi, he sits upon his throne of judgment, Vicharabhu. He is assisted by his recorder and councillor,

Chitragupta, and waited upon by his two chief attendants and custodians, Chanda or Mahachanda, and Kala-pursusha. His messengers, Yamadutas, bring in the souls of the dead, and the door of his judgment-hall is kept by his porter, Vaidhyata.

Yama has many names descriptive of his office. He is Mrityu, Kala, and Antaka, 'death;' Kritanta, 'the finisher;' Samana, 'the settler;' Dandi or Dandadhara, 'the rod-bearer;' Bhimasasana, 'of terrible decrees;' Pasi, 'the noose-carrier;' Pitripati, 'lord of the manes;' Pretaraja, 'king of the ghosts;' Sraddhadeva, 'god of the exequial offerings;' and especially Dharmaraja, 'king of justice.' He is Audumbara, from Udumbara, 'the fig-tree,' and from his parentage he is Vaivaswata. There is a Dharmasastra which bears the name of Yama.

YAMUNA: The river Jumna, which rises in a mountain called Kalinda (Sun). The river Yamuna is personified as the daughter of the Sun by his wife Sanjna. So she was sister of Yama. Balarama, in a state of inebriety, called upon her to come to him that he might bathe, and as she did not heed, he, in a great rage, seized his ploughshare-weapon, dragged her to him and compelled her to follow him whithersoever he wandered through the wood. The river then assumed a human form and besought his forgiveness, but it was some time before she could appease him. Wilson thinks that "the legend probably alludes to the construction of canals from the Jumna for the purposes of irrigation." The river is also called Kalindi, from the place of its source, Suryaja, from her father, and Triyama.

YASKA: The author of the Nirukta, the oldest known gloss upon the text of the Vedic hymns. Yaska lived before the time of Panini, who refers to his work, but he was not the first author who wrote a Nirukta, as he himself refers to several predecessors.

YATUS, YATUDHANAS: Demons or evil spirits of various forms, as dogs, vultures, hoofed animals, etc. In ancient times the Yatus or Yatudhanas were distinct from the Rakshasas though associated with them, but in the epic poems and Puranas they are identified. Twelve Yatudhanas are named in the Vayu Purana, and they are said to have sprung from Kasyapa and Surasa. They are associated with the Dasyus, and are thought to be one of the native races which opposed tho progress of the immigrant Aryans.

YAVANAS: Greeks, the Yavanas of the Hebrew. The term is found in Panini, who speaks of the writing of the Yavanas. The Puranas represent them to be descendants of Turvasu, but they are always associated with the tribes of the north-west frontier, and there can be no doubt that the Macedonian or Bactrian Greeks are the people most usually intended by the term. In the Bactrian Pali inscriptions of King Priyadarsi the word is contracted to Yona, and the term Yonaraja "is associated with the name of Antiochus, probably Antiochus the Great, the ally of the Indian prince Sophagasenas, about B.C. 210." The Puranas characterise them as "wise and eminently brave." They were among the races conquered by King Sagara, and "he made them shave their heads entirely." In a later age they were encountered on the Indus by Pushyamitra, a Mauryan general, who dethroned his master and took the throne. In modern times the term has been applied to the Muhammadans.

YAYATI: The fifth king of the Lunar race, and son of Nahusha. He had two wives, Devayani and Sarmishtha, from the former of whom was born Yadu, and from the latter Puru, the respective founders of the two great lines of Yadavas and Pauravas. In all he had five sons, the other three being Druhyu, Turvasu, and Anu. He was a man of amorous disposition, and his infidelity to Devayani brought upon him the curse of old age and infirmity from her father, Sukra. This curse Sukra consented to transfer to anyone of his sons who would consent to bear it. All refused except Puru, who undertook to resign his youth in his father's favour. Yayati, after a thousand years spent in sensual pleasures, renounced sensuality, restored his vigour to Puru, and made him his suecesser. This story of Puru's assuming Yayati's decrepitude is first told in the Mahabharata. The above is the version of the Vishnu Purana.

YOGA: A school of philosophy.

YUDHISHTHIRA: The eldest of the five Pandu princes, mythologically the son of Dharma, the god of justice. With the Hindus he is the favourite one of the five brothers, and is represented as a man of calm, passionless judgment, strict veracity, unswerving rectitude, and rigid justice. He was renowned as a ruler and director, but not as a warrior. Educated at the court of his uncle, Dhritarashtra, he received from the family preceptor, Drona, a military training, and was taught the use of the spear. When the time came for naming the Yuvaraja or heirapparent to the realm of Hastinapura, the Maharaja Dhritarashtra selected Yudhishthira in preference to his own eldest son, Duryodhana. A long-standing jealousy between the Pandava and Kaurava princes then broke forth openly. Duryodhana expostulated with his father, and the end was that the Pandavas went in honourable banishment to the city of Varanavata.

The jealousy of Duryodhana pursued them, and his emissaries laid a plot for burning the brothers in their dwelling house. Yudhishthira's sagacity discovered the plot and Bhima frustrated it. The bodies of a Bhil woman and her five sons were found in the ruins of the burnt house, and it was believed for a time that the Pandavas and their mother had perished. When Draupadi had been won at the swayamvara, Yudhishthira, the eldest of the five brothers, was requested by his juniors to make her his wife, but he desired that she should become the wife of Arjuna, by whose prowess she had been won. Through the words of their mother, Kunti, and the decision of the sage Vyasa, the princess became the common wife of the five brothers. An arrangament was made that Draupadi should dwell in turn with the five brothers, passing two days in the separate house of each, and that under pain of exile for twelve years no one of the brothers but the master of the house should enter while Draupadi was staying in it. The arms of the family were kept in the house of Yudhishthira, and an alarm of robbery being raised, Arjuna rushed there to procure his weapons while Draupadi was present. He thus incurred the pain of exile, and departed, though Yudhishthira endeavoured to dissuade him by arguing that the elder brother of a fatherless family stood towards his juniors in the position of a father.

After the return of the Pandavas from exile and their establishment at Indra-prastha, the rule of Yudhishthira is described as having been most excellent and prosperous. The Raja ruled the country with great justice, protecting his subjects as his own sons, and subduing all his enemies round about, so that every man was without fear of war or disturbance, and gave his whole mind to the performance of every religious duty. And the Raja had plenty of rain at the proper season, and all his subjects became rich; and the virtues of the Raja were to be seen in the great increase of trade and merchandise, in the abundant harvests and the prolific cattle. Every subject of the Raja was pious; there were no liars, no thieves, and no swindlers; and there were no droughts, no floods, no locusts, no conflagrations, no foreign invasions, and no parrots to eat the grain.

The neighbouring Rajas, despairing of conquering Raja Yudhishthira, were very desirous of securing his friendship. Meanwhile, Yudhishthira, though he would never acquire wealth by unfair means, yet prospered so exceedingly that had he lavished his riches for a thousand years no diminution would ever have been perceived. After the return of his brother Arjuna from exile, Yudhishthira determined to assert his supremacy by performing the Rajasuya sacrifice, and this led to a war with Jarasandha, Raja of Magadha, who declined to take part in it, and was in consequence defeated and killed. The dignity which Yudhishthira had gained by the performance of the sacrifice rekindled the jealousy of Duryodhana and the other Kauravas. They resolved to invite their cousins to a gambling match, and to chcat Yudhishthira of his kingdom. Yudhishthira was very unwilling to go, but could not refuse his uncle's invitation. Sakuni, maternal uncle of Duryodhana, was not only a skilful player but also a dexterous cheat. He challenged Yudhishthira to throw dice with him, and Yudhishthira, after stipulating for fair-play, began the game. He lost his all, his kingdom, his brothers, himself, and his wife, all of whom became slaves.

When Draupadi was sent for as a slave and refused to come, Duhsasana dragged her into the hall by the hair, and both he and Duryodhana grossly insulted her. Bhima was half mad with rage, but Yudhishthira's sense of right acknowledged that Draupadi was a slave, and he forbade Bhima and his brothers to interfere. When the old Maharaja Dhritarashtra was informed of what had passed, he came into the assembly, and declaring that his sons had acted wrongfully, he sent Draupadi and her husbands away, imploring them to forget what had passed. Duryodhana was very wroth, and induced the Maharaja to allow another game to avoid war, the condition being that the losers should go into exile for thirteen years, and should remain concealed and undiscovered during the whole of the thirteenth year. The game was played, and loaded dice gave Sakuni the victory, so the Pandavas went again into exile. During that time they rendered a service to Duryodhana by rescuing him and his companions from a band of marauders who had made them prisoners. When Jayadratha, king of

Sindhu, was foiled in his attempt to carry off Draupadi, the clemency of Yudhishthira led him to implore his brothers to spare their captive's life. As the thirteenth year of exile approached, in order to keep themselves concealed, the five brothers and Draupadi went to the country of Virata and entered into the service of the Raja. Yudhishthira's office was that of private companion and teacher of dice-playing to the king. Here Yudhishthira suffered his wife Draupadi to be insulted, and dissuaded his brothers from interfering, lest by so doing they should discover themselves. When the term of exile was concluded, Yudhishthira sent an envoy to Hastinapura asking for a peaceful restoration to the Pandavas of their former position. The negotiations failed, and Yudhishthira invited Krishna to go as his representative to Hastinapura. Notwithstanding Yudhishthira's longing for peace the war began, but even then Yudhishthira desired to withdraw, but was overruled by Krishna.

The death of Krishna at Dwaraka and regrets for the past embittered the lives of the Pandavas, and they resolved to withdraw from the world. Yudhishthira appointed Parikshit, grandson of Arjuna, to be his successor, and the five brothers departed with Draupadi to the Himalayas on their way to Swarga. The story of this journey is told witb great feeling in the closing verses of the Mahabharata.

Yudhishthira had a son named Yaudheya by his wife Devika; but the Vishnu Purana makes the son's name Devaka and the mother's Yaudheyi.

YUGA: An age of the world. Each of these ages is preceded by a period called its Sandhya or twilight, and is followed by another period of equal length called Sandhyansa, 'portion of twilight,' each being equal to one-tenth of the Yuga. The Yugas are four in number, and their duration is first computed by years of the gods:-

1. Krita Yuga,	4000	
Sandhya,	400	
Sandhyansa,	400	
		4,800
2. Treta Yuga,	3000	
Sandhya,	300	
Sandhyansa,	300	
		3,600
3. Dwapara Yuga,	2000	
Sandhya,	200	
Sandhysnsa,	200	
		2,400
4. Kali Yuga,	1000	
Sandhya,	100	
Sandhyansa,	100	
		1,200
		12,000

But a year of the gods is equal to 360 years of men, so

4800 × 360	=	1,728,000
3600 × 360	=	1,296,000
2400 × 360	=	864,000
1200 × 360	=	432,000
Total,		4,320,000

years, forming the period called a Mahayuga or Manwantara. Two thousand Mahayugas or 8,640,000,000 years make a Kalpa or night and a day of Brahma.

This elaborate and practically boundless system of chronology was invented between the age of the Rigveda and that of the Mahabharata. No traces of it are to be found in the hymns of the Rig, but it was fully established in the days of the great epic. In this work the four ages are described at length by Hanumat, the learned monkey chief, and from that description the following account has been abridged :-

The Krita is the age in which righteousness is eternal, when duties did not languish nor people decline. No efforts were made by men, the fruit of the earth was obtained by their mere wish. There was no maliee, weeping, pride, or deceit; no contention, no hatred, cruelty, fear, affliction, jealousy, or envy. The castes alike in their functions fulfilled their duties, were unceasingly devoted to one deity, and used one formula, one rule, and one rite. Though they had separate duties, they had but one Veda and practised one duty.

In the Treta Yuga sacrifice commenced, righteousness decreased by one-fourth; men adhered to truth, and were devoted to a righteousness dependent on ceremonies. Sacrifices prevailed with holy acts and a variety of rites. Men acted with an object in view, seeking after reward for their rites and their gifts, and were no longer disposed to austerities and to liberality from a simple feeling of duty.

In the Dwapara Yuga righteousness was diminished by a half. The Veda became fourfold. Some men studied four Vedas, others three, others two, others one, and some none at all. Ceremonies were celebrated in a great variety of ways. From the decline of goodness only few men adhered to truth. When men had fallen away from goodness, many diseases, desires, and calamities, caused by destiny, assailed thern, by which they were severely afficted and driven to practise austerities. Others desiring heavenly bliss offered sacrifices. Thus men declined through unrighteousness.

In the Kali Yuga righteousness remained to the extent of one-fourth only. Practices enjoined by the Vedas, works of righteousness, and rites of sacrifice ceased. Calamities, diseases, fatigue, faults, such as anger, etc., distresses, hunger, and fear prevailed. As the ages revolve righteousness declines, and the people also decline. When they decay their motives grow weak, and the general decline frustrates their aims.

In the Krita Yuga the duration of life was four thousand years, in the Treta three thousand, in the Dwapara two thousand. In the Kali Y uga there is no fixed measure. Other passages of the Mahabharata indicate "that the Krita Yuga was regarded as an age in which Brahmins alone existed, and that Kshatriyas only began to be born in the Treta.

YUYUTSU: A son of Dhritarashtra by a Vaisya handmaid. On the eve of the great battle he left the side of the Kauravas and joined the Pandavas. When Yudhishthira retired from the world he established Yuyutsu in the kingdom of Indraprastha.

n

ON & CULTURE

(New)	250/-
)	250/-
ɛ Mythology (New)	250/-
	250/-
ew)	250/-
	250/-
	250/-
	250/-
	250/-
Goddesses	250/-
his times	125/-
ayana	125/-
	250/-
e	250/-
	250/-
	250/-
	250/-
	250/-
	250/-
	250/-
	250/-
	250/-
ıda	250/-
	250/-
	250/-
	250/-
	250/-
ıdgita	125/-
	80/-
ne	125/-
Iome	125/-
iily	75/-
ıs Powers	95/-
	150/-
	225/-
	195/-

ıs
PRESS

, 2nd Floor, 4735/22,
ng,Ansari Road, Darya Ganj,
2903912, 23280047, 09811594448
@sify.com, www.lotuspress.co.in